A PLUME BOOK

THE MASCOT

MARK KURZEM studied at Melbourne, Tokyo, and Oxford universities. He served as international relations adviser in Osaka, Japan. This is his first book. He lives in Oxford, England.

"This is a book to keep you up at night." —*The New York Times*

"The astounding details emerge piecemeal and chronologically; they are so numerous that only an incomplete précis can be accommodated here. . . . Here the reader, eager to learn what bombshell will land next, rushes past all obstacles. The book becomes quite spy-thrillerish, featuring a former Israeli agent, sinister encounters, telephoned threats, and a break-in at Kurzem's house." —*Chicago Sun-Times*

"Part thriller, part psychological drama, part puzzle with a strange twist, *The Mascot* is one of the most astonishing stories to emerge from the Second World War." —*The Telegraph* (London)

"Stunning. So emotionally cataclysmic and poignant it makes your hair stand on end." —*The Sunday Telegraph* (Australia)

"The author proves himself an indomitable investigator equal to unearthing his father's identity. Transcriptions of Alex's harrowing recollections are augmented by research into his origins, a task in which his son is assisted by Holocaust experts from Melbourne to Minsk. The author also offers fascinating insights into his father's psychology, including storytelling as catharsis . . . An emotionally shattering detective story." —*Washington City Paper*

THE MASCOT

UNRAVELING THE MYSTERY OF
MY JEWISH FATHER'S NAZI BOYHOOD

MARK KURZEM

℗ A PLUME BOOK

PLUME
Published by the Penguin Group
Penguin Group (USA) Inc., 375 Hudson Street, New York, New York 10014, U.S.A. •
Penguin Group (Canada), 90 Eglinton Avenue East, Suite 700, Toronto, Ontario, Canada
M4P 2Y3 (a division of Pearson Penguin Canada Inc.) • Penguin Books Ltd., 80 Strand,
London WC2R 0RL, England • Penguin Ireland, 25 St. Stephen's Green, Dublin 2, Ireland
(a division of Penguin Books Ltd.) • Penguin Group (Australia), 250 Camberwell Road,
Camberwell, Victoria 3124, Australia (a division of Pearson Australia Group Pty. Ltd.) •
Penguin Books India Pvt. Ltd., 11 Community Centre, Panchsheel Park, New Delhi – 110
017, India • Penguin Group (NZ), 67 Apollo Drive, Rosedale, North Shore 0632, New
Zealand (a division of Pearson New Zealand Ltd.) • Penguin Books (South Africa) (Pty.)
Ltd., 24 Sturdee Avenue, Rosebank, Johannesburg 2196, South Africa

Penguin Books Ltd., Registered Offices: 80 Strand, London WC2R 0RL, England

Published by Plume, a member of Penguin Group (USA) Inc. Previously published in a
Viking edition.

First Plume Printing, September 2008
10 9 8 7 6 5 4 3 2 1

Copyright © Mark Kurzem, 2007
All rights reserved

 REGISTERED TRADEMARK—MARCA REGISTRADA

CIP data is available.
ISBN 978-0-670-01826-0 (hc.)
ISBN 978-0-452-28994-9 (pbk.)

Printed in the United States of America
Set in Janson Text with Kraftwerk
Original hardcover design by Daniel Lagin

BOOKS ARE AVAILABLE AT QUANTITY DISCOUNTS WHEN USED TO PROMOTE PRODUCTS OR SERVICES.
FOR INFORMATION PLEASE WRITE TO PREMIUM MARKETING DIVISION, PENGUIN GROUP (USA) INC.,
375 HUDSON STREET, NEW YORK, NEW YORK 10014.

In memory of my mother, Patricia Kurzem (1937–2003)

CONTENTS

CONTENTS

PART III

MAPS APPEAR ON PAGES X AND 245.

AUTHOR'S NOTE

The story of my father, the mascot, is a true one. In order to protect the privacy of some of the individuals and organizations I encountered during my research over the years, I have altered various names and identifying details.

I have also condensed the chronology of my research in order to enhance the narrative flow of the book, but the actual sequence of events remains true and accurate. I beg my readers' indulgence of these alterations, for they were made with their reading pleasure in mind.

In addition, there are various accounts of the Second World War, and, almost inevitably perhaps, discrepancies among historians' versions of certain incidents in matters such as dates, locations, and the troops involved. An important case in point is the precise date of the Slonim massacre, which still remains unclear, as does whether my father witnessed the massacre, as reflected in this book. I also encountered inconsistencies in the recollections of some individuals who were direct witnesses to the events. Furthermore, there were considerable variations in the spelling of place-names. In the interest of clarity and consistency, I have adhered to one version at all times.

I have done my best to navigate these discrepancies throughout.

North-central eastern Europe.

THE MASCOT

PART I

CHAPTER ONE
THIS IS ALL THAT I KNOW

I f I'm ever asked, "What's your father like?" a simple answer always escapes me.

Even though I can look back on a lifetime spent in his company, I have never been able to take his measure: One part of him is a shy, brooding Russian peasant who shows a certain air of naïveté, if not gullibility, with strangers. Then there is another side: alert, highly gregarious, and astonishingly worldly.

His unexpected appearance on my doorstep in Oxford one May afternoon in 1997 left me more mystified than ever.

I was walking back to my digs, weighed down by books that I'd just bought at Blackwell's bookshop. I was looking forward to getting home and immersing myself in a new purchase, the door of my study closed to the world for several hours.

As I let myself in I noticed a scrap of paper that had been slipped under the door. It was the stub of a boarding pass for a flight from Melbourne. Written on its margin was "OVER AT DAPHNES DAD."

I immediately recognized my father's handwriting: he wrote only in capital letters and without any punctuation. He had always formed his sentences like this; he'd grown up in eastern Europe during the Second World War and had had no formal schooling.

I was taken aback. I had spoken to my father on the phone only a couple of days earlier. He had been at home in Melbourne, watching television with my mother, and when I had asked how their week had been, all he would say was, "Oh, it's been the same as usual here, son. Nothing much happens in this neck of the woods."

His tone had not altered in the slightest nor had his voice missed a beat when I asked what they were planning for the coming week: "No plans, really."

At that moment a slight clicking sound indicated that he had just turned on the speakerphone so that my mother could join in the conversation. He did this every time I called.

The three of us chatted on the phone for some time about things that had happened during the past week in Oxford, where I was a research student. We touched upon my plans to visit Tokyo—where I'd be for about four months, conducting research on a *matsuri*, or ritual festival—in about a month's time.

My father didn't have much to say about this, so the conversation drifted into silence. While he and my mother were always supportive of my path in life, the intense connection I'd always felt toward the culture and history of Japan slightly baffled them: it had become something of a family legend that as a child I would insist on dressing up as a miniature samurai before going to the corner shop to buy the milk and bread.

I promised to call my parents again before my departure. Then, just as I was hanging up, I heard my father give a nervous little cough. This was often a sign that something was troubling him. I hesitated, but before I could ask him if all was well he had put the phone back on the hook. Throughout our conversation he'd given no other indication of the dramatic scenario that was forming in his mind.

My eyes fixed on the note again: "OVER AT DAPHNES DAD." Although it had to be true, I still couldn't quite believe that my father was here, and I felt a rising unease. What was he doing here? Ever since I'd been a student at Oxford I'd wanted him and my mother to visit me. My mother had been keen to do so but had always been held back by my father's reluctance: he hadn't been back to Europe since leaving in 1949 and was adamant that he didn't have the slightest interest in returning.

"That's the past," he'd insist fiercely, "there's nothing there for me. Australia's my home now."

As I was growing up, he often made such assertions, but none of us, family or friends, ever gave them much thought. We never asked him why he felt this way, and he never volunteered any particular explanation. Just like him, we were absorbed in the business of living in the bright and healthy sunshine of the "lucky country," as it was so often called.

I made my way over to Daphne's. Daphne was my elderly neighbor from across the street, and she must have been peeping through the curtains in her front room, because the door opened gently before I'd even knocked on it. She stood wide-eyed on her front step and pointed excitedly toward the back of her house. "It's your father!" she said, seemingly as astonished as I was. "But he seems to be nodding off," she whispered. "Come in quietly."

Daphne led me down the narrow hallway and opened the door to her living room. From the doorway I could see my father, his legs stretched out in front of him and his head resting against the wing of the chair so that his eyes were concealed from view. His arms were folded across the small brown case sitting on his lap.

I tiptoed farther into the room and whispered a thank-you to Daphne for taking my father in and looking after him. We'd been facing away from my father to avoid disturbing him. But from behind me I heard him stir, and I felt his eyes on me. I turned around. He had raised his head slightly and fixed his strong blue eyes on me with curiosity. I took in his familiar impish features: his arched eyebrows and his high and rosy cheeks gave him a permanently mischievous air. But I was struck by something else—it was as if I'd captured his image in a photograph and glimpsed an aura of sadness. But this quickly sank beneath the surface of his mobile features.

I can't pretend that I wasn't alarmed by his impetuousness, but his presence didn't entirely surprise me. Over the years, I'd become accustomed to his highly impulsive and quixotic nature. He often made decisions on the spur of the moment without much regard for our likes or dislikes.

"Marky!" my father exclaimed warmly.

"Dad?"

"Open your ears. Daphne offered you a drink."

I wanted to start questioning my father there and then. But I didn't want to make a fuss in front of Daphne, who seemed to have sensed that I was thrown by my father's appearance. She cut in with her own effort to keep the atmosphere calm. "Let's have a beer. A Foster's," she said cheerfully, then added, "mate!" That ubiquitous Aussie term of affection made my father and I both smile despite the fact that I rarely thought of myself as an Aussie. Not only was I not a blond, blue-eyed surfer boy, or a "footy" player, but my years in schools away from the sunburnt country had left my body with an academic pallor.

"To Melbourne!" Daphne toasted.

"To Melbourne," my father responded with a sheepish grin in my direction.

It was early evening before we finally made our way back across the street. In the half-light I fumbled with the door key while my father waited patiently behind me, coughing.

The door open, I turned to help him. I reached down to the small, battered brown case beside him, but his hand shot out immediately, snatching the case from my grasp. "Let me take that," he said emphatically.

He had always been protective of his case—it was an unstated rule that nobody apart from him should ever lay hands upon it. He took it with him everywhere, clasping it so closely under his arm it might have been grafted to his rib cage.

It was all he'd brought with him from Europe at the end of the Second World War. In it he carried his few meager belongings: mementos from his childhood in Russia and Latvia.

For as long as I could remember the case had been a feature of our family life. Although we knew that it contained photographs, documents, and other remnants of his past, none of us had ever been allowed to see inside it. Instead we'd have to wait until he decided to display its contents to us. My mother would sometimes chide him for his secretiveness, exclaiming, "For God's sake, Alex, you guard it as if it's Fort Knox! What have you got in there, the Crown Jewels?"

When he was at home, my father invariably kept the locked case in the bottom of his wardrobe, hidden beneath my Catholic mother's family Bible to give it extra and somewhat superstitious security. He kept the keys to the case in his pocket and out of the reach of me and my brothers, Martin and Andrew, at all times. Of course, his air of mystery gave the case an almost totemic power over our imaginations that was never more strongly felt than when my father decided to tell us a story from his past, using the case as a prop.

Once or twice a month, after my mother had done the dinner dishes and we had all settled down in front of the "telly," absorbed in some police drama or thriller, my father would take up his position on the floor in front of the fireplace—regardless of the season—and my mother would sit in her armchair close to the hearth. It always seemed as if the deepening silence among us as we became absorbed in the "idiot box," as my mother liked to call it, created in my father the urge to assert himself as the center of the household. He seemed to be tacitly saying, "I have a much better story to tell than the one you're watching now."

He would become visibly restless, raising his head slightly as if he were straining to hear something. Then his eyes would begin to dart about the room, unfocused, as if he were staring into another world, quite spellbound by what he saw there. Above all, it was his slight, barely audible clearing of the throat, as if he were struggling to release his trapped voice, that would alert us all to what was coming.

He would rise from the floor and disappear from the room while we silently prepared ourselves for his return. With a nod from our mother, one of us would turn off the television. Even if we'd been on the point of learning who the villain was in *Homicide* or *Consider Your Verdict*—our favorites—we never uttered a word of protest. We were all much more riveted by what was coming.

If we were lucky, my mother would even pass us each a small bar of chocolate. Fidgeting and wiggling about on the couch, my brothers and I would wait impatiently for our father's return, case in hand, some moments later. He would place it gently on the floor in the center of the room. With a small flourish he would draw out a photograph or a document creased and frayed around the edges and yellow with age. Then he would abruptly close the lid on the case, placing the selected item on top.

Whatever he chose was used as a prop around which he would weave a tale about his life during the war or, more frequently, about his adventures on freight trains in the Australian outback or with a traveling circus in the 1950s. As the story unfolded, we would sit in rapt attention, licking our chocolate bars. From time to time he would reach back into the case to fetch another memento and would slowly turn it over as if doing a conjuring trick. Like a magician plucking one rabbit after another in quick, precisely timed succession from his hat, my father never had to lower his eyes to locate his next prop. He would draw out each one as if by divination. We were always enchanted by his stories and the artful way he related to his battered old case.

Apart from his love for eastern European foods, the case seemed to provide my father with his only connection to his past—the only one he seemed to want. From the moment he'd set foot on Australian soil in December 1949, my father had embarked with unabashed enthusiasm on his journey toward becoming an authentic Aussie—dinky-di—through and through. Quickly he came to believe he was one: for example, if someone cut him off when he was driving, he would curse the "bloody new Australian" driver, forgetting that he himself—cursing in broken English with his thick Russian accent—was pretty far removed from being "true blue" in the minds of many Anglos.

My father's love for Australia extended far beyond the footy, and it was rare that anything ever compared favorably to the place he had called home since his arrival as a refugee on board a ship called *Nelly*. He even carried a photo of the *Nelly* in his wallet as a measure of his attachment, five decades later, to the vessel that had ferried him away from war-torn Europe to the haven of Australia.

"From the moment they set foot in Australia," he would say, "people are free to be who they are, without persecution, and to make something of themselves." Then, raising his eyes to the heavens theatrically, he'd exclaim, "Why on earth would I want to go back to Russia? The poverty, the weather. God forbid! You'd have to be crazy!"

He would put himself forward as an example: "Look at me. If I'd not come to Australia I'd be stuck in a freezing field somewhere in the middle of nowhere in Russia, looking after pigs. Here, I've built up my own business." His tone was not boastful but rather grateful. To him, his adopted country was the "best little place on earth." I'd always admired my father's attitude, but it set him apart from many of my friends' immigrant parents, who would often complain about how much better life had been back in the mother country.

The outer western suburbs of Melbourne where I grew up were predominantly immigrant areas populated by Italian, Maltese, and Greek families, among others, and many of them seemed dominated by

The *Nelly*, which brought my father to Australia in late 1949.

a longing to return to their homeland. They would cling tenaciously to their own language, even as it began to atrophy, and use just enough English to make themselves understood. They would surround themselves with clothing, foods, religions, and customs that helped keep their pre-émigré world alive.

Not my father. He never showed any interest at all in his Russian origins, and because he didn't, we didn't, either.

Despite my father's determination to be an Aussie in every sense of the word, we didn't bond over footy or any other sport or "mateship" rituals that would have been typical of a father-son relationship in Australia in the 1970s. Rather, it was the image of my father with his case that created a bond between us. Whenever I picture my father in my mind's eye, he is invariably holding the case. Yet I still hadn't seen inside it.

I reached across and picked up, instead of his case, the small travel bag at his feet, the type that you would take for a weekend break, not a trek

Our house in Altona.

halfway around the world. We made our way down the dark corridor and into my tiny living room. My father remained standing, taking in his surroundings.

"So this is where you live," he declared rhetorically. "Small," he added, raising his eyebrows melodramatically, "like a cave or a bunker." Then he declaimed, glowing at the thought, "Not sunny like Australia."

I observed him as he stood there in the half-light of my living room. His features had suddenly crumpled, and he seemed tired from the long flight.

"Dad," I said as gently as I could, "do you feel like talking about this at all?"

"About what?"

The question provoked him to shift away from me to the other end of the room, where he began to examine the prints on the walls and the Japanese porcelain arranged on the mantelpiece.

"What do you think, Dad?" I said, baffled. "Why you're here, of course."

"What's the matter with you?" he retorted innocently. "I told you I would visit you one day. To see what kind of life my number one son has made for himself."

He stopped at the window, peering out at the small rear courtyard. Mollified a fraction, all I could manage was, "A bit of advance warning would have been nice, Dad."

"How much notice do you need?" he said lightly. "I won't take up much space."

Space wasn't the issue, of course, but it was clear he wouldn't harbor any further discussion about his sudden appearance. He turned toward me, and, for the first time, I noticed a gaping hole where his front tooth should have been.

"Your tooth!" I said, pointing to the gap.

"It fell out on the way here. Somewhere over India, I think," he said, "but the rest of me got here okay."

Despite his glib remark, the gap made him seem vulnerable—wounded, even—and I was reluctant to push him for an answer.

Over supper in the kitchen he suddenly confessed to me that my mother had no idea that he was with me in Oxford. He had told her a "fib" about going to Sydney to see Otto, an old friend from the circus who was in poor health. My father said that he had promised to call my mother every day, and he was ready to do so now. I led him to the phone in the study but then immediately went to the living room, afraid that listening in would make me a collaborator in this unfathomable charade.

But my collusion was inevitable. Even as I waited in the other room I tried to avoid making noises that might betray my father's scheme to my mother. Through the partly opened door I could hear him chatting amiably with her, and I tried to keep track of their conversation.

"Yes, I'm okay, luv. The doctor said Otto will be fine. He just needs rest," I heard him say. "I think it would be better if I stayed here a few more days to keep him company, to get things organized for him."

The tone of my father's voice as he explained his plan to my mother sounded just as convincing as his words. In fact, I was sure my mother would have no doubts about the situation in Sydney; extending his visit to Otto would have seemed to her to be perfectly natural behavior for her husband. He was a caring person who over the years had always gone to great lengths to help his friends, often putting their needs before his own. Sensing this, my mother often complained that people were taking advantage of him, but he would always just shrug and say gently, "That might be so, luv, but don't be hard on them. Anyway, I'd rather be kind to someone, even if they don't deserve it, than turn my back on them."

I peeped into the room to see if my father was uneasy about having to lie to my mother. If he was, it was not obvious to me. He was casually moving around the study, still holding the handset and pretending to be in Otto's home. "Nah, between you and me," he whispered into the mouthpiece, "it's not much of a place, luv. Dark and dingy. Poor chap."

In the days that followed, my father seemed reluctant to move, as if, having reached Oxford, he was seeking refuge there and was content to lie low. We made occasional trips into town, wandering from college to college, as I pointed out places and objects of interest. My father was attentive, yet someone who knew him well, as I believed I did, would have noticed that he still seemed distracted, as if he had some unfinished business to address.

One evening toward the end of that week, we sat in silence over dinner. We had run out of small talk, and it was becoming increasingly difficult to skirt around the larger question of his entirely unexplained appearance in Oxford. The evasive dance we'd been doing all week was proving more and more difficult to sustain.

Out of the blue, he announced that he had decided to return to Australia the following evening. I was dumbfounded and found it hard to believe that the visit might now come to an end without my having the slightest understanding as to what had instigated it.

"So that's it then, Dad?"

"What?" He looked up at me, perplexed.

"You've made up your mind to go home? Just like that?"

"Well, I've got to go home sometime." He laughed. "Mum will be wondering what I'm up to in Sydney. That reminds me, I'd better check the weather there in case she asks me." He clicked his fingers at me. "Check in the newspaper for me, luv," he demanded.

I grunted in a halfhearted way, unsure whether even doing this small favor for my father was tantamount to complicity with him.

He always had affectionate names for me—"number one son" and "Marky" were his favorites—but often he would use the endearment "luv" quite casually and without conveying any of its usual cloying overtones. Despite these surface intimacies, however, I never felt that he was taking me into his confidence. He was a man who kept his own counsel.

"Go on," he pressed me.

I gave in and reached for the newspaper. Mystified, I decided that a change of scenery might have a salutary effect on us both and perhaps even help to break our odd impasse. Still partly hidden behind the broadsheet, I suggested that we spend his final day in London, at the end of which I would put him on the subway to Heathrow in time for his departure to Melbourne. He readily agreed and we began to make a plan that included having lunch at the Café Daquise, an old Polish restaurant in South Kensington known for its traditional eastern European food, which had always been my father's favorite.

During my childhood, my father would sometimes decline to join us as we sat down to our Australian meals of roast lamb or fish and chips, preferring instead dill pickles, rye bread, and—even now I shudder at its sight and smell—raw herring. I hoped that the Daquise might remind him of the cafés and delicatessens of Acland Street, one of the few places in Melbourne in the 1960s and '70s where he could indulge in these delicacies, the kind of world where he could relax.

As a child I used to love going to Acland Street with my father to buy cheesecake from one of its eastern European bakeries. I would stand next to him, holding his hand, as he stared into the front windows laden with pastries stacked high on display trays. One recollection came unexpectedly to mind. I had forgotten it completely, so I was a little perplexed at its sudden appearance. The memory seemed to have forced itself to the surface in order to point me toward an explanation for my father's visit.

On the occasion in question I had noticed him staring intently between gaps in the trays into the darker recesses of a pastry shop. I followed his gaze and saw that he was peering into a world I had never seen before: an exotic scene of somewhat alien-looking women, dressed to the nines, with vividly painted lips and exaggerated eyebrows. My father seemed captivated by their masklike faces and the studied and individual way in which they ate—their hands delicately poised, their fingers, laden with gold rings and bracelets, lightly touching their cheeks as they brought forks laden with moist cheesecake to their lips. In some way these women were afterimages of an arcane world that my father recognized and was enchanted with.

I suddenly remembered another incident from one of those visits to Acland Street. One day, as we stood before the window of a cake shop, I noticed that my father had become distracted by something reflected in the window. It was the image of a man behind us who was leaning on the hood of a car parked directly opposite. The man's arms were folded across his chest, and he gazed frankly, and with a friendly smile, at my father. I noticed that when his eyes met the man's my father seemed to freeze to the spot, even though the stranger continued to smile broadly, even giving my father a gentle wave. My father gripped my hand tightly and abruptly moved on, as if eager to escape from something. In retrospect, it seemed that even though the man did not know my father, he recognized something about him.

While my father was clearly attracted to these denizens of Acland Street, he also seemed to be slightly afraid of them. Sometimes I saw him cock his ear, sparrowlike, as if to listen for something. It was as if what he saw through the shopwindows were the landscape of another life, part of a web that threatened to ensnare him, as if he belonged to them and they to him.

CHAPTER TWO

THE HEMORRHAGE

The train into London was almost empty, and we found ourselves alone in our carriage. My father sipped his coffee and stared out at the measured English landscape. For a second I caught sight of his reflection in the carriage window and saw that he'd been staring at me, evaluating me. His expression softened when my eyes met his.

"You've done well, son. You're an educated man," he said. I felt a little embarrassed to see him beaming with such pride. It was not his habit to praise me or my brothers. I turned my head to look out the window, mumbling, "Thanks, Dad."

"I've never been to school, what with the war and things," he continued.

"But you told me you were at school in the displaced-persons camp outside Hamburg."

"Yeah, just for about a year. But I didn't learn one single thing. None of the teachers could control me—I was a little devil. I just wouldn't settle. I must have been restless from the war."

These comments had come out of the blue and without any obvious connection to our trip to London. I was intrigued because he had never been willing to discuss his schooling before, cursorily dismissing any questions we posed. But before I could engage him any further, he abruptly raised his newspaper and hid behind it, lowering it only when we had safely reached Paddington Station.

———

The sunlight was blinding as we emerged from the underground at South Kensington. It was not yet 11:00 a.m., and I hoped that the émigrés who usually settled themselves at the Daquise midmorning would by now be there in full force: drinking coffee, eating cheesecake, and chatting volubly. If we got there any later, the cacophony of eastern European languages, especially Polish and Russian, would be supplanted by the lunchtime rush of local office workers, and I wanted everything to be undilutedly nostalgic.

We made our way to the café. I stood back as I watched my father peer through the front window. He put on his glasses, perusing the posted menu.

"Look, Marky, they've got latkes as well! I'm starving. Let's eat," he declared as if he couldn't wait another moment. He gripped me by the elbow, trying to hasten me inside. "Open sesame," he chuckled with relish as he pushed open the door. We stepped across the threshold.

From her stool behind the cash register the matronly owner, precisely coiffed, cast a disdainful look at us. She raised her bulk from her stool just enough to pass menus across the counter in a desultory fashion. With a barely detectable nod, she indicated that we should sit wherever we could find a table. It was what I imagined a typical eastern European welcome to be, a sour melancholy passing for enthusiasm.

We settled in a corner at the rear of the café. My father looked around the room, taking in his surroundings. Customers sat huddled at tables, drinking coffee, gesticulating, seemingly engaged in debate. At other tables, men or women sat alone, smoking, staring into space, or immersed in foreign newspapers.

"God forbid. Where have you brought me, son?" he joked somewhat edgily.

"I thought you'd like it here, Dad. Just like Acland Street."

He smiled at me, seemingly touched by my consideration, then visibly relaxed. I noticed that he was guarding his battered case as closely as ever, and again I offered to take it.

"Give it to me, Dad. I'll put it against the wall behind me. Next to your weekend bag."

"It's fine here, son," he said, gently dismissing my fussing.

"C'mon, I'm not going to steal it or anything."

He shook his head emphatically. "It's more than my life is worth, your life, too," he declared. "It's your inheritance."

We both laughed, knowing that it was true: he really did have little else but his case to leave me.

"Is that all I'll get?" I shot back with mock disappointment.

He grinned at me. "Be grateful for whatever comes your way."

I signaled to the elderly waitress, who waddled over to take our order and gave a contemptuous snort in response to our indecisiveness. For an instant I feared that this unfriendly reception would dampen my father's interest in the surroundings, but I needn't have worried. He found her behavior amusing and stared after her, making light of her moodiness. "We must have got her on a good day," he whispered, a twinkle in his eyes.

Just as on our visits to Acland Street years ago, my father was alert to the sounds of the various eastern European languages he could hear around him—Polish, Russian, and even a smattering of Yiddish. He glanced over his shoulder, stretching to see who owned the voices. Clearing his throat, he turned back to me. The sounds seemed to have triggered something inside him.

"Before I went to Riga when I was a child . . ." he started.

"You mean when you were lost in the forest?"

"No. Even earlier than that," he said quietly.

"I thought you couldn't remember anything from that time?"

"There is something I remember." He paused for what seemed an inordinate amount of time. Then he leaned forward to confide in me. "I have these two words locked away inside of me. I've never forgotten them." Then he was silent. I waited.

"One is 'Koidanov,'" he said finally, "and the other is 'Panok.'" He repeated the words. "Panok. And Koidanov." Immediately after they left his lips, he seemed distracted by them.

"Are they the names of people? Places? What do they mean?"

He leaned even closer across the table toward me. Then he shook his head, grim-faced, and shrugged. "No idea." Then just as suddenly, he was energized by a thought: "But you know what I think, son? Those words are the key to who I was before the forest, before the Latvian soldiers . . ."

"When you were with your Russian pigherd parents?"

He fell silent, again seemingly lost in his thoughts. Then he said quietly, "If that's who I am."

"If that's who you are?" I blurted out sharply. "What on earth do you mean, Dad?" I shot him a questioning look, but his eyes darted around, avoiding mine. I tried another tack.

"You've remembered these words all your life?" I asked more gently. "Have you told anybody about them?"

He shook his head. He stared at his hands, which rested on the table.

"I can't understand that, Dad."

His head was slightly bowed, perhaps under the burden of what he had just revealed or in a vain attempt to deflect my line of questioning. But I persisted. "Why did you keep them secret?"

He gave a shrug, then abruptly pulled away from me, back to his side of the table. "It wasn't a secret," he said. "I just thought that there was nothing to say about them. I didn't know what they meant and I didn't know how I could find out what they were." He seemed exasperated by my puzzlement. "And besides," he smirked, "Mum and I were busy raising you three boys. I didn't have time to think about anything else."

I suddenly pictured my mother sitting alone in the living room in Melbourne. "Does Mum know about this?" I asked.

"I don't want her to know," my father said, "for the time being. I just don't want to worry her."

"Why tell me then? And why now?"

"I want you to do something for me, son." Though he tried to seem offhand there was an underlying note of urgency in his voice. "I want you to find out what these words mean."

He leaned further back in his chair, folding his arms in a gesture of finality, as if all he wanted me to do was to discover the significance of the words and not trouble myself with his reasons for keeping them secret.

"I want to know who I am. I want to know who my people are before I die," my father said. Leaning forward across the table again, he added pensively, "I want to place a flower on my mother's grave. Wherever that might be."

I fell silent. I was shocked.

"Please, son," he said, as if he needed to convince me.

While I was thrown by his request, unable to recall a time when he'd asked me so directly for my help, it went without saying that I would help him, even if what he wanted still seemed so vague. I pulled out a piece of paper. "Tell me how to spell the words—"

We were interrupted by the waitress who arrived with our meals and slapped the plates down on the table. We ate in silence, my father bent forward, as was his habit, with one arm curled around his plate, protecting the steaming cabbage rolls as he devoured them greedily.

I had lost my appetite, however, and thought about his brown case again. It was true that I saw the case, despite its battered exterior, as something filled with riches, and all the stories it contained, especially all the tales of my father's life since his arrival in Australia, as my inheritance. They were the kind of enchanting stories of human bravado that would make any child proud of his father. I felt more ambivalent about the stories of his childhood in Europe during the war. I could never get a clear picture of what had gone on because my father painted that time in the broadest of brushstrokes.

We enjoyed one particular story my father often told us more than the others, about the time he spent wandering alone in a dark, overgrown forest at the age of five or six when he had become separated from his parents, who were Russian pigherds. He could never remember how this had actually occurred, he said, but he always believed that the trauma of it, together with his time alone in the forest in the freezing winter— for weeks and perhaps even months—caused him to forget both his name and his origins.

My father told us that at night he would tie himself inside the forks of trees to survive the wolves, whose howling he could hear in the distance. As he sat high above the ground, shaking with cold, swinging his tiny legs, and waiting for the first light of dawn, he sometimes imagined that he could hear his mother's voice calling out to him. But he could never remember her words. This part of the story prompted our avid inquiries.

"Weren't you afraid, Daddy?" we would ask. "Could you see the wolves' eyes glowing in the dark?" He would dismiss any questions that suggested he'd been at all vulnerable and respond as if he'd always been brave, confident, and readily equipped for any contingency. "Nah, boys," he'd say, "I'd just make sure that I'd tied the knot tight enough."

As if by an agreed-upon formula, one of us would usually exclaim insistently, "But, Daddy, you must know where you come from. Everyone does!"

When he would deny that he did, it only made us more insistent. "You must know, Daddy!"

My mother was always very protective of my father, and she would usually step in at moments like these, when our naïveté made us ruthless and we pressed him too much. "Boys! Leave your father alone," she would insist gently. "Settle down now and let him get on with his story."

As the years passed and he retold this story, my mother, my brothers, and I all came to accept the ground rules he set: sit in silence and ask nothing. But in my imagination I would create my own childlike images of my father as a little boy, a Mowgli-like creature wide-eyed with fear, despite what he'd said about his courage, being chased down dark, twisting forest trails by some large, shadowy figure, possibly half-human, half-beast.

My father told us that the turning point in his life came when he was found by Latvian soldiers in a forest on the outskirts of a deserted village somewhere near the Russian border in 1942. They had fed him and tidied him up. It was then that two figures surfaced who would play important roles in his future. The first was Kārlis Lobe.

Lobe was the commander of the Latvian police brigade whose

soldiers had discovered my father and taken it upon themselves to give the boy a new name. They called him Uldis Kurzemnieks. Uldis was a common Latvian first name, much like John, and Kurzemnieks literally meant "one from Kurzeme." Kurzeme was a region in the west of Latvia from which many of the soldiers had come. (My father would abbreviate Uldis Kurzemnieks to Alex Kurzem to spare his fellow Australians the pain of pronouncing the tongue-twisting foreign name.)

Lobe later gave my father a false birthday, November 18, chosen for him because it commemorated Latvian National Day. Eventually he made another key decision about my father's life, arranging for him to be removed from the potential dangers of armed conflict at the front and taken to the safety of Riga and the home of a Latvian family called Dzenis, who ran a chocolate factory.

I looked around at the other tables in the Daquise, and the sight of many elderly European gentlemen of a certain bearing led me to reflect on my father's account of his life with Lobe. My father was always circumspect, even evasive, whenever I asked him about Lobe. His response never varied: "He was a good soldier. He was firm with me, but always fair." When I would try to draw him out further on Lobe's appearance in those days, he became dismissive: "He looked like a soldier. That's all. Nothing special." I could never get my father to say anything more than that, so over the years I came to picture Lobe as tall and upright, with an aristocratic, almost Prussian, manner. I formed a mental snapshot of Lobe holding my wildly laughing father, then a small boy, aloft in the air. Somehow this image became my own private expression of gratitude to the man who had "rescued" my father from the wolves. Now, having just learned of a new element to my father's past, I began to wonder what other revelations might follow.

After we left the Daquise we wandered the streets of South Kensington, slightly disoriented. It was just as well that we had no special plans for the remainder of the afternoon. It seemed as if the little crack that had appeared in the surface of my father's demeanor less than an hour ago had now somehow resealed itself. He was content to walk in silence, as was I.

Eventually we came to the underground tunnel that took us beneath Exhibition Road. Its tiles provided cool relief from the unusually stifling humidity of this late May afternoon. The tunnel was deserted, and as we moved into its deepest section, the sound of the overhead traffic became muted. In the stillness our footsteps echoed back at us. This had a disquieting effect on my father. The rat-a-tat of our steps made his body stiffen as if he'd heard something I could not.

Suddenly he stopped and stared at me.

"Something terrible happened," he said. I waited for what he was going to say next. He studied my face but then turned away from me and faced the wall. "No. Forget it," he said. "It's nothing, really."

"What do you mean, 'nothing'? You just said something terrible happened. What was terrible, Dad?"

He turned to face me again. "Forget it, son. You wouldn't understand."

I could see only his silhouette against the light from the other end of the tunnel. I moved closer to him. His face was pale and his features had become inexplicably gaunt. He breathed more heavily than usual, as if trying to expel some inner tension.

"It was terrible what they asked me to do!"

"Who are 'they'? What did they make you do?"

He was distracted by the sound of someone else entering the tunnel and stiffened again at the echo of approaching steps. I was baffled by his response and instinctively reached out to grasp his arm in an attempt to soothe his nerves. I was surprised by my own gesture: neither my father nor I were physically demonstrative with each other.

A man in a suit hurried past us, with his head down. My father gave him an embarrassed smile. We must have made a strange scene—two men standing in silence in the dark center of the tunnel.

By the time the figure had faded into the distance, my father seemed calmer. I could almost feel his heart slowing down. "Tell me, Dad," I said gently. "Are you in trouble? Is something the matter in Melbourne?"

He shook his head. "Nah, son. It's not worth worrying about. Just something that came into my mind. Out of nowhere." He repeated the words "out of nowhere" and then seemed genuinely perturbed by what he'd just blurted out, as if he'd given too much away.

"I won't force you, Dad," I persisted, "but if you feel like telling me . . ."

He stared at me with a blank face. Finally, he spoke. "C'mon, Marky, I feel like an ice cream. Where can we get one?"

He loved sweets and desserts, especially chocolate and ice cream, but I knew immediately that this abrupt change of topic was nothing more than a ploy to try to make light of what he had just said. Yet such was the force of his personality that I felt compelled to go along with the diversion.

"Let's get out of here," he said, taking charge. "This place makes me feel"—he clicked his fingers as he habitually did when he was trying to search for a word in English—"claustrophobic." He chuckled lightly at finding the right word so quickly. He put his arm around my shoulder affectionately—again uncharacteristically—and began to move us both toward the light at the far end of the tunnel.

We surfaced into the hubbub of the street above. My father, who had always had keen eyesight, spotted a gaudy, pink-striped ice-cream van farther down the road, and after queuing for his favorite— "Strawberry. I love strawberry"—we made our way to a park nearby. As we walked along I cast a furtive glance at him. His face lit up with child-like pleasure in his ice cream.

A small crowd had gathered in the park, enjoying the late-afternoon sun. We found a bench and silently observed the children playing on the grass nearby. My father must have quietly drawn his case onto his lap because suddenly, out of the corner of my eye, I noticed that he was fumbling in his pocket for something. He pulled out the well-worn key and inserted it into the case's lock. As always, he opened the case just wide enough for his hand to slip inside. He pulled out a flat envelope and carefully closed the lid of the case before passing the envelope to me.

"What's this?" I asked in a low voice.

"Something you should see, son."

I felt a sense of trepidation and hesitated to open it. As I made a move to do so, he suddenly snatched it back.

"On second thought, let me do it!" He opened the envelope and slowly withdrew a small photograph. He gripped it firmly, grimacing as if in pain.

I drew closer to him and gazed down at the photo. Although the image had discolored with age, it was relatively sharp. I saw a small boy no more than six or seven years old. Dressed in a military uniform that must have been made especially for him, he was posing proudly in front of a gaily decorated Christmas tree.

My eyes focused on the uniform, and for a moment I caught my breath. On the lapels and sleeves of the high-necked jacket the uniform bore the lightning insignia that identified the SS. The boy was a miniature version of the stereotypical Nazi one sees in war movies. It was my father.

I scanned the image of the boy-soldier, my father, beaming at the camera. What was my father doing dressed like this? What sort of people would let a child dress in this fashion? Who took this photograph? When was it taken? And why take a photograph like this? Myriad questions ran through my mind at once. Where was it taken? In Russia? In Latvia? Was it connected to Koidanov or Panok? It didn't make sense. My father had never mentioned being a soldier. Only a Boy Scout of sorts.

I began to move even closer to my father in order to scrutinize the details. But before I could, he abruptly shoved the photograph back into its innocent white envelope. He slid the envelope back into the brown case. "It's awful, son," was all he managed to say.

"Is this why you're here?" I asked. "Is that what you've been hedging around all week?"

He avoided my eyes. "It's a complicated story. We'll talk another time."

"Where did it come from, Dad?"

"It's from the war." He said nothing else.

The photograph my father showed me in London in 1997.

At that moment my feelings about the case, my so-called inheritance, shifted. I resented it and felt an inexplicable disgust toward it and even toward my father. I shrank away, wanting to escape from both. I wondered what else the case might contain. Was there something even darker, if that was possible, than what I had just seen? I found myself questioning how much he'd left out of the stories he'd been telling us all our lives. What hadn't he told me, or my mother, or my brothers about his childhood? I began to see the battered case as a Pandora's box: now that it had been truly opened, it might never be shut again. I couldn't help wondering whether he'd be quite as protective of it now that he had intimated what secrets it might contain.

It seems absurd now, but instead of pressing him further I looked around me, worried that someone nearby might have caught sight of the photograph and identified my father as the boy in it—or indeed observed any resemblance to me. But nobody had noticed anything. The family on the neighboring bench were chatting happily among themselves. I began to act as if nothing had happened. I glanced at my watch. The afternoon was almost gone. "C'mon, Dad, you've got a plane to catch. I'll take you to the subway."

I grasped his free hand and rose, barely giving him time to secure his case, and headed off in the direction of South Kensington station.

The platform was crowded with commuters. The train appeared suddenly.

The doors opened directly where we were standing and passengers began to pile out. I eased my father out of their way and to one side of the carriage doors. By now, his head had dropped forward, making him seem even more dispirited than before, almost lifeless. I feared saying anything at all to him, even a simple good-bye or a bland "Safe journey, Dad."

In a flash, however, his listlessness evaporated. Above the din of the platform he shouted at me breathlessly, "It was Lobe and Dzenis—something they wanted me to do years ago—Dzenis made me do it—Dzenis said, 'Tell everyone you saw nothing—that Lobe did nothing.' But it's not true! It's not true! I did see things."

The words spilled out of him in a torrent, as if some old scar tissue had burst open to reveal a festering wound.

"Dzenis told me that they had saved my life and now it was my turn to repay them. I didn't want to, but I felt that I had no choice. Dzenis had already written it, so I just signed it. I did wrong."

He was beside himself in a paroxysm of fear, anxiety, and shame, and yet he seemed driven by the need to speak.

A voice over the loudspeaker warned us to mind the closing doors.

"Dad, step back!" I shouted. But before I realized what was happening, he had grabbed his bags and squeezed through the doors as they slammed shut. We stood facing each other, separated by glass. My father's eyes were wide open, almost bulbous, as if he'd been starved of oxygen. He seemed to be in shock, astonished by his own involuntary outburst. I was appalled by his transformation but could do nothing. A railway guard's whistle warned me to back off for safety.

The train began to move away. I followed the carriage, breaking into a jog to keep pace with it. Through its window I saw my father find a seat and settle down, delicately nursing his case. As the train gathered speed, his carriage moved away from me. He raised his hand in a tentative farewell. For just an instant I glimpsed in him the boy in the uniform. Then the train was gone, swallowed up by the tunnel, leaving only the rattling of the tracks.

I remember very little of my return journey to Oxford. The train soon left behind the outer suburbs of London and began to weave its way through the countryside that I normally found so comforting. Now as the certainties of my life fell by the wayside, it seemed quite alien.

What had my father seen that he had not mentioned to our family before? What had the chocolate-factory manager Dzenis wanted my father to lie about? He had mentioned Lobe, but what was the lie about Lobe? It seemed from his sudden emotional convulsion that the roles Dzenis and Lobe played in my father's life were far more complex than I'd ever been led to believe. And, as much as I tried, I could not erase the image of that photograph from my mind's eye. I regretted that I hadn't had the presence of mind either to pull him back out of the carriage or to jump onto the train with him. And now, of course, there was no way that I could persuade my father to explain himself.

When I reached home, I headed straight to bed, curling up fetuslike under the covers, feeling vulnerable and exposed by the bewildering events of the afternoon. Yet sleep eluded me as I imagined my father at this moment. He would be airborne by now. I pictured him perched upright in his cramped airplane seat, still nursing his case, many of whose secrets I now suspected had tormented him for most of his life.

It dawned on me that I was losing my father and would never have him back again in the same way that I had always known him. As Dad. The comfort and safety that this term of affection had supplied throughout my life had suddenly been undermined, as if the family nest with its familiar twigs and eggs had been scattered to the four winds.

CHAPTER THREE
EARTH TREMORS

fter my father had returned to Australia, I held back from calling him until he'd been home for nearly a week.

As I dialed my parents' number, I wondered if by now he would have confessed to my mother where he'd really been and imagined he might now explain to me his cryptic outbursts. I couldn't have been more wrong.

When he answered the phone, my father greeted me in his usual fashion, almost immediately turning on the speakerphone so that my mother could listen in. Jovial and relaxed, he asked me what I had been up to and how my week had been, careful not to indicate that he had been with me only days earlier. Clearly he'd been maintaining the charade with my mother.

When I put the phone down, I realized that he hadn't imparted a single piece of information, certainly nothing that related to the dramatic climax of his visit.

Two weeks after my father's visit, I had spoken with him two or three times, yet he still acted as if nothing had happened. On one occasion he even affectionately echoed my mother's oft-repeated question: "When are you coming home for a visit, Marky? It's been ages since we've seen you."

I decided to take matters into my own hands. I called a travel agent and booked a flight for the following evening to Melbourne. My research trip to Tokyo would have to wait.

My father was waiting for me in the arrivals terminal at Melbourne airport. We were both bleary-eyed—me from the journey, which had taken nearly twenty-four hours, and my father from having to rise so early to meet my 5:00 a.m. flight. But he bore no other sign of surprise at my unexpected arrival. I suspected that he knew why I was there.

I hadn't seen my father in just over three weeks, since his brief visit to Oxford. I felt very strange to be in his actual physical presence, self-conscious and even a little ashamed, as if my arrival was a demand for access to his secrets. But I also felt that what had transpired in Oxford and London had been a tentative invitation to be his companion. To the outsider my father may have seemed emotionally intense—paradoxically making him appear gruff rather than sensitive at times—but I had gotten used to it. He did want to express his emotions, but they seemed trapped. He said, "What are you doing here, son?" then stretched out his hand to shake mine while I opened my arms to embrace him, bungling our greeting.

"What are you doing?" my father exclaimed, attempting to smooth over the awkwardness. "Trying to push me over or something?"

With that, he grabbed my luggage and headed for the parking lot, with me following behind, benumbed and disoriented. It took me several moments to notice the familiar scent of the pungent eucalyptus trees, the dawn chorus of birds—kookaburras, rosellas, wild parrots, the slightly ungainly pink and gray galahs that often thumped into trees for no reason—and the vast high Australian sky. I gave an involuntary shiver.

We drove home in silence. Somehow the incident on the subway in London had become the lodestone of our relationship, and until it was mentioned we wouldn't have much to say to each other.

I rolled down the window and stared out at the passing landscape of sprawling suburbs, built when the Australian dream—the triple-fronted brick house nestled on a quarter-acre plot—was in full bloom. The "brick veneers," as they were called, dominated either side of the freeway. Even as a child I knew I didn't ever want to live in one, though I had envied their atmosphere of proper Englishness. They all seemed so quiet and ordered compared to the chaos of my own arid childhood suburb, Altona, in the west. Altona was in essence a vast, open volcanic plain, full of dry scrub and tiger snakes, on which were dotted little pockets of newly built homes, some still incomplete, with dry, weedy gardens. When I was growing up, the roads were largely unpaved and the sewage was not yet connected, so the inhabitants would have to wait for the "dunny man" who came weekly to change over the smelly metal toilet tanks.

Altona was the site of the city's petroleum industry and had been named after the German Altona, a sister oil town in Germany. The town surrounding the industrial complexes had been built to support the factories.

As we drove, my father drew my attention to some new buildings under construction. "Melbourne's really coming on, isn't it?" he said, obviously searching for a neutral topic. I didn't respond but instead gazed at his profile, which was reflected next to me in the passenger window. I saw him turn his head briefly in my direction before facing the road again.

As he turned into the main artery leading into Altona and then into a smaller road that took us directly to our street, a familiar sight came into view—the oil refinery complex, with its spidery web of pipes rising high into the sky. A single flame burned continuously from the top of a slender pipe at its upper end and cast a thin glow over the houses that otherwise lay in the refinery's shadow.

When I was a child, this flame had always comforted me—like an Olympic torch or the eternal candle on a church altar—sending me off to sleep, safe in the knowledge that it was giving off its protective light. Sometimes, when I awoke during the night, I would raise my blinds and peer out of the window, just to make sure that it was still burning.

At the other end of our street lay the abattoirs, whose smell of freshly slaughtered carcasses added to the acidic taste of petroleum that regularly coated the inside of our mouths. Always upwind of our neighborhood, the stench would blow down and settle over the street by midmorning. Sometimes it was so bad you would have to cover your mouth and nose with a handkerchief.

We turned into the driveway and came to a stop. My mother was already standing on the front porch.

"Go and say hello to Mum," my father said, unlocking the trunk of the car. "I'll look after your bags."

"You didn't feel well enough to come to the airport, Mum?" I asked as I kissed her.

"Sorry, luv," was all my mother replied. She was not averse to complaining about her various aches and pains—her Irish stock was not a sturdy one—but now her stoic response made me think that something more serious may have been affecting her.

The house was full of familiar smells.

"I've got your breakfast on," she called across to me from the stove. "A full Aussie fry-up. How many snags do you want?"

"Two sausages are fine, Mum," I answered.

"Oh, you call them sausages now, do you?" she said, teasing me. "That's your posh Oxford way of talking, is it?"

I sat down at the kitchen table. After my father had taken my luggage through to my old bedroom at the back of the house, he joined us. He poured himself some coffee and sat down opposite me, pretending to immerse himself in the morning paper. My mother served me my breakfast and sat down beside me.

Just as she sat, my father rose, gulping down the remains of his coffee.

"Well," he announced gruffly. "Some of us have work to do. I'll be in the workshop if you need me."

"Workshop?" my mother snorted, winking at me conspiratorially. "Is that what you call it? It's a junk heap. He hasn't tidied it since the day we moved here in 1963."

He pretended not to have heard her and turned his back on us. "He's never gonna do it!" she silently mouthed across the table, shaking her head in a gesture of mock disgust. I laughed, suddenly pleased to be home.

A short while later, I took my breakfast dishes over to the sink where my mother was standing. I came up next to her, gazing with her into the backyard. We could see my father tinkering in his workshop, an old ramshackle garage that was literally falling down around him.

She began to wash my breakfast dishes. "It's a bit of a surprise," she said, "you coming home like this."

My mother expressed herself in her typical low-key fashion, but I felt her eyes intently examining me for clues.

I tried to shrug her off. "Things are a bit slow moving in Tokyo. My research won't begin for some time yet," I said, being deliberately vague. "Thought I'd come and see how me old mum and dad are."

My mother laughed lightly before her expression became serious. "Just as well you did," she murmured, looking down into the sink.

I shot my mother a questioning look, which she must have sensed.

"It's your father," she said. "I can't explain it at all. He's been in a strange mood the last few weeks. Ever since he went to see an old friend in Sydney."

"Any idea why?" I asked. I hated lying to my mother like this.

She shook her head. "He's not said a word. In fact, it almost seems like he doesn't want me here. He doesn't want to do anything, not even go out on Sundays." Sunday had always been their day together.

"Perhaps he'll talk to me," I said. "After all, I've come halfway across the world to visit."

My mother stopped what she was doing and seemed to reflect on my answer for some moments before responding.

"Give him time, luv," she said in a way that conveyed the modest wisdom I always associated with her. "In good time we'll learn what this is all about." Then she changed the subject. "You must be wrecked," she said. "Why don't you have a nap?"

When I awoke it was just before lunchtime. I lay on the bed staring at the ceiling. Everything was just as I had left it years earlier, when I had left home for the first time. I sensed that my mother had never given up hope that I would return permanently, and on every visit home she would always ask me at least once, "Do you ever think you'll come back home to live?"

I usually took this line of questioning as her test of my attachment to family life with them, but I wondered now if instead it betrayed a fear of being left alone with an unknown quantity. My mother was a highly intuitive woman—she knew something was wrong.

A light tap on the door roused me from my thoughts. My father poked his head in. "Lunch, son," he said and went away again.

I was acutely conscious of the fact that my father had avoided me all day. I wondered how I was going to broach the topic when he seemed so determined to remain silent.

Almost a week had passed since my return to Melbourne, and during that time my father and I had resumed the bizarre pas de deux of our time together in Oxford and London. But this time the dynamics of our choreography had subtly altered. He still set its terms, but now that we were under the same roof he could escape only as far as his workshop, and he couldn't stay there forever.

In the meantime, I spent my time catching up with my brothers, aunts, and old friends. Everybody was surprised by my unexpected visit, but I would just shrug in response to their probing. It was as if a bomb had been dropped into the midst of my family that had yet to explode. Only I knew about it, but couldn't warn them.

Pulling into the driveway late one night toward the end of my first week home, I noticed a faint light coming from the kitchen of the dark house. I let myself in quietly. I could hear my mother snoring gently along with her radio in the front bedroom. I was tiptoeing across the living room toward the kitchen to get a glass of water when I heard my father's nervous cough. I opened the door a fraction to see what he was up to.

My father was seated at the kitchen table. His reading glasses were perched on the end of his nose, and his head was bent down over his case. He was rummaging through it with the lid wide open, but from where I was standing I couldn't get a clear view of its contents.

For several moments I stood at the door, but he must have sensed my presence. He turned abruptly and caught me hovering there. He snapped the case shut and laid his arms across its lid protectively.

For a moment I was offended. It was as if I were an enemy threatening to intrude on his territory.

"How long have you been there?" he asked suspiciously.

"Only a moment," I replied.

He chose to accept my response, though I sensed that he suspected otherwise. "I didn't hear you come in," he said.

I walked over to the sink and poured myself a glass of water. "What are you still doing up at this hour?" I asked. "It's nearly one in the morning."

"Can't sleep," he said wearily.

I sat down opposite him.

"You're in late tonight," he said. He set his case casually on the floor next to him, trying to make it as inconspicuous as possible.

"What were you looking for just now?" I asked, nodding in the direction of the case on the floor.

My father stretched his arms above his head, feigning nonchalance as if the case were of little significance to him.

"Nothing," he answered casually, but his nervous cough betrayed him.

"Nothing?" I said evenly. "Always the same thing. Nothing!"

My father looked at me with sharp, appraising interest, but he didn't say a word. I was too tired to pursue a game of cat and mouse at this hour. I rose and walked over to the sink to deposit my empty glass. My back was still to him when I heard him mumble something. I turned around and saw that he had again brought his case to the table and was opening its lid.

"Sorry, Dad, I missed that," I said, approaching him as he began to rummage in the case.

"My identity paper," he said, looking up briefly.

"What do you want them for at this hour?" I asked.

He shrugged and unfolded the yellowing paper. "Uldis Kurzemnieks," he read.

"Don't forget—Alex Kurzem," I added.

He gave a bitter laugh. "I've got more names than most people, but I don't know my real name."

I nodded my head grimly. I decided to grasp the opportunity. "But you know who you were at least—a little pigherd boy," I said, suspecting since his outburst in London that this was not likely the case.

My father shook his head. "Not at all, son," he said. "Not at all."

"Tell me, Dad," I prodded gently.

"I wouldn't know where to begin," he said.

"Start anywhere," I almost pleaded. "I promised you in London that I would help you find out the significance of those words. But I need more to go on."

He looked up from the identity paper he still held in his hand. His face suddenly looked drawn. "But they are only pieces . . ." he said.

"Don't worry, Dad," I urged him.

"It was terrible." My father paused reflectively and then began in earnest. "It started during the night. We were in the kitchen. I was playing on the floor with my little brother. I can see my mother now. She was sitting quietly in the candlelight, watching us with a worried, shell-shocked look on her face. She was nursing my baby sister. Suddenly the door flew open and two soldiers stormed in, shouting crazily. They had truncheons. They began smashing up the place. My mother didn't make a sound, but my brother screamed. She must have been quick-witted because somehow she scooped us all up in her arms and dashed to a stool and sat down. She pushed my brother under her skirt and then I saw her thrust the baby under there as well. She tried to cover me with what was left of her skirt but there wasn't much space. Then things went quiet. They must have stopped smashing up the place. From where I was I heard the soldiers' footsteps coming closer and felt my mother freeze. I heard this thudding sound and every time I heard it, I felt my mother's body shake. They must have been hitting her over and over with their truncheons. She took all the blows. I just gripped the two little ones tightly, praying that they wouldn't make a sound.

"I must have blocked the rest out because the next thing I remember it was quiet again. Not a single sound. The soldiers had gone.

"At first I was too scared to come out. I just waited there, holding my brother and sister and gripping my mother's leg. Then I heard my mother whimpering softly.

"Slowly I put my head out from underneath her skirt. I put my head in her lap and gripped her tightly around her waist. I felt something strange on my forehead. It was wet. It ran down my cheek and trickled onto my lips. It was warm but I had no idea what it was.

"Then my mother moved. She got up from the stool, and I saw that her face was covered in blood. Then I understood what the sweet taste in my mouth had been. My mother's blood. I had tasted my mother's blood. But she seemed oblivious to her injury. The little ones were now screaming in fear and panic, and she took them both in her arms and tried to calm them. She began to sing to them.

"Suddenly I heard screams coming from our neighbors' homes and I ran to the door to see what was going on. But my mother called to me to stop and close the door. I tried to, but the door had been half torn from its hinges by the soldiers. I remember that rain was pouring in through the doorway and the wind was bitter."

I was struggling to grasp what my father was describing, but I didn't dare interrupt him.

"Later that night I was sitting in the kitchen alone. I remember looking at my feet swinging backward and forward. My mother was in the next room—just a small space divided off by a curtain—still singing to my little brother and baby sister. Try as she might, she couldn't calm them after what had happened; they hadn't eaten all day and were hungry. I remember that empty feeling, too, like rats gnawing at your insides."

"When did this happen to you?" I asked.

"I'm not sure," my father replied. "I guess I was about five, possibly going on six."

"What year did this happen, then?"

My father shook his head.

"Do you remember what time of the year?"

"Autumn? Perhaps it was early autumn. I have this vivid memory of leaves all over the ground.

"Finally," my father continued, "my brother and sister must have gone to sleep. I must have dozed off as well, right where I was, in the kitchen chair. When I opened my eyes, my mother was sitting opposite me in the dark. She was very quiet. I could only see her silhouette, but I felt her looking at me. She beckoned me over gently. She pulled me onto her lap, hugging me. She stroked my hair, over and over. I remember the rhythm of it, her fingers moving gently. Then she said, 'We are all going to die tomorrow.'"

My father fell silent. A moment or two later, he raised his eyes toward me, looking mystified.

"You know," he said slowly, "my mother called me by my name, she must have done so, but, for the life of me, I can't remember it. I can hear her voice speaking to me but I just can't hear my name."

"Do you remember any names at all? What about your family name?" I asked.

My father shook his head despondently.

"Your brother or sister, what about them?"

"No names. Nothing at all."

"How old were they?"

"They were younger than me. My little brother was just beginning to walk—he would toddle about. My sister was still a baby in my mother's arms." My father paused and a slight smile crossed his lips at the memory.

"My mother told me that I was the head of the house because my father had gone . . ."

"Where was your father?"

"He was dead."

"How did he die?"

"I don't know. My mother told me one day that he was dead. That's all I remember. I just have this vague impression of him not being there."

"When was this?"

"I'm not sure."

I was now growing slightly impatient with my father's inability to recollect all the details. He, too, seemed frustrated by the gaps in his memory.

"Let's go on," I suggested and then reminded him, "you were in the kitchen with your mother . . ."

My father began to speak slowly and meticulously. "My mother said to me that we would all die tomorrow."

"How did she know?" I asked, unnerved by the harshness of my tone.

"I have no idea. I only remember what she said to me. But I don't see why it's important how my mother knew."

My father seemed to retreat into his shell. Then, after some moments, he went on. "She said that I mustn't be afraid."

"But you must have been."

"I don't know how I felt. I suppose I didn't want to die. Of course, I didn't really know what death was. But I knew it was something bad. I'd seen my father kill chickens and things like that.

"My mother said that I must stay with her. She said I should help her with my little brother. She said that the soldiers would take us down the hill and not to be afraid. 'I will have the baby with me,' she said, 'so I want you to take your brother's hand and not let go. No matter what happens, stay beside me with your brother so he isn't frightened. Then when I tell you, just close your eyes and hold on to me. Don't be afraid.'

"My mother helped me into bed then. My brother was already asleep in the same bed. She sat on the edge of the bed and put a blanket over me. She bent down, kissed me on the cheek, and then, whispering gently, urged me to go to sleep. I watched her climb into her own bed with my baby sister. I think it must have been the moonlight coming through the window because I could see her silhouette cuddling the baby. I can see it now.

"I must have dropped off to sleep after that, because the next thing I remember was waking up. I opened my eyes. It was still dark outside. I could hear my mother's breathing across the room. I lay there and suddenly this thought came into my head—'I don't want to die'—as if someone were whispering it into my ear. I just didn't want to die like the chickens in the back garden. I didn't want anyone to wring my neck. And then I couldn't get rid of that thought until I did something about it."

My father's voice dropped to a whisper. "I got up as quietly as I could and got dressed. I walked across to my mother's bed. I looked down at her face. She was asleep. I didn't want to wake her. But I bent down and kissed her good-bye."

My father could now barely get the words out.

"I kissed my mother good-bye," my father said again, falling completely silent. After a moment he continued, "I went through the dark house and out of the door. I stood on the doorstep. I remember rain falling on top of me. There were big drops coming off the edge of the roof. It was dark . . ."

"You said just now that the moon was shining."

He looked at me as if my comment were absurd.

"Well, perhaps it had gone behind the clouds or something. But there was no light at all," he replied, and then continued unperturbed. "Nothing was moving. It was so quiet. I went down the back garden, past the apple tree that I always played in with my friend—"

"Do you remember his name?" I interrupted.

My father shook his head.

"I came to a fence at the back of the garden. I knew a way out. There was a loose plank that I would sneak through when no one was looking—coming and going from our house secretly. I began to climb through but suddenly I was trapped. Something was holding me back. I panicked. I thought that one of the soldiers had sneaked up behind me and grabbed me by the pants. I struggled alone, lashing out in the dark, and somehow I got myself free. When I was through onto the path on the other side I could tell that there had been no soldier there, only my fear. My pants had been caught in the fence.

"I was frightened. But then suddenly something came into my

mind—a safe place at the edge of the village, a field where I used to play with my friend. If I could get there first of all, then from there I could go on farther to the hill behind it where there were lots of trees. It must have been in my mind that I could hide there. I must have had my wits about me. And at that age! Hardly born!"

My father shook his head in a mixture of pride and disbelief.

"By day I knew all the pathways. But now I was like a blind man. I couldn't see anything. But somehow or other I got to the village hall. I remember seeing a movie there, a silent one. It might've been Charlie Chaplin, or the other person—Buster Keaton." He smiled nostalgically. "I remember being there with my friend, having an ice cream. My father must have given us some coins. They used to have dances there, too. All us kids would be there laughing at our parents' dancing!"

I was torn. This was likely the first time my father had ever shared these memories with anyone, and I wanted to hear more. But first I wanted to know what had happened that night.

My father seemed to have read my mind.

"After that I kept walking. It was only a couple of minutes from the village hall to the edge of the field. I knew I had to cross it to get to the hill and the trees. I was frightened then. It was the noise this time, not just the dark. I could hear someone crying. It was a woman. But I couldn't see where she was. I waited until she quieted. Then when I thought it was safe to do so, I started to walk across the field. It was tough because the rain was almost torrential. A couple of times I got stuck. I couldn't lift my feet and kept falling over in the mud. Then the rain stopped. I wasn't sure how far I'd got, but I mustn't have been as quiet as I thought I'd been, because suddenly I heard a groan as if I'd woken someone up. I froze to the spot. After some time—I am not sure how long I stood there—the groaning stopped. Slowly I took a step; there was no sound, so I began to take another one when all of a sudden a voice called out to me. 'You!' It was a woman's voice. I just stood there unable to move, like a statue.

"I was petrified. Then the woman spoke again. This time her voice was softer. 'Help me! I am over here!' I don't know why but I trusted the voice. I took a step to where it was coming from. And then I saw it. I could just make it out. An arm. Coming out of the ground. It was waving to me. I couldn't understand. How could an arm rise up out of the earth?

" 'Can you see my hand, boy? I can see you! Don't be frightened,' she said to me gently, just like my mother would. 'Come here!'

"I took another step toward the arm. And then another. I could hear her breathing heavily now. In and out. I kept my eyes on the arm. I put one foot in front of another when suddenly the arm disappeared as if it had been sucked back into the earth. I went closer to where I thought it had gone. Then you know what happened? It shot out of nowhere. It grabbed me by the wrist and yanked me forward. I was tumbling over, dragged down, sucked into the earth."

My father began to breathe heavily, slightly out of control, as if his memory had taken over and was forcing the words out of him. I made a move to help him, but he waved his hand to stop me.

"I was struggling, kicking and fighting," he said. "Suddenly I stopped falling. I was lying on top of someone. The lady."

"Terrifying," I said gently.

My father shifted his gaze slightly to look at me.

"No. It wasn't. It was beautiful. I was lying against her. She had her arm across me. She was so soft and warm. I could feel her breathing, her chest was rising and falling. She was like my mother. I don't know how long I lay there like that.

"I know that sounds strange now that I understand what was really going on. I was in a sort of big hole in the ground. And it wasn't only this lady and me. There were lots of other people there. Now that I was nearer to them I could also hear their groans and other squeaking, wheezing noises.

"I must have fallen asleep because the next thing I remember was her arm shaking me. She was crying, 'Wake up! Wake up!' She told me that I had to help her out of the hole. She told me to climb out first. I don't know how long it took me, but I got out in the end. Then she told me what to do.

"I lay on my stomach at the edge of the pit and stretched my arms out to her. I could just make out her hand in the darkness. I clasped it in my two hands, and when she told me to, I pulled as hard as I could. She tried to raise herself up as I tugged. But it was in vain. I wasn't strong enough.

"Then, without warning, the lady's arm went limp. She whispered to me in a weak voice, 'Leave me!' But I didn't want to. I had to help her.

"I don't know, perhaps I went crazy, I was tugging at her arm over and over, but it was limp. I realized much later that she had died there and then with me yanking stupidly at her. But then at that time I just didn't understand. I felt that I'd let her down; I didn't want to leave her alone but in the end I did. I just got up and ran. I didn't stop. I didn't look back."

Even now my father looked distressed by his inability to help this woman. I wanted to offer him words to ease his guilt. All I managed was a limp "What else could you have done, Dad?" before urging him to continue with his recollections. "Where did you run to?" I asked.

"There was a thin light now so it must have been around dawn. I ran up the hill and into the trees. I didn't know what to do. I just wandered among the clump of trees for some time. Eventually I found one that looked comfortable and curled up in a hollow in its roots.

"I must have fallen asleep because a terrifying noise woke me up. It was like a crack of thunder. Then I heard the sound of people screaming, shouting, crying out, women's and children's voices. I knew something dreadful was going on, but I had no idea.

"I was very quiet. I didn't want anyone to find me. I moved from tree to tree until I was near to the top of the hill and could see down to where I'd been with the lady and where the noises were coming from. I peeked around a tree trunk."

My father lowered his head, shaking it repeatedly. He seemed disconsolate and his voice got very quiet. "If only I hadn't looked."

He let out a deep sigh and shrugged. Finally he looked up. He squinted and spoke steadily, carefully.

"Blood was everywhere. And mud. And people, naked, in a big pit. Most were dead. But some of them must have still been alive, because the whole pit seemed to be moving; it was rising and falling like a wave.

"Then it dawned on me that's where I had been the night before. In the pit. Where I had slept with the lady. They must have killed some people the day before.

"There were soldiers everywhere with guns. They were making women and children stand in front of the pit. Then I heard the cracking noise again and all the people fell forward into the pit.

"The soldiers were killing them with their rifles, with their pistols. Later I understood what was going on, but I didn't get it at that time. All I knew beyond doubt was that what was happening was terrible. I must have been able to sense fear and terror."

"Who were these people?"

The expression on my father's face tightened as he tried to remember.

"People from the village. Some faces I knew. There was one man. I'm sure that he had come to our house. I remember sitting on his knee. He had this very long beard. His clothes had smelled musty. Then I saw this other lady, one of our neighbors. She would march up and down the street with her umbrella rain or shine. She was always telling off me and my friend, but she was nice, really. Sometimes she gave me a plum from her tree."

For just an instant my father seemed to recollect a happy moment from his childhood. "I remember," he said gently, as if caressing the pleasurable memory itself. The reverie dissolved in the next instant: "They just looked like ordinary people to me. But now I am sure they were Jewish."

At this point my father tensed his shoulders, as if bracing himself for an even more shocking revelation. His voice came out in a hoarse whisper.

"I could see the soldiers forcing more people down the hill using bayonets on the tips of their rifles. Then I saw that my mother, brother, and sister were among them, and other members of my family. I can't remember who they were, but I know I belonged to them somehow." My father looked ahead, transfixed by the memory.

"I wanted to call out to my mother; I wanted her to know where I was. I wanted to show her I was okay. But I was too far away from her. I wanted to go to her but somehow I knew that I couldn't. If I joined them, the same thing that was happening down the hill would happen to me."

He spoke these words as if he were hoping for some sort of absolution, a comforting word that might tell him that it was all right, that the situation would have made it impossible for him to do so. But I was mute with shock.

My father was pale. "I have this terrible impression from those moments. I don't know if it is memory, but what else could it be?" He hesitated.

"Go on," I urged him.

My father cleared his throat. "Well, while all this was going on I noticed other people from the village in the distance. I can see them now just as they were then. They were standing on the balconies of their houses. They seemed lighthearted, smoking and talking, some even laughing. I wanted to get them to do something to stop this. They just stood there, watching.

"I couldn't understand why they didn't help my mother, my brother, my sister, and all the other ones. I felt like I was burning up inside . . ." My father's face reddened now, as he seemed to relive his hopeless frustration.

"I saw my mother again. By then she was at the bottom of the hill. I could see her struggling to hold on to my brother. Then I remembered I'd promised to take my brother's hand. I felt guilty that I'd let my mother down."

My father maintained his matter-of-fact tone.

"The soldiers shot my mother. They put the bayonet into my brother and sister. I cried out and then bit my hand to stop myself. So that no one could hear my scream. I kept thinking, 'Don't let anyone hear you, or they'll do the same to you.'

"I saw it all," he said evenly. "All day. The shooting went on all day. I covered my ears to block out the noise. The horror went on and on. I believe I must have gone mad, coming in and out of consciousness."

An eerie stillness descended on my father, and he stared blankly into space for several moments. I realized that he'd never spoken about what he'd seen, and that while his manner seemed composed he was struggling to find the right words to describe the extermination of his family. Then he leaned forward in my direction.

"Sometimes I wished I'd died with them that day," he said. "Held my brother's hand like I'd promised my mother. Gone into the pit and died with them. Even now." The remorse and despondency in my father's voice shocked me, as did the revelation that he had lived with this guilt throughout his life.

His face betrayed his turmoil, and finally he asked, almost pleading, to stop for a moment.

I felt the same way. It was as if I had been transported from the safety of the family kitchen to a cold autumn morning in Russia more than fifty years before.

I filled the kettle at the sink and put it on the stove. I remained standing where I was, wanting to separate and reclaim myself from my father, who remained frozen on the other side of the room.

I placed a mug of tea on the table before him. He gulped from it so greedily that for a moment I was afraid that he might burn his throat, but the hot liquid revived him almost immediately. He stared at me resolutely and began to speak again.

"I was there all day, among the trees, watching what went on," he said, picking up where he had left off. "All the time I kept biting my hand, rocking back and forth like I was having a fit.

"I know it's frustrating," he said, "but I don't have any choice about what I can remember and when. My memories are here inside me like vipers inside my bones gnawing their way out."

My father had accurately read my concerns. Some of his memories were unnervingly acute while others were no more than vague impressions containing many gaps. Still, he was only a child at that time.

I looked at him now, suddenly shocked by the coolness of my appraisal: I still recognized him as my father even if I had never seen him in this state before. It was as if the face I had known all my life had been peeled back to reveal the unadorned man, the raw human being.

I glanced at the clock on the wall. It was after 2:00 a.m., but my father showed no signs of flagging. I waited for him to continue.

CHAPTER FOUR

INTERROGATED

When I woke up among the roots of the tree it was dark. I crawled back to the edge of the wood. The moon was out, so I could see back down to where"—he paused, lowering his voice—"it had all gone on.

"That place," he added pointedly, "was all covered up now, and I couldn't hear any sound. I didn't know what to do. I simply stood there. Then suddenly I heard a twig snap, and turned and ran back through the trees. On and on, away from my village—my home—I kept on running, too frightened to look back.

"It got colder and a heavy mist had descended to the level of my neck. I didn't want to be caught, so you know what I did? I crawled along under the mist. I couldn't see much, but I knew nobody would be able to see me, either."

My father seemed pleased by the recollection of his ingenuity.

"I was freezing. That's what I remember more than anything in those first days. I'd run away from home with only what I had on—short trousers and a jumper. I couldn't stop my entire body from shivering. Sometimes I had to grip my jaw to stop my teeth from chattering. My feet were really burning, as if the ice were eating into them."

I thought of my father's feet now. He was in his early sixties, and ever since I could remember his feet were gnarled and badly swollen, which doctors later attributed to the cold and damp of the forest penetrating his delicate child's bones.

"How long were you in this forest?"

"I have no idea. I was lost. I just wandered. Then I would fall asleep, wake up, scavenge for food, and go to sleep again."

"What kind of food did you eat?"

"Plums. Wild plums. Berries. I didn't know which ones were suitable. I ate them to fill the hole in my belly. Once or twice I ate poisonous ones and got so sick I thought I would die. I just lay on the ground, throwing up, and at those moments I couldn't have cared less who or what found me—bears, wolves, monsters. Then I would have to force myself to get up and keep walking.

"Not that the berries or the plums were ever enough. There were days when I couldn't find anything at all to eat, and I would chew on the sleeve of my jumper. That made me feel safe and helped me get off to sleep.

"It was not long before the first snow appeared. From then on I had to be careful about leaving trails of footprints. As the snow became heavier, I left the small paths that I had been following, and I went deeper into the forest where nobody would be able to spot my tracks so easily.

"I had to keep walking to stay as warm as I could, but I soon realized that I was going in circles. I came to the same cottage in a clearing more than once. I would peek at it from behind a tree. But I never approached it.

"Anyway, it turned out to be a good move to go deeper among the trees, because one day I had a great stroke of luck that saved my life.

"I was crawling on all fours through some undergrowth. I put my hand forward and it suddenly touched something: I immediately knew it was human. I jumped backward. I was petrified and panting with fear. I expected that whoever it was would grab me and that would be the end of me.

"I found a stick nearby. I crawled back through the bushes. I could see a man lying there. I wasn't sure if he was dead or alive.

"I reached out and poked him gently with the stick. He didn't move. I jabbed him again, harder this time and on his chest, but he didn't stir at all. That restored my courage. I stood above him. I could see he'd been a soldier. He was still in his uniform. There was a stream of blood coming out of his body. It was brown and congealed on top of the snow.

"I crouched down next to him. His eyes were closed. Then suddenly it crossed my mind that he might be like that lady stuck in the pit. You know, everyone must've thought she was dead, but she was alive.

"I commanded him in a loud voice, 'Wake up, mister, wake up!' so that I could be sure that he would hear me. When he didn't answer I was a hundred percent certain that he was dead.

"I sat down next to him. Despite the fact he was dead, I started talking to him. I hadn't spoken to anyone for a long time, and, well, he was better than nobody. I wanted to tell him what had happened to me. I told him those words I remembered, the ones that I told you: Koidanov and Panok. Even then they were already fixed in my mind. Perhaps my mother had drummed them into me, told me not to forget them—"

"Why would your mother say that to you?" I cut in. "If she thought that you were going to die, then why would she tell you to remember something?"

My father paused, looking puzzled. "I don't know," he said and then went quiet as if something were dawning on him for the first time.

"What's wrong?" I probed.

"Well," my father said, "what if somehow or other, my mother knew that I was going to escape?" He stared at me. "You know," he continued slowly, "she might've put me up to it."

"What do you mean?" I asked. "That's not what you said before."

"No, that's true," my father admitted. "I can't remember every detail of that night. But perhaps somehow because she knew what was going to happen the next day, she hoped that one of us—me—might stand some chance of getting away. It would have been impossible for her to escape with the two little ones. Perhaps she did say something to me, like 'Get away, son' or 'Go now while you can!'—something like that . . ."

We sat in silence. Then my father seemed to set aside the thought and, sipping on the dregs of his cold tea, returned to what he had just been describing.

"I started to examine the dead soldier more closely. I noticed his overcoat, and then I thought to myself, 'Take it! He doesn't need it!' I tugged away at it for ages. His arms were so heavy, but somehow or other I managed to get them out of the sleeves.

"The hardest part was getting the back of the coat from underneath him. He was a big man, and I had to keep pushing at him, trying to get him over onto his side and then to flip him over completely. But I had no luck since I kept falling over in the snow. I hunted around for a bigger stick and soon found one that I used like a lever. I pushed it under the soldier, and with all my might I managed to raise his body onto one side. And when it was raised high enough, I pushed my whole body against the soldier's back. Quick as a flash he'd rolled over facedown, and I'd freed the coat. I was exhausted and sat down, leaning against his side for quite a while.

"Then the real problem began," he went on. "I had to get the coat on. But it was so enormous that I could hardly lift it off the ground. Somehow I managed to get my arms into the sleeves. Of course, I couldn't see my hands and most of the coat was in the snow rather than on me. It was like a wedding dress where the back of it drags behind. But I didn't care. I eventually tied most of it round me with the belt it had. I was warm for the very first time.

"Then I thought, 'His boots! Take his boots!' The soldier had tied them up in such knots that my icy fingers couldn't get them undone. But finally I tugged them off and I took his socks, too. It was heaven having them on. They went up beyond my knees. The boots were far too big for me, too, but that didn't matter, either. The shoes I had left home in had almost fallen apart by then. I put my new boots on and wound the laces round and round my skinny ankles. I remember thinking that I looked like a clown with such big feet stretching out in front of me.

"There was one last thing: the soldier's cap to keep my ears warm. Lifting it off was the worst thing of all: I had to touch his face.

"When I put the cap on it sank down over my eyes so that everything went black for a moment. I pushed it back off my face and for the first time my head wasn't freezing cold."

My father gave a slight chuckle. "God knows what I looked like, paddling through the snow, half-buried in all that stuff. But only one thing I am certain of: that dead soldier saved my life."

"How could anyone survive this?" I wondered aloud, aghast at the picture my father was painting. He leaned forward.

"I can tell you about that," he said. "Don't think about survival, just survive. That's the answer. Once you start thinking, that's when the trouble starts."

"You were a very resourceful boy," I said.

My father nodded, grateful for my admiration.

"I was always alert to a noise, even the slightest one—the break of a twig, the rustle of some leaves. Anything could indicate danger. I had to be on guard every moment. It was when the sun started to go down that I would become most frightened. All sorts of sounds would start up in the forest. Things rustling in the undergrowth nearby. Wolves in the distance. A sound that still gives me goose bumps.

"I had to be quick-thinking. You know how I'd escape from them?" he asked me. Without waiting for a response he said, "I would climb as high up as I could in a tree and wedge myself into the fork of one of the branches. I had learned to climb our apple tree when I was little. Now I could climb any tree I wanted and the wolves were never able get me, even if I fell asleep!

"Again, I owed it all to that dead soldier. I'd use the belt from his overcoat—I'd wind it around my waist and then round and round the branch—so that I didn't fall down. I'd wake with a start if I slumped forward too far or when the flaps of the coat had fallen open and I was too cold. Then I'd pull the coat around me and tighten the belt again to make sure that I didn't lose my balance.

"Sometimes I couldn't sleep at all. I could hear noises below me in the darkness. I'd wait patiently until the sun came up. It seemed as if daylight would never come."

As he spoke of being frightened, I formed a different picture of my father. This version had none of the bravado of his fireside tales.

"Those long nights would eventually turn into day when I could walk and scavenge, walk and scavenge, but then the dark would come back again. So that was my life and I owed it to that soldier"—he hesitated a moment and added—"and the other dead people I came across."

"There were others?" I cut in.

My father nodded.

"How many?"

My father shrugged. "Quite a few. Whenever I came across one—they were mostly men—there was always something good growing around them. Much later, when I was with the soldiers and the weather was warmer, I'd often find wild strawberries growing around or underneath the bodies. And they were the biggest, juiciest strawberries you would ever see! I guess the bodies fertilized the soil as they decomposed."

"Did you come across any living people?" I asked.

"Sometimes I did," my father replied. "There were occasions when I heard voices in the distance or the sound of footsteps on one of the paths nearby, but I'd move away as quickly and quietly as possible and hide in the undergrowth. They must've been peasants or woodsmen, I guess.

"But I did meet someone once. Properly. And that day my life was to change forever. I told you before that I was wandering in circles and that I kept coming across the same isolated cottage that I would watch from the safety of the trees. Well, one time I saw this old woman come out. She was a babushka all rigged out with her colored head scarf. I watched her as she gathered up some logs from a woodpile. Then she went back inside with them. I crept over to the window of her cottage. I was just tall enough to peep in. I could see that she was alone, cooking something in a big pot on the fire.

"I moved across to the door and I knocked. I was nearly mad from cold and hunger. Her face appeared at the window and she rushed to open the door immediately. I remember her words exactly.

" 'What in God's name?' she said. I stood there, shivering. But then she bent down and took my face in her hands. I hadn't felt anything like the touch of another human being in a long time. Certainly not one who was alive. Her hands were covered with hard calluses, but they were so warm.

'You're freezing!' she exclaimed. 'Come.' I allowed her to usher me in. She sat me down by the fire and began to rub me up and down vigorously.

" 'Whatever were you doing out there?' she asked. 'You must be starving,' she added. She prepared me some soup from the pot. I don't know how many bowls I ate. I just ate and ate. At one point she took the bowl away from me. 'That's enough,' she said. 'You'll be sick.'

"My reaction was terrible. I was like a wild animal. I growled at her and made a dive for the bowl, trying to snatch it back. I must have frightened her, because she took a few steps back. 'Have it your own way,' she said. Then she went to the other side of the room and sat down there, watching me. I calmed down eventually, and she slowly edged the stool closer to me until finally she was next to me again. I must have looked and smelled disgusting because I saw her flinch. She reached out her hand and touched my hair. She said that she would give me a wash. She took off my clothes and gave me a thorough wash down. I didn't mind. I can't tell you how happy I was at that moment.

"She put some old clothing on me and threw my rags into the fire. She made such a face as they burned. We had a struggle, though, about the overcoat and boots. She wanted to toss them into the flames. She didn't understand what they meant to me—they were my survival.

"She chased me round the cottage for them, that poor old babushka. I wasn't ever letting go of them." My father chuckled. "I wish I could see her again," he said. For the first time my father's eyes moistened slightly.

"So how long did you stay with her?" I asked.

"Only that one night. She'd settled me down on the floor near the fire, wrapped up in a thick woolen blanket. It was the first time I had felt this degree of warmth in such a long time. I felt myself nodding off, exhausted profoundly by all my time spent tied into trees. And then something happened that changed everything in a flash. The door flew open, and this enormous hulk of a man stormed in. I thought he was an ogre from a fairy tale that my mother had told me. He was filthy and smelly.

"He threw down the basket he was carrying and made a beeline for me. Before I knew what was happening, he'd grabbed me by both ears and dragged me out of the blanket. He lifted me off the floor so that my feet were dangling in midair. The pain in my ears was excruciating. I must have looked like a rag doll or a dead puppet.

"The babushka tried to intervene: she seized his arm, pleading with him to put me down, but he shouted at her violently. She retreated to the far corner of the room, looking worried and frightened. I heard him call her 'Mother,' and then I understood why he'd barged in—it was his home and he was in charge of it.

"Finally he released his grip on my ears, but I was still immobilized by his enormous hand tightly grasping me by the scruff of my neck. I was petrified and moved as far away from him as possible, despite his grip on me. He yanked me closer. 'So what have we got here? Let's get a good look at you!' He laughed out loud, looking me up and down very slowly and coldly, like a wild beast evaluating its prey. 'A little forest creature? No. We've got ourselves a little Jew here.'

"I knew I was in danger because his tone was so threatening. The babushka must have sensed it, too, because she chose that moment to put a big bowl of soup down on the table for her son. He grunted, and for a split second he was distracted.

"I knew I had to get out of there. I made a dash for the door. But he just reached out and grabbed me around the neck and then savagely kicked me across the room like I was a football. I lost consciousness.

"When I came to, the pain was so bad. There was this terrible ache in my hand. While I was out of it, he'd tied my hands together with rope and then tied the rope to the leg of the table. His feet, in big heavy boots, were resting on my back, pinning me to the floor. I tried to move to relieve the pressure, but he dug his heels into my back. 'Stay there,' he warned me. I did as I was told while he went on eating his soup.

"When he'd finished he undid the ropes and yanked me up by the arm. Then he lifted me into the air as if I were a rag doll and put me into his wooden basket. He tied me tightly in. I couldn't believe it. I struggled to free myself but it was pointless.

"He sat down by the fire and glared at me with a hideous smile. 'Tomorrow,' he said in a whisper, and then he indicated his throat being cut. I understood his meaning.

"When I woke before dawn I was still tied into the basket. I remained there silently, listening to the ogre's snores. I dozed on and off. The babushka was pottering by the fire.

"I saw her look furtively at her son. Reassured that he was still sleeping, she then moved nearer to me and slipped me a piece of bread. But he stirred at the next moment and, fearful of him, she snatched the bread away and retreated to her corner of the room.

"The son rose and then slung the basket with me still in it onto his back and set off from the cottage. As we moved away I saw the babushka's face at the cottage window. She waved to me and then with a somber expression she made the sign of the cross. I had no idea where we were going.

"By this time I'd been in the basket for hours. The pain was excruciating. I again struggled to free myself. He stopped, looked over his shoulder, and raised his hand, saying, 'Do you want this again?' I held my breath, even though I wanted to groan from the pain.

"After quite some time he stopped abruptly at a gate. We'd come to a small yard next to a tiny schoolhouse. It was dusty but there was a smattering of snow on the ground. He slung the basket down and untied me. The next thing I saw were people slumped against the rear wall. They were mainly men. Of all ages.

"A moment later I was able to take in the entire situation. On the opposite side of the yard there were about a dozen soldiers. Some were squatted down on the ground, smoking, laughing and joking among themselves, and swigging something from a big flagon.

"Another soldier appeared. His face was grim. He said something to the soldiers, but it was in a language I'd never heard before. The soldiers slowly got up.

"They all had rifles with bayonets. They began to line up. Two of them prodded the people by the wall with the tips of their bayonets, shouting and kicking at them. At that moment the babushka's son seized me around the waist, strode across the yard, and tossed me down in front of the soldiers. He laughed and said, 'Another one for you! From the forest.'

"I cowered before them. All I could see were the soldiers' boots. I waited, unsure what would happen to me, and then I decided—I don't know why—to raise my head up so I could get a clearer view of their faces.

"I was surrounded by them. Smiling, but not in a friendly way, they all stared down at me. One of them started to kick me, forcing me to crawl toward the wall to join the others. I sat beside an old man. I felt his arm go around my shoulder. He spoke the same language as me and told me not to be frightened.

"I held on to him. One of the soldiers ordered us all to stand up straight. Then another shouted an instruction and the other soldiers raised their guns. I knew what was to come next. I'd seen this before, in my village."

My father paused and then said, "I thought, 'I'm hungry. If I am about to die, then I want something to eat before that. I want to taste bread.'

"At that moment my eyes met the eyes of one of the soldiers, the one who appeared to be in charge. I broke away from the old man and I ran toward him, exclaiming defiantly, 'Bread! Give me bread!' I don't know what prompted me to do it—something much more than hunger, I suspect.

"One soldier hurtled toward me and roughly propelled me back into the line. The old man tried to pacify me, but something got into me. I dashed forward again. This time another soldier came at me, pointing a pistol at my head. Even now I'm sure he was going to shoot me, but before he could pull the trigger I heard the lead soldier shout out so that he lowered his weapon and the soldiers all lowered their rifles, too.

"A few of them began muttering among themselves, seemingly resentful because the lead soldier had intervened and they couldn't get on with the shooting.

"Instinctively I knew that I had to do something at that moment to make the atmosphere less tense. I stepped forward and thrust out my distended stomach to emphasize how hungry I was. To make sure they all understood, I started to mime eating a piece of bread, all the while chanting, 'Bread! Bread! Give me bread!'

"It must have looked comical because I saw the glimmer of a smile cross the lead soldier's face. I was scared but I trusted him. He had warm eyes. I started to think of him as the good soldier. Then some of the other soldiers burst out laughing. They were distracted by my jigging about. Out of the corner of my eye I noticed that some of the prisoners had begun to sidle away. I hoped they'd escape. But just then the good soldier noticed them, too. Immediately he fired his pistol in the air and everything went deadly quiet. The other soldiers rounded up the escapees.

"At that point, the good soldier took me by the wrist and led me across to the building. Even though I felt I would be safe in his hands, I still struggled against him, digging my heels into the ground. He yanked me even harder until we reached the entrance. Then he turned back to the soldiers and indicated that they should hurry up with their task.

"The good soldier pulled me farther into the schoolhouse and threw me down onto the floor. I kicked out at him wildly and he tried to slap me but I ducked. The soldier chuckled and then I began to laugh as well and this broke the tension. 'So, you want bread?' he asked me. He spoke to me in my language. I nodded.

"He pulled out a dirty cloth from his pocket and unwrapped it. It contained a piece of bread. He held it out to me. At that moment it was more precious than gold! I made a lunge for it and scampered away with it to the corner of the room, where I gnawed away at the rock-hard lump like a rat.

"The soldier tried to cajole me into parting with the bread. He stretched out his open hand to me, all the time staring me in the eye. I gripped it close to my chest. But one part of me trusted this soldier, so that eventually I passed him the bread. The soldier pretended to eat it, which drove me to spring up at him, trying desperately to rip it out of his hand, but he held me back at arm's length, dangling the bread in his other. Then the sound of his laughter made me realize that it was nothing more than a game, and my rage gave way to pleasure. I was giggling in a way that I had not done since I was with friends back in my village.

"The soldier tore the bread into morsels and passed them to me one by one, indicating that I should chew them more slowly. Then he passed me his flask and I took a big swig, thinking it was water. But it was alcoholic. It burned me up inside and I nearly passed out.

"Then all of a sudden there was a sound like a cracking of thunder. I'd heard this sound before: the day my family died. I was petrified and ran to the schoolhouse window, hoping to escape that way, but he dragged me firmly back across the room. 'Stay!' he barked angrily. I did as instructed and watched as he paced back and forth: something else was clearly bothering him. Suddenly he stopped and stared at me. I thought I was done for and that he had decided to take me outside to be shot.

"He came closer and grasped me by the shoulders, telling me to stand up straight. He crouched down beside me and slowly began to remove the rags that I had on. I flinched."

My father suddenly seemed shy and embarrassed.

"The soldier looked reluctant, but he indicated that I had to lower my pants. I did what I was told. He inspected me, only for a moment, then he turned away. I hastily covered myself. He kept his back to me but was shaking his head, saying, 'No good, no good, no good!' I looked inside my pants. 'What is no good?' I wondered.

"I knew something was seriously wrong, so I tried to copy the soldier's stern expression, just to make him laugh, but he wouldn't. My childish antics only seemed to fuel his annoyance so that he began shaking me and whispering harshly, 'No good. Stupid.'

"Slowly he calmed down. He sat down on an empty crate and lit up a cigarette. Then he pulled me onto his lap. He seemed to be considering something. This time I waited quietly.

"After several minutes he stood me up in front of him. He was grim-faced. 'Never let anyone look at you!' he warned me. He nodded his head in the direction of—you know—what's down below, and then shook his head sternly. Again he said, 'No good,' and then he held his pistol to his head, pressing the business end of it several times against his temple in order to rub in the point.

"I mimed holding a pistol to my head, with my other hand pointing at my groin, again wanting to believe it was all a game. The soldier finally had had enough of me and jerked me across to the window. He lifted me up so that I could see that the prisoners were now all lying on the ground.

"None of them moved and the soldiers were stumbling about among them, checking them for valuables. Then the good soldier turned his head and looked at me in this very forbidding way. It was then that I understood the seriousness of what he was warning me about—that this could be my fate, too, if anybody saw what was 'no good' about me.

"He told me to wait in the schoolhouse. When he left I heard him bar the door behind him. I dragged a stool to the window and watched as he rejoined the other soldiers, who quickly formed a circle around him.

"The good soldier seemed to be trying to convince the others about something. I saw him point to the schoolhouse. It dawned on me that he was talking about me.

"The soldiers were not happy and from where I was I could hear raised voices. They shook their heads vehemently and kicked at the ground, raising dust everywhere.

"The horrible soldier, the one who'd wanted to shoot me, broke away from the circle, spitting on the ground. Then another soldier joined him. I saw the good soldier quiet everyone down with his hand. He spoke again, and this time some of the soldiers nodded. They seemed to be coming round to whatever the good soldier was suggesting.

"I jumped to the floor and moved about the room, which was piled up with furniture. That's when I noticed something in the corner: an enormous crate. I decided to look inside. The lid was hard to lift, but I managed to shift it just enough to get a look inside. It was full of rifles. Without a moment's pause, I said to myself, 'I'll shoot them all. I'll work

out how to use the guns and then I'll shoot them all from the window!'"
My father seemed astonished by what he'd tried to do.

"I dragged one of the guns out of the crate and across to the window.
It weighed almost as much as me. I couldn't work out how to use it and
quickly gave up on the plan. I decided to snatch another peek from the
window. It was lucky I did because at that exact moment I saw the soldiers nodding and then the good soldier suddenly turned and headed
back toward the schoolhouse. I ducked quickly before anybody saw me
at the window and hurried to hide the gun behind the crate, but I wasn't
quick enough because just then the soldier came in. Fortunately, he had
no inkling of what I'd been planning and instead he told me that soon
he'd teach me how to take aim and shoot.

"With that, he lifted me up onto his shoulders and off we marched
back into the sunlight. We joined the other soldiers, who were now
swaggering about aimlessly. I was frightened by their drunkenness, and
even though I was now safely on the good soldier's shoulders I sensed
that some of the soldiers were uneasy about my presence.

"The horrible soldier scowled in my direction. Suddenly, he began
howling like a wolf, obviously to frighten me, which he did. A few of the
others joined in. It must have been the alcohol that turned them into
beasts.

"I was still perched on the good soldier's shoulders, and I could
sense that he was nervous. He took a stronger grip of my legs. He used
his free hand to reach for his pistol and suddenly fired a shot in the air.
Everybody went quiet. We were all motionless for what seemed like an
eternity.

"Then the good soldier looked around the circle of men, still brandishing his pistol. Nobody made a move against him, so he eventually
lowered it.

"The matter of my presence had been settled for the time being, but
I had no idea how long I would remain protected by the good soldier. I
must have come that close to death and knew I would have to be cautious
in the future. But for the moment I felt as if the good soldier had become
my guardian."

"Why do you think he did this?" I asked.

"Who knows. Perhaps I reminded him of another boy he knew. Perhaps he pitied me. After all, what decent person would let harm come to a child? He saw that I was a human being, even though I looked feral after all that time in the forest.

"Mind you, the soldiers weren't much different. They looked like they hadn't washed in ages. Some of them had green teeth, like moss was growing on them. But that was more than I had. Most of mine had dropped out by then."

My father returned to the scene in the schoolyard. "After that the soldiers gathered up their weapons and packs, and we set off in silence. As we did so, I glanced back at the prisoners lying dead. What was strange were the butterflies that had suddenly descended out of the sky in a swarm. I was hypnotized by how beautiful it all was."

"Beautiful?" I must have sounded slightly appalled, because my father quickly added, "Of course, I was sorry for them, especially the old man who'd tried to protect me, but they were dead. What could I do? I had to think about myself. For the first time I felt safe. No, that is not the right word. I also knew I had to be very, very careful, as the good soldier had warned me. I felt I had a chance to survive if it wasn't found out that I was circumcised. In those days it indicated you were Jewish." My father blushed.

"So you believe you are Jewish?" I asked.

My father nodded.

I wondered what that made my brothers and me. To what extent and in what way were we Jewish.

"Do you have any other memories of being Jewish?"

"I have one memory of a man, you know, like a priest with a long beard, coming to our house . . ."

"A rabbi?"

"Yes, that's it, a rabbi. He came for a ceremony that had something to do with my little brother. Perhaps a circumcision."

"Do you ever consider yourself to be Jewish?" I asked.

My father shrugged and looked slightly bewildered. "In truth I've never known what to call myself," he said, raising his eyes to the ceiling. "I was born Jewish. What happened to me happened because I was Jewish. But then the Latvians had me baptized a Lutheran. I am Russian, but all my life everybody has believed I'm a Latvian. God forbid!"

"So what happened after you went with the soldiers?" I asked, steering my father back to his memories. I did not want to surrender the intimacy of the darkened room.

"I was soon back in the forest," my father said. "I was still scared, but not in the way I was before. Of course, I was now worried that what was 'no good' about me would be discovered. All my old fears in the forest about wolves and things had been swept aside for a new and much darker one.

"That first night the soldiers made a camp with a fire. They sat around it, drinking. All the soldiers seemed hypnotized by the flames and the crackling of the fire. I sat quietly next to the good soldier, in fact I was almost cuddling him: I was hungry for human warmth. At one point I noticed the horrible soldier staring at me from the other side of the fire. He was smiling at me, but his eyes were hard. I looked away, pretending that our eyes hadn't met.

"But in truth I was quivering inside. I was desperate to stay alive and suddenly feared that now that the soldiers, even the good one, had had time to think about their decision to take me with them, the more uncomfortable they might begin to feel about it.

"My body must have been shaking as well because I then felt the good soldier's arm tighten around my shoulder. He hadn't noticed the stare of the horrible soldier and didn't understand what I feared. 'Cold,' he said, taking off his scarf and wrapping it around me.

"Sometime later, as I was nodding off, I heard the bad soldier call out. 'Hey boy,' he said. I roused myself and looked across at him. He was now sitting upright and looked alert. He called out to me again and this time beckoned me over.

"I had no idea what he would do to me, but I didn't want to make him angry in any way. I went over to him. I half-expected a slap from him since just the sight of me seemed to aggravate him. Instead, he pointed at his chest. 'Vezis,' he said and then repeated it. At first I didn't understand. Then it dawned on me; he was telling me his name. The bad soldier was called Vezis.

"Then the good soldier beckoned me back over to him. He pointed to himself and said, 'Kulis.' I immediately tried to pronounce it. 'Kulis. Kulis. Kulis,' I said, savoring it a bit. 'That's right!' he said, pleased. I felt as if I had done something wonderful. Then the others joined in. I went around the circle learning all their names. There was, let me see, Rozes, Upe, Ozols, and Dzintars.

"There were about three or four more soldiers whose names I can't recall. Kulis called for bread and alcohol, which they made me drink. It nearly knocked me out. 'Samagonka,' they called it: if you had just the right amount it was like an anesthetic."

"Did you tell them your name?"

"They kept pointing at me, showing me that they wanted to know who I was, but there was nothing that I could tell them. I couldn't remember my name.

"The soldiers talked among themselves for quite a while and then finally they seemed to agree on something. Sergeant Kulis stood me up before him and pointed to my chest, saying 'Uldis Kurzemnieks.' He ordered me to repeat it, but I found it hard to pronounce. Every time I mispronounced it they'd boisterously push at each other and slap each other on the back, laughing. That set me off. I did a little jig around the fire while chanting the words to a tune I made up as I went along. That's how I became Uldis Kurzemnieks.

"Exhausted, I flopped down and dropped off to sleep next to Sergeant Kulis. I woke up before dawn. The others were still asleep except for the sergeant. 'Hurry, get up,' he said to me. He had a small bucket in one hand and led me by the other into the surrounding woods. We came to a stream and he showed me how to collect water, which we took back to the camp. He showed me how to stoke the fire and prepare tea. By that time the others had stirred. I went around pouring tea into their mugs. One or two of them even tousled my hair and smiled at me. I realized I had a job and I could make myself useful.

"Later that morning, I learned how to collect kindling wood for the fire in the evening. The sergeant gave me a forage bag that I wore over my shoulder so that whenever I came across some wood I could collect it. I was a quick learner. I started to make myself more and more useful to the soldiers in those early days with them. After the sergeant had taught me about the water and the fire I could do it all alone. I would be up and about before all of them, preparing their tea. And I'd learned so much from my time alone in the forest that I would pick berries for them that they could eat safely. They were impressed with me. I became more certain that I had found my place in the group.

"I also picked up Latvian quickly. Whenever a soldier handled an object or saw me doing something, he would call across to me, naming it in Latvian, and I would repeat it until I remembered it perfectly.

"During daylight we moved through the forest. The soldiers were always on the hunt for *partizani*, they called them. I heard that word constantly, but for some time I had no idea what *partizani* was. We never seemed to see any.

"Then, no more than a few days after I'd been taken, Sergeant Kulis told me the troop was returning to base camp. 'S,' they all called it. Even though the babushka had tried to clean me up, I was still dirty and smelly when they captured me, but they hadn't paid much attention to that. Now, suddenly, Sergeant Kulis was obsessed with cleaning me up. He scrubbed my face and hands and combed my matted hair.

"Then he and the others tried to teach me how to march like a soldier, but of course I couldn't master that. I still had my clown boots on. They taught me how to salute and click my heels together, at the same time shouting my name, 'Uldis Kurzemnieks.' It felt silly but I knew that they were deadly serious about all this. In the end they were satisfied with my performance. One of the soldiers hoisted me onto his shoulders— they all took turns carrying me now and would even bicker with each other about whose turn it was—and off we went.

"We passed through a village en route to the base camp. There were a few people going about their business, but when we marched by they became very quiet. One man took a furtive look at us, and I could see that he was shocked by the sight of me, this little boy, marching along with the soldiers.

"Finally we reached base camp in a school on the outskirts of a village."

"Its name?" I asked.

"I remember 'S,' that's all," my father answered.

"You've forgotten it?"

"No. The soldiers only ever referred to it as 'S,' as if they were talking in code."

"Why would that have been?"

My father shrugged. "The base was where I met the commander of the unit for the first time. Sergeant Kulis took me to his office set up in a schoolroom in the main building. We stood outside the door for a moment. He leaned down, tidied my hair, and made me practice my salute and greeting one more time. Then he told me to wait there on the doorstep until I was summoned.

"As I stood there a few soldiers spotted me and called out, 'Hey! Kurzemnieks!' I had never seen them before, but obviously they'd already heard about the new member of their troop.

"Just then the door opened and Sergeant Kulis ordered me inside. Once I'd entered, I immediately clicked my boots together, saluted, and stated my name proudly. I stood at attention, waiting to hear a return greeting and to be dismissed. Instead I heard a roar of laughter. I dropped my pose and stared across the room. A man was seated behind a desk. As he stood up, I could see that he was a short man and a bit plump. He was wearing a uniform—it looked brand-new: sharply creased with shiny buttons and a high collar. But it was its color that hypnotized me. It was a gorgeous light blue like the color of the sky.

"The commander came around to my side of the desk. I saw that he wore black boots up to his knees. They shone like a mirror so that I could see myself reflected in them. He saluted me. Then he leaned against the edge of the desk and lit himself a cigarette. He smoked the cigarette slowly and sized me up through half-closed eyes. He was formidable. I could tell that he was important. 'Just be still and don't stare back,' I told myself. It was an instinctive reaction, but I felt that I didn't like him.

"After several moments he beckoned me closer. I flinched slightly.

"Sergeant Kulis must have sensed my hesitation. 'Hurry up!' he whispered in my ear, giving me a quick shove from behind. Now that I was closer, the commander made a grab for me and hoisted me up in midair so that I hovered above him. I stared straight ahead, still not meeting his gaze.

"'Little man,' he said directly to me so that I had to look down and meet his gaze. His eyes were like steel, even though he was smiling up at me. 'Do you know who I am?' he asked. I was surprised because he spoke my language perfectly. I shook my head. 'I am your commanding officer,' he said. 'Commander Lobe. Can you say that?' I remained hovering in midair as he made me repeat his name several times until I had mastered it perfectly."

"Commander Lobe? Remember when I went to Stockholm to meet him?" I asked.

"That's right," my father said.

I had gone in search of Commander Lobe in the early 1980s and found he was living in Stockholm. My intent was to thank him in person for his kindness toward my father during the war. However, my encounter with the commander and his wife had gone awry, and I left bewildered and disturbed by Lobe's terrifying behavior. I had never told my father exactly what transpired during that visit, but in light of his revelations to me now I began to understand why Lobe had reacted the way he did.

"Then finally he put me down on his couch in the corner of the room and sat down next to me. He produced a pencil from somewhere and twirled it around between two fingers before making it disappear. I was mesmerized by his magic trick. I lost all my reserve with him and tugged at his jacket, trying to find the missing pencil. 'Show me. Show me Commander Lobe,' I pleaded with him, hoping that if I pronounced his name perfectly again, he would let me in on his secret. And he did.

Slowly the pencil edged its way out of the sleeve of his jacket as if it were alive. And I laughed at how I'd been fooled.

"My attitude toward him changed for a moment. I was captivated, as if we shared a special bond. It felt nice. I can't find another word for it, just nice to be there on his lap feeling the warmth of his hug.

"Then he reached across for a piece of paper and wrote something down on it. Still cradling me on his lap, he pointed at what he'd written and said, 'Kurzemnieks.' He put the pencil into my hand, but I didn't know how to hold it. I'd never been to school, never learned to read or write. Commander Lobe was surprisingly gentle with me: he positioned the pencil in my hand and wrapped his hand around mine, trying to guide it to copy my name. He was patient with my clumsiness as I slowly began to master the first few letters.

"Then he indicated that I should try it by myself. I occupied myself with this—full of a desire to see both men pleased with my efforts and mastery—while they talked across me.

"As their conversation continued, I could tell that it had become serious and urgent. I kept my ears pricked, and even though it was in Latvian I got the gist of it; the sergeant was trying to convince Commander Lobe that I should stay with his troop.

"The commander listened closely to Sergeant Kulis's words. Sometimes his face looked doubtful, and at other times he smiled, nodding in agreement. Occasionally I could feel him staring into the back of my head, again coldly appraising me.

"Suddenly the commander slapped his thighs and gave me a tight squeeze around the waist. I sensed the sergeant's relief. Then the commander got up, and Sergeant Kulis indicated that I should salute again. I jumped to attention, determined to be the perfect soldier.

"The commander dismissed us from the room, and in my last glimpse of him that day I saw him reaching for the telephone on his desk with an absorbed look on his face.

"When we got outside, the sergeant lifted me onto his shoulders and galloped around the yard like a horse so that the other soldiers there also joined in making whooping noises until it reached a crescendo.

"I laughed out loud. I knew that something momentous had been decided—they were not going to line me up and shoot me—that Sergeant Kulis had been planning something for me and Commander Lobe had agreed to it. But at that stage I had no idea what it was that lay in store for me."

CHAPTER FIVE
THE SEDUCTION

I screamed the place down. The corporal—he was called Rozes—had lifted me into a metal tub full of icy-cold water and was trying to get my underpants off. I gripped them for dear life and firmly stood my ground, fending him off. I couldn't get Sergeant Kulis's warning out of my head. I went wild so that there was water splashed everywhere. I hated water. In the months in the forest I'd got used to living in my own filth. It made me feel secure"—he chuckled to himself—"and there was no way I was going to give up that little comfort. Eventually he got fed up with my antics. 'Very well,' he said. 'Have it your way. Leave them on!'"

My father was explaining an incident that had happened after Commander Lobe had decided to let him stay with the soldiers. His story had begun to take on momentum and I remained largely silent.

"I was covered in soap and shivering," he continued. "The corporal knelt beside the tub with his shirtsleeves rolled up and attempted to scrub me.

"Suddenly the door to the washroom flew open and Sergeant Kulis stormed in. 'Quiet down!' he snapped at me. 'The entire barracks can hear you.' Sergeant Kulis then dismissed Corporal Rozes, who seemed pleased not to be responsible for me anymore, and drew up a stool next to the washtub.

"I was still grimly gripping my wet underpants. He gave me a broad smile and then said, 'Good.'

"He lifted me out of the tub and began to dry me vigorously with a towel. I liked that. My body felt alive and tingling, just as when my mother dried me. For a moment I forgot everything, all the misery I'd experienced.

"Sergeant Kulis was happy and laughing, too, as he rubbed me down. Then he wrapped the towel around me.

"At that precise moment Commander Lobe entered. I hadn't seen him since the day he'd agreed to let me stay with the soldiers. He instantly noted my wet underpants. For a moment he seemed perplexed by the sight of me: he looked me up and down and was on the point of saying something when Sergeant Kulis suddenly leaped to attention in a very exaggerated way.

"I knew that the sergeant was trying to distract him, and it did the trick because Commander Lobe seemed to have a change of heart about me: he gave the sergeant a curious look, telling him to relax, and then turned to me. He gave me a broad smile and looked genuinely pleased to see me.

"The commander had a parcel under his arm. He told me that it was a gift for me. I followed him into the next room, where he set the package down.

"I removed the wrapping, then the lid. It was a pale blue jacket. Then it dawned on me that it was a uniform just like the soldiers' but in miniature. It was in the same color blue as theirs, with all the same flashes, buttons, and badges. Underneath it were shiny black boots and jodhpurs as well.

"The commander ordered me to put on the outfit there and then. It had been made especially for me and fitted perfectly.

"We struggled a little to get my swollen feet into the shiny black boots, but eventually we succeeded. I looked sleek and elegant. I was no longer a clown in my oversized boots and my overcoat. I had become a miniature version of Commander Lobe.

"Then the commander produced something else for me. It was a thick leather belt. He buckled it around my waist, and from his jacket he drew out a small, glistening pistol. He made a great show of placing it in a holster that was attached to my new belt. Then he stepped back from me, appraising me. I felt proud, but I was also uneasy about what he had turned me into. Deep down, I knew this was not me. The commander was pleased with what he saw and saluted me formally. When I tried to return the salute, I stumbled in the heavy uniform, belt, and pistol, which all together probably weighed more than I did. I felt like the awkward, clumsy boy I was and not the strong soldier I was pretending to be.

"Sergeant Kulis watched us from the doorway and as the commander led me over to a full-length mirror. I barely recognized myself. In fact, I had no memory of ever having seen my reflection before.

"The commander took a box camera from his military holdall and positioned me against the opposite wall. He made me pull my shoulders back and thrust my jaw forward into the air. I had to hold the pose while the camera clicked over and over. There was no satisfying him. 'Turn this way,' he told me, 'now turn that way.' The camera clicked some more. 'Take the gun out!' he ordered. 'Point it there! Stand nice and still!' More clicks! I was exhausted after all this.

"That night the soldiers took over a small café in a town nearby for a celebration. I was the guest of honor.

"I sat at the head of a long table on Sergeant Kulis's knee. The table was overflowing with food and drink, and the soldiers made sure that I had enough of everything I desired. Needless to say they all got drunk and high-spirited very quickly. They were singing patriotic songs—some non-sense about wild eagles flying over Latvia and the bears in the forest—and clapping and cheering loudly, disturbing the other customers."

"So on the one hand you loved being with these men, but on the other hand you thought they were fools?" I asked.

"Well, not fools then, just very strange. They weren't like any people I'd known before. They were . . ." My father raised his eyes to the ceiling as he sought out the word that would satisfy him. Then his face brightened. "Oafs. That's it! They were clumsy oafs.

"You say I loved being with them. That's not correct, either. I was grateful to them, and I had to be sure that they could see how grateful I was. I laughed and clapped with them.

"Commander Lobe arrived later and immediately snatched me off the sergeant and stood me up on the table. He made a toast to me, and the soldiers raised their glasses. They all looked up at me as if I were the most important person in their lives." My father broke into a smile. "So I did a little jig there and then on the tabletop, to please them. They clapped for me wildly, as if I were a star.

"Then the commander must have noticed that a customer at a neighboring table was watching me out of the corner of his eye. Not surprising, if you picture me there on the table dancing in my blue uniform. The commander said something harsh to the man, and the man quickly got up to leave. As he passed our table, the commander ordered him to stop and bow to me before letting the frightened man scurry away. I felt terrible—the commander's attitude was wrong. I knew that. But of course I couldn't utter a single word of protest.

"I clambered down off the table. The soldiers had been feeding me capfuls of vodka and I must've fallen asleep because the next thing I recall was the sergeant tucking me, still in uniform, into my bunk in the barracks.

"I woke early the next morning with a terrible hangover. I wanted to stay in my bunk and not move a muscle, but one of the soldiers came to drag me out of it. On the way to the mess hall he joked that I'd have to learn to hold my liquor if I was going to be a soldier. Fortunately, the tasteless breakfast gruel and the strong black tea fortified me.

"Later that morning we set off on patrol. We trudged on and on in the forest without a break. It was tough going and gradually I lagged behind. At one point the sergeant dropped back next to me and took me by the hand. 'Keep up,' he told me. 'Behave like a proper little soldier. Look at the special uniform you've been given.'

"I nodded enthusiastically. I didn't want to make any of the soldiers fly off the handle at me. In the short time I'd been with them I'd quickly learned not to do anything that would make them irate."

"What sort of things made them angry?" I asked.

"I couldn't predict. More often than not they lashed out when they were drunk, but I had to be on the alert always. I was forever telling myself to stay out of their way."

He continued, "By the middle of the day we'd reached a railway siding. A goods train with supplies bound for the front line was gearing up to go.

"Sergeant Kulis explained that our job was to keep a lookout for *partizani* and stop them from blowing up the train. I was immediately anxious. I didn't know what *partizani* looked like. They could have been anybody.

"There were about ten of us soldiers, and most of them had already perched themselves on the roofs of carriages. Sergeant Kulis hoisted me onto his shoulders and then into the grasp of another soldier who was up there.

"The soldier tied me to his waist with a rope, so I wouldn't fall. Then he thrust a rifle toward me—it was almost larger and heavier than me—and told me to take charge of it. It was ridiculous: how on earth could a child hold it up, let alone fire it? Besides, I didn't have any idea how to use it. When he realized this, the soldier positioned me between his knees and, holding the rifle up for me, showed me how to take aim. Then he pulled the trigger himself.

"The force of the shot was like somebody had kicked me in the shoulder. I panicked at the explosive sound—it reminded me of that day in my village. For an instant I had the strength of Samson. I broke the soldier's grip and, still on my leash, I tried to scramble away on all fours. If I hadn't been tied to him I would've jumped off the roof—I wouldn't have cared whether I broke every bone in my body—and then escaped into the forest. They wouldn't have caught me there. I knew the forest better than they did—it had been my home. But I couldn't. I was trapped, tied to the soldier like a dog on a leash, and there was nothing I could do. The soldier reined me in, laughing derisively and mocking the terrified expression on my face. When I was back wedged between his knees he gave me a clip across my ear for good measure.

"He had no inkling of what had unnerved me.

"The train gathered speed and I held on for dear life, as they say. We must have been traveling like that for at least two hours, and we never came across a single *partizani*. Then the train came to a halt in another town."

"Do you remember the name of the town?"

My father shook his head briefly. "My first impression was that it was larger than 'S.' There were many more soldiers milling around the station. Some of them noticed me and gathered just below my carriage; they were curious about me, and when they caught sight of the rope still tied around me they laughed. I was humiliated and tried desperately to release myself, but to no avail.

"I had to wait until my captor untied the rope. When I was on the ground, I heard somebody call out, 'What's your name, soldier?' For a moment I was stumped—perhaps because of shock. I looked across at Sergeant Kulis, who called back to the crowd, 'Private Uldis Kurzemnieks. Latvian police brigade.'

"At that, many of the soldiers surrounded me, wanting to shake my hand or take their photos with me. You see, there was a man there with a tripod and a large camera for some reason. Perhaps he was an official army photographer.

"In any case, he set up the camera and then positioned me in front of it. Somebody slung a rifle over my shoulder. Things became a bit unruly as the soldiers scrapped with each other to pose with me. One group of soldiers formed a half-circle around me, posing proudly. I remember that one of them thrust his pistol into my belt and put his arm around me. Once a photo had been taken, they were ordered into town and another group took their place. This went on for quite a while. I didn't mind. In fact, I enjoyed being the center of attention.

"Eventually Kulis called a halt to the photos. He crouched down to my level, staring into my face with a serious expression. He said '*partizani*' again. Then he took me by the hand and we started to march into the town. Other soldiers were also heading in the same direction. I knew something was up because they were passing flasks between each other, gulping down *samagonka* as they swaggered along. There was no discipline.

"It was eerie because the soldiers were noisy, yet underneath this noise it seemed to be deadly quiet. There wasn't a single soul about. The townspeople had retreated inside their homes. I saw curtains in windows twitch slightly as we passed by.

"I was frightened by then and didn't want to be at the front with Sergeant Kulis. I let go of his hand. He didn't seem to notice. He was so intent on what lay ahead.

"I let myself fall behind until I found myself at the rear of the troops.

"Eventually we reached a crossroads. I peered through the forest of soldiers' legs. On the opposite side there was a building set back a little from the road. It was taller and wider than any building I'd ever seen before—it may have been two or even three stories high.

"There were hundreds of people waiting outside—old people, women, and children huddled together. I could just make out some of their faces. They reminded me of people I'd known in my own village. Worse than that, they wore the same expression of fear that I'd seen on the day of the killings. That petrified me even more, but I was confused, too, because Kulis had called them partisans.

"I edged away slowly and was about to turn on my heels and flee when a soldier guarding the rear caught sight of me. He called me over, and when I reached him he gripped me by the shoulders and spun me around in front of him so that I was facing forward again.

"I was too frightened to close my eyes and get in trouble again. I tried as much as I could not to see anything, pretending that the sun was blinding me and squinting my eyes. I couldn't avoid glimpses of what was going on. Soldiers were prodding people into the building while others were hammering big planks of wood across the windows.

"Then I heard the outside doors being bolted. Soldiers put bunches of burning sticks and dead tree branches up against the building. In a flash it caught fire. For a minute or so it was deadly quiet, apart from the crackling of the fire as it took hold. The flames spread quickly and then terrible screams and wails began. And the louder the screams became, the more silent the soldiers were. Nobody laughed. They were hypnotized by the flames that rose higher and higher into the sky. Even the soldier I was with had forgotten about me. He, too, was frozen to the spot and entranced by the flames."

My father paused again and took several steadying breaths. "Maybe they saw their own souls burning at that moment," he said in a low voice.

"Then something snapped me out of it." His voice was barely audible. For a moment he seemed to panic and gasped in air as if he were about to suffocate.

I gently encouraged my father. "Go on, Dad. Tell me what you saw."

"Suddenly there was a movement from the building. It was a woman . . . my God!" My father let out a muted cry, as if he were seeing her at this moment.

"She was on fire. She dashed out from the huge wall of flame. Two children ran behind her. They were also on fire. They didn't make a sound, as if I were watching a silent film.

"Then, before I knew what was happening, I heard cracking sounds and the woman and the children fell to the ground. They didn't move. I knew they were dead. But the flames still rose from their bodies.

"I looked to where the noise had come from. I saw Sergeant Kulis and two other soldiers lowering their rifles.

"Kulis turned in the direction of the watching soldiers. Even though I was at the rear of the crowd, his eyes found me. He smiled and waved to me, shouting, 'Partizani,' as if to explain his actions.

"Without any thought, I turned and fled. I heard the sergeant call after me, but I ignored him. I didn't dare look back. I ran through the streets until I reached the outskirts of the town, where I came across a small farmyard. I saw a shed there and crouched down behind it and covered both my ears with my hands. I didn't want to hear the screams, which had reached a crescendo and could be heard even where I was now hiding.

"At that moment I hated Kulis and all of the soldiers. I wanted to be free of them. Then in the next moment I felt defeated. Where could I go? I slumped down, wishing death would take me, too. I wanted to be free from this misery.

"I looked up into a man's face that was full of rage and hatred. It must have been the farmer who owned the shed. Before I could make a move to escape, he kicked me so hard that I went flying across the yard. But I didn't feel any pain. I was numb inside and felt like I deserved his kick. For being with the soldiers, and for being in uniform."

My father paused briefly and then went on. "I had no choice but to return to the soldiers," he said. "I know I said that I would have preferred to be alone in the forest, but deep down this was not true. I was a frightened little boy.

"I made my way back along the road into town. The troops were where I'd last seen them—in front of the remains of the building. The screams had ceased. There was only the crackling and hissing of the wood as it smoldered and then collapsed.

"I can still hear the screams of those poor people as they clawed at the burning doors trying to get out."

My father was again silent for several moments.

"Sergeant Kulis spotted me, and came over. He put his hand on my shoulder. I froze inside. I didn't want him to touch me. I hated him. He'd done what other soldiers had done to my family. He was no different from them.

"Slowly the soldiers headed back to the station. Corporal Vezis, who always seemed so disciplined, went crazy, chasing some farmer's chickens that had strayed onto the road and kicking at them like they were footballs."

"Where did this happen?" I asked, half regretting that I'd urged my father to tell me the story.

"The soldiers never mentioned any names in front of me. We could've been anywhere. It was more than likely somewhere in Russia, given that later the soldiers told me that I was picked up in Russia, but I have no idea how far I had wandered in the forest before I was handed over to the soldiers. And how far did they take me in order to reach their makeshift barracks and then later their main camp? How far did we go on the train that day? No idea."

"What time of the year was it?"

"Not long after I was picked up by the soldiers," my father replied. "They told me later that they had found me in late May 1942, so it must have been early June the same year."

"That would have made it summertime."

"Exactly, and that is where I am confused, because my impression is that it was cold, and that there was snow on the ground."

"They might've lied about when they picked you up," I suggested.

"But why would they?" my father said, genuinely mystified.

"Perhaps to hide their involvement in this massacre," I mused. "If only there was some way to find out more about the movement of Latvian troops."

"Perhaps 'Koidanov' or 'Panok' is the key to where I was born. If that were the case, we could learn a lot about my movements and the soldiers as well."

"What about this building?" I asked. "What was it?"

My father shrugged. "At that time I didn't recognize the building as anything in particular. But I wonder now if it was a synagogue."

"That's what I was thinking," I replied. From my limited knowledge of the Holocaust, I knew that it had been a commonplace occurrence. "The people were likely Jewish," I added.

My father looked momentarily bewildered. "Sergeant Kulis used the word 'partizani.'"

"The Nazis often used that term for the Jews they hunted in the forests. They also called them Bolsheviks."

"I didn't know," my father said, visibly shocked. "To be honest, I wouldn't have had the slightest idea who was Jewish and who wasn't, even if they were my people. I was only five or six." Then he added: "All I thought was that they looked like people from my village. Certainly now, looking back, I am sure that they were Jewish."

Another photo of my father, this time in his Wehrmacht uniform, 1943.

I was curious about the photographs and asked my father if he had any in his case.

"No, not a single one. The soldiers must've kept them as souvenirs for themselves. But nobody thought to give me one. I have another photograph," my father said, eager to please. He reached across for his case. I heard the familiar clicks of its locks before he began to rummage inside it. After a few moments he held up a photograph. This one was a head-and-shoulders shot of my father in a military uniform I'd never seen before.

"Good God!" I heard myself say.

"You can't tell because the photo's in black and white," he said, "but the uniform is blue—a pretty blue color like the sky. My first uniform. I loved it more than the other ones with their drab colors."

"There were other uniforms? Other colors? How many uniforms did you have?"

"Three altogether. First of all the blue one, then we changed to a light brown one—"

"When was this?"

"I can't give you dates," my father answered, "but the first change must've been about six months after I got the blue one. Each time, a new miniature uniform was prepared for me.

"I remember being told that we were no longer 'policemen' and that we'd become members of the Latvian army and part of the Wehr-macht."

"And that one was light brown, you said?"

My father nodded.

"How long were you in that?"

"Until . . ." My father squinted, trying to recall. "It must have been in the summer of 1943, when Commander Lobe decided to take me north with his new brigade. That's when I had to change to a green one, like khaki green, only lighter."

"How long were you in the green uniform?"

"Until I left Latvia in 1944."

"Just a moment," I said, raising my hand. I repeated the details of uniform changes to myself, committing them to memory. It occurred to me then that much like a detective I was in dire need of a notebook to record the minutiae of my father's story.

After a short silence my father spoke. I could sense his unease.

"There were other times"—he hesitated—"when I saw things . . . other atrocities committed by the soldiers. Sometimes when I was shunted to the rear of the troops I could only hear things. That was bad enough, but I guess they thought they were protecting me . . . as if I could be protected in any way from their brutality."

My father fell silent. I could see that he had again become despondent. "I knew that the soldiers were doing wrong. If only I'd done more—"

I cut my father off. "What could you have done?"

"I should've tried to stop them."

"What? You were a child."

My father didn't respond. I could tell that he was not convinced.

"Dad," I said, "your life must have been hell with the soldiers."

"I got used to it."

I wondered silently how one got used to hell. Was it any easier for a child who had little memory or experience of anything better?

My father's voice interrupted my train of thought. "They used me to get girls from the local villages when they wanted to have a party. They thought that because I was a small boy and so cute that the girls would be more willing to join them.

"One time we stopped for the night in a barn. The soldiers were already pretty drunk and unruly. They'd made this primitive distillery that they carried about with them on patrol in order to make *samagonka*.

"That evening they set up the contraption and had me watch over it until the bootleg was ready. Then it was my job to keep the soldiers' tin cups topped up. Some of them forced me to swig the stuff so that before long I was as unsteady on my feet as the rest of them.

"A young girl, no more than fourteen or fifteen years old—she must have been the farmer's daughter—came in with food for all of us. As she was passing it around, Corporal Vezis tried to kiss her. She laughed and pushed him away playfully, but I could tell she was frightened. She got out of there quickly. The other soldiers joked among themselves, saying that that was exactly what they needed—some girls.

"I kept on pouring the *samagonka*, but as much as possible stayed out of the way. At one point I felt Corporal Vezis's eyes settle on me. He called me over and straightened my uniform. Then he got up and told me to follow him. I didn't want to. I wanted to sleep. But he and another soldier pushed me out of the barn and down the path toward the village. On the way he made me pick some wildflowers—pretty ones.

"When we got to the village square, we hid behind a cart. Corporal Vezis and the other soldier quietly watched the comings and goings of people in their houses. Then a young woman appeared on the doorstep of one cottage. That's when Vezis pushed me out into the open. In a whisper he ordered me to present the flowers to the young lady. I didn't want to, but I didn't dare disobey him, what with his violent temper.

"The girl was so surprised to see me, a boy in a uniform, swaying drunkenly at her door. I held out the flowers and she seemed touched. Then I nodded my head in the direction of Corporal Vezis.

"From a distance, the two soldiers must have looked harmless enough—just like any country boys courting girls—despite their uniforms. They waved at her in a friendly way, and she took me by the hand and went over. For a short while they talked and laughed among themselves, forgetting all about me. I was still drunk, silently willing myself to stay upright.

"Then the girl disappeared back across the square. Soon she returned with three other young women in tow. Together we all headed back to the barn.

"The party got into full swing very quickly. The women sipped on *samagonka*, and before long they were a little drunk as well. They began to dance for the soldiers. A few of the soldiers got up and were staggering around, trying to join in with the women, while other soldiers clapped and laughed at the way their comrades made fools of themselves.

"It had been more or less good-humored when suddenly the atmosphere turned nasty. Corporal Vezis tried to force one of the girls to sit on his knee and she resisted. Instead she gave a breathless laugh, pulled me onto her lap, and gave me a big cuddle. In a jealous rage, the corporal yanked me off the girl's knee, almost ripping my arm off, and tossed me violently across the room.

"He then made a lunge for the girl, attempting to kiss her. She struggled with him, and when she broke free he made a grab at one of the other girls. All the while, the other soldiers looked on, clapping and cheering.

"You can imagine what happened after that," my father said quietly, shaking his head in disgust. "I hid in a corner. I didn't want to see what was going on, but I couldn't block out the panting and the screaming, which seemed to come from all corners of the barn. My memories of what happened next are vague."

My father seemed to be in pain and screwed up his eyes as if torn between his duty to visualize something more clearly and the desire to forget whatever it was he had witnessed.

"I must have fainted," he said. "When I came round I could only hear the soldiers' snoring. I peeped out and they were all asleep, scattered around the barn, wherever they'd collapsed in their drunken stupor.

"Then I saw that the girls were still in the far corner of the barn trying to clean themselves up. Their clothes were torn and they had been badly beaten.

"I wanted to help them. All I could think of was to offer them water. I tiptoed over to them. They backed away from me as if I were one of the soldiers, and then, without a word, they all slipped out of the barn.

"I stood there for a moment. I was bereft. They were repelled by me even though I felt I was on their side. I wondered if I should follow them and find refuge with them. I imagined I'd be able to tell them who I was: that I wasn't one of these men, that I wasn't anything like them. But then I thought: 'Who would want me after I'd been with these devils?'

"Now, of course, I understand that the soldiers had been using me to lure the girls to the barn. I feel responsible for what had happened to them, even now."

My father stared bleakly into space.

I shuddered.

I pictured my father moving amiably from one drunken soldier to the next, smiling as he solicitously poured the anesthetizing *samagonka*. I saw him on the doorstep of the young woman's cottage holding the bunch of wildflowers.

I was overwhelmed by the vulnerability of this child immersed in a world of arbitrary and deliberate brutality. How had he managed to steer himself through it? He said himself that he tried not to stand out or attract any attention, never daring to disagree with the soldiers or recoil from their pornographic forays, which must have been unfathomable to a child of no more than six or seven.

I wanted to know more about these men, these soldier-puppeteers, who had controlled and exploited my father.

Yet it was not only the horror of my father's experiences that had overtaken me; it was anxiety for my father and the possibly incredible dimensions of his story. Would people be able to accept the predicament of a child's memory, lacking comprehensive details of names, dates, and locations? Could I? Thus far my father had revealed a handful of names and the letter "S" to add to the mystery of Panok and Koidanov. The remainder were impressions and sensations about incidents seen through the eyes of a child, shaded by bloody violence and an all-consuming fear of being discovered.

I looked at the clock on the wall. It was nearly 4:00 a.m. The house was silent. Even my mother's snoring had ceased. It felt as if the very walls of the house were listening to my father's story in rapt silence. And now, like me, they waited to see if he would continue.

I rose and stretched my tired body, catching a glimpse of my face reflected in the darkened kitchen window. Opposite me, my father also stood to stretch. He smiled shyly at me, and his eyes betrayed no sign of fatigue. Instead their usual intense, vivid blue shone as if he'd just risen from a long sleep.

CHAPTER SIX
THE DZENIS FAMILY

My father and I sat down at the table again, as if recommencing a formal interview.

"How long were you with the soldiers on patrol?" I asked.

"From when they picked me up, which they later told me was in May 1942, until toward the end of 1943," he replied. "I wasn't on duty all the time. Sergeant Kulis sometimes took me to visit Riga, the capital of Latvia."

"How often?"

"At least twice, perhaps even three times; whenever he was given leave."

"Does the length of time the soldiers claim you were with them make sense to you?"

"It does," my father said, "because I spent one winter alone in the forest before the soldiers captured me, and then I was on patrol with them for a second freezing winter before I was taken to Riga for a short time in the late spring of 1943."

"Do you remember much of 1943?"

"I do," my father answered, "especially after reaching Riga, where life was more stable. When I was with the soldiers on patrol, nobody paid any attention to dates and times as far as I could tell. It was chaos. And I was older in Riga. I remembered when people mentioned dates, and I was learning to read, so I could follow details in newspapers and magazines."

"If these dates are correct, the extermination of your village, wherever it was, must have taken place in 1941."

"Late in 1941," my father said.

"Why late 'forty-one?" I asked.

"It was getting cold and the nights were drawing in when it happened in my village."

"I am trying to picture where your village might have been in Russia," I said.

"They never mentioned where we were, apart from insults . . ."

"Insults?"

"Yes, you know, curses and swearing. Incessant."

"Such as?"

My father's face turned red with embarrassment. He coughed and looked around.

"If you'd rather not say," I said.

My father nodded gratefully. I realized that I had rarely, if ever, heard him swear. Perhaps his aversion stemmed from his being forced to listen to the soldiers' abuse.

I changed the subject. "How far was the 'S' camp from Riga?"

"I couldn't say, but the train journey to Riga with Sergeant Kulis seemed to take forever. But then everything does for a child. We would have to change trains at least once and also spend one night on board—it was always uncomfortable, and I would cuddle up to the sergeant, who'd wrap me inside his big army coat."

"What did you do in Riga?"

"It was a real treat for me." My father's face lit up.

"Even though things must have been scarce during wartime they treated me very well. I did all the usual things that kids like doing. Sergeant Kulis would take me to stay with his mother and father, and we'd spend lots of time with his fiancée, Wilma, as well. We'd go to one of the parks if the weather was fine. That always attracted a lot of attention, especially from other children. Boys in particular were envious of my uniform. 'How can we join the army?' they used to ask me all the time.

"Once the Kulis family took me to see a movie, and before it there was a newsreel about the war. Believe it or not, I didn't like it: it was just propaganda. I'd been at the front. I knew the difference between what really went on and what was on the screen, which was just fantasy. I was a real soldier.

"The more time I spent in Riga, the more well known I became. One day Sergeant Kulis and Wilma took me to a café for ice cream. When I entered holding Wilma's hand, the entire café seemed to recognize me and several people rose from their seats and applauded.

"I can taste it now, that ice cream. Strawberry, it was." My father smiled nostalgically. "I hadn't had ice cream since I was a child in my village."

"It sounds as if you no longer hated Sergeant Kulis."

"I'm not sure what I felt. I never forgot or forgave what he'd done that day when the building was burned down. But Commander Lobe had put him in charge of me, and I just made the best of it, trying to get along with him and everybody, for that matter. I was a quick learner, too, so it wasn't long before I was chattering away in Latvian with the soldiers and people I met in Riga."

"You were turning into quite the little Latvian," I joked.

My father gave an uneasy laugh. "No," he said. "I wasn't one of them. I could feel them loving me, but I didn't want any part of it. Deep inside me I wanted to be free of them. Always. Anyway, it was in the late spring of 1943 when Sergeant Kulis told me that he and I would be making another journey to Riga. I imagined that it was going to be one of our typical visits together and began to anticipate the many treats that I knew would be coming my way.

"But as soon as the train pulled into the main station in Riga, I had an inkling that something was up. Wilma was not there to greet us as she'd been on other occasions. Instead an enormous shiny black limousine waited at the curb outside the station exit.

"The sergeant gathered my knapsack and ushered me toward the car. A chauffeur dressed in a soldier's uniform stood to attention and held the door open for me. I couldn't believe the luxury inside the car; the seats were covered in leather and there was even a small cocktail bar. The engine was almost inaudible as we wove our way smoothly through the streets of Riga. I gazed out from the passenger window, but I didn't recognize anything I saw—we were in a different part of Riga.

"I stared across at Sergeant Kulis, who was still gripping my hand. 'Where are we?' I demanded with a growing sense of panic. 'We'll be there soon,' he said, and I could tell that he, too, was uneasy about something. This visit seemed to be going very differently from other visits when he took me by bus to his family home.

"Then the car turned, and moments later we pulled up outside a building that seemed to tower above the street. I was a village boy, and I'd never seen anything like it before. I peered up at it through the car window. I was enchanted: I thought that it was a magical palace, with all its colored lights and its pretty lit sign above the entrance. The sign said LAIMA CHOCOLATES.

"It was then that I noticed a man was standing in the shadow of the building near the entrance. I stared intently at him, but I couldn't quite make him out.

"The chauffeur came around and opened the door on my side, at which point the mysterious man stepped forward into the bright morning light. He wasn't a soldier. Instead he was wearing a well-cut suit of a fine shiny material. He seemed very formal: he stood very erect and rigid with his hands held behind his back, and I thought that he must be a well-bred sort of person.

"He came toward the car and stretched out his hand to shake mine, but I held back. I waited for Sergeant Kulis to join me, and when he did I instinctively tried to take his hand. But he shrugged me off and instead shook hands with this superior man. Then he turned to me. 'This is Mr. Dzenis,' he said. 'Say hello.'

"I hid behind Sergeant Kulis's leg. He tried to nudge me out to the front, but I had frozen to the spot. Then the sergeant said, 'Mr. Dzenis is going to look after you.' My heart sank. My intuition that something was wrong had been right, but I had never imagined that I was going to be given away.

"Sergeant Kulis nudged me again, trying to get me to greet this forbidding man, but I remained mute.

"Suddenly, before I even understood what was happening, the sergeant lifted me off the ground and gave me a hug, as if I were a child and not a soldier. 'Farewell, my little friend,' he said. With that he put me down and strode away. I lost control, again forgetting that I was a soldier, and began stamping my foot. I set my jaw stubbornly. I wanted Sergeant Kulis and not this Mr. Dzenis, even if he did live in a beautiful palace. I have always remembered that moment and the sergeant's parting words to me.

"Mr. Dzenis literally began to drag me back toward the limousine. I was kicking and screaming, but then I got hold of myself. I told myself not to make any trouble. I'd learned better than that.

"For a moment we paused on the pavement, and I got one last chance to search the street with my eyes. By then there was no sign of the sergeant. At that moment I didn't think I would ever forgive him for deserting me."

"Why were you reluctant to leave the soldiers?" I asked.

"I'd gotten used to them and the way they cared for me," my father replied. Then with a shrug of his shoulders he added, "Besides, I had nobody else."

"The limousine set off again. This time I was in the company of Mr. Dzenis. Like Mr. Dzenis himself, the part of the city we passed through somehow seemed more well-off than where I usually went with Sergeant Kulis. There were shops with bright and colorful displays in their windows, and the ladies walking on the pavement appeared happy and fine-looking.

"Eventually we turned off a main road and into a narrow street. There was a sign that said VALDEMARA IELA. Shortly after that, we came to a halt outside a well-kept apartment block. It was as impressive as the palace I'd just seen. There was a long path leading from the curb up to the front door. On one side of the entrance the Nazi flag—a giant swastika—was flying, and on the other, the Latvian flag.

"I climbed out of the car and waited for Mr. Dzenis to join me. He took my hand as we headed up the path and entered the building. We were in an elegant foyer, and for a moment I was transfixed by a chandelier that hung from the ceiling and sparkled like a jewel. Then I was seduced by the overpowering scent of a spray of beautiful flowers that sat on a side table.

"Mr. Dzenis told me that we should hurry. 'Everybody is waiting for you,' he said. I was curious—who was everybody, and why were they waiting for me? But another part of me was confused and angry—I was still thinking about my duties and my comrades in the troop. 'What could be more important than that?' I thought to myself.

"We climbed the stairs to the top floor and outside the door to the apartment Mr. Dzenis smoothed my uniform and hair.

"The door opened and we stepped inside. The entrance hall was softly lit by lamps that seemed to flicker—like the Aladdin's cave of my imagination—and the moments after that were equally dreamlike. Out of nowhere a beautiful made-up face bent down to my level and smothered me in kisses. There was the scent of perfume; I can't describe it, apart from saying that it was like I was falling down a deep well lined with cotton wool. In the next moment I was being hugged by another beautiful lady, who made cooing sounds and smiled at me with moistened eyes.

"Suddenly it was all too much for me. I squirmed free of her arms and stood to attention, saluting wildly at her. Mr. Dzenis gave me a stern look and warned me to behave with proper manners. When I had calmed down, he introduced me to the first lady who had kissed me so much. She was Emily, his wife. 'Call me Auntie,' she said and then made way for the other woman who'd fussed over me already.

"She was tall and glamorous-looking, perhaps about eighteen years old. Her name was Zirdra and she was Mr. Dzenis's eldest daughter. She had a beautiful laugh that tinkled like water in a stream. I felt instantly that she had a gentle nature.

"Another girl hovered in the background. She must have been about five years older than me. Immediately I could tell that she was a completely different kettle of fish from Zirdra. She had no intention of welcoming me in any way and instead frowned down at me contemptuously. She turned out to be Ausma, Mr. Dzenis's youngest daughter.

"Auntie told me that Zirdra and Ausma were going to be my big sisters and that I had another sister, the middle one, called Mirdza, who was unwell and confined to her room for the evening. Later I learned that Mirdza had suffered from polio when she was younger and, though not disabled in any obvious way, her body was racked with inexplicable pains and aches. I also learned later that the three girls were all from Mr. Dzenis's first marriage, which had ended in divorce, and that he and Auntie had no children from their own marriage.

"That first night the Dzenises gave a lavish party in their apartment. I was the guest of honor. But it was not without drama beforehand. Zirdra had tried to give me a bath and, of course, I'd not forgotten Sergeant Kulis's warning. It was mayhem. Zirdra chased me around the room, wanting to undress me for the bath, and I was ducking behind chairs, under the table, wherever I could wriggle into. In the end she gave up, but only because the guests were due to arrive.

"The party was a great success for the Dzenis family. When I entered the room for the first time, yet again everybody stood and applauded me. I knew what was expected of me: I stood as erect as I could and proudly saluted in all directions. Everybody seemed very amused by this.

"Many of the guests were in uniform: there were Latvian and German officers with their wives. One of the German officers stepped forward and made a great show of giving me the Nazi salute. It was then that Mr. Dzenis whispered in my ear how much I should appreciate such an important soldier taking an interest in me. He told me to return the special salute, which I did. This caused another round of applause.

"Later Commander Lobe appeared."

"So you were reunited with Lobe at the Dzenis party?"

"Yes," my father answered. "He was in a jolly mood and seemed pleased to see me. He pulled me onto his knee and chatted to me in Latvian. He was impressed that I had mastered the language so quickly.

"At one point in the celebrations two men arrived. They hovered by the door and Commander Lobe went over to join them. One turned out to be a journalist called Arnold Smits, and a photographer whose name I didn't hear. They wanted to take some shots of me at the party, and they got Zirdra to crouch down to my level and hug me for the camera, but I squirmed shyly. All the guests thought that this was hilarious except for me—I still wasn't relaxed in the company of women. The commander told me that I'd better get used to being photographed with glamorous women because he had great plans to make me into a star. I didn't understand what he meant but thought to myself, 'I don't want to be a star if it means being kissed by women all the time.'

"That's all I can remember about the commander that night, but in the coming months I was to spend a lot more time with him and got to know him much better." My father's words sounded ominous, but instead of telling me more he lapsed into a lengthy and impenetrable silence. I had no idea what he might have been thinking.

"Anyway," he said suddenly, "you know what kids are like at parties. I got bored and I was curious, too, about where I was to live. I decided to explore the apartment, leaving the adults to their merriment. The main hallway had doors leading off in all directions. The first door led into a study. I had never seen anything like it. It was full of books, and there was a large desk by the window. It smelled of leather and polish. It seemed so rich.

"After that I returned to the party. Zirdra spotted me slipping quietly back into the room and gave a little wave. I joined her on the sofa, and she immediately began tickling and cuddling me. After the long journey to Riga and meeting so many new people, I actually fell asleep on her lap. Later, when I awoke, the guests had gone and the maid was cleaning up. But I was still on the sofa, nestled in Zirdra's arms.

"For a moment I remained hypnotized by the warmth of Zirdra's body but then, as I came to, I sprang to my feet. I was angry with myself and everybody around me. 'I must return to my comrades,' I shouted. I'd become obsessed with the idea of being a soldier.

"Zirdra reached out to calm me down, but I pushed her aside and dashed across the room. I wanted to escape, no matter where I ended up. I struggled to open the heavy door.

"Mr. Dzenis must have heard the ruckus because at that moment he opened the door from the other side. His body blocked my way. 'Wait. You live here now. With us,' he said firmly. This only threw me into a deeper panic. I burst into tears.

"Zirdra hurried over to me and tried to comfort me again. 'Don't worry, I'll look after you,' she whispered gently. 'I'm your sister now.'

"There was kindness in her voice and instinctively I trusted her, but at the same time the word 'sister' must have triggered something in me. I sobbed uncontrollably. 'I want my own sister. My brother. Not you!' I wailed. Suddenly there was a stony silence in the room.

"Zirdra looked into my face. 'You have a family?' She was astonished. 'Where are they? Do you know?'

"You could have cut the tension in the air with a knife. Then, unimaginably, things took another turn for the worse. Ausma was fed up with my tears. 'Why do we have to have him here?' she complained. Then she added, 'Let's send him back to his real family, if he has one.' Then something else occurred to her. 'Besides,' she said petulantly, 'he's probably a little Yid . . .'

"Mr. Dzenis sprang across the room and slapped her hard. She fell back into the sofa, holding her cheek and shrieking. Mr. Dzenis was shaking with rage. 'Stupid!' he spat at her so violently that both Ausma and I stopped crying, and the entire room fell into shocked silence.

"It was Zirdra who broke the spell. 'Time for bed,' she said, wiping my eyes with her scented handkerchief. Then, taking my hand, she led me to my room and sat me down on the bed. 'Don't you worry,' she said. 'We're just looking after you until your family comes back. We'll find them for you.' I was forlorn at the thought. I had witnessed what had happened to my family. They were all gone. I knew that there was not a single person who would come back to me."

I saw grief flash across my father's face, but in the next instant he endeavored to mask his pain with a bright smile. Quickly he dived back into his story.

"Zirdra reached under the pillow and pulled out a small blue bundle. 'New pajamas!' She smiled warmly. 'Let's put them on you.'

"After all those months sleeping rough on patrol I couldn't have wished for more. Soft, warm, and clean bedclothes. But, of course, I wouldn't let Zirdra near me. From what had just happened with Ausma unwittingly suspecting I was Jewish I knew with more certainty than ever that I would have to be on my guard. Always. Nobody would ever learn the truth about me no matter what happened in the future.

"Zirdra struggled to undress me for some time, but in the end I was stronger—I gripped my trousers with an incredible stubbornness—so that finally she gave up. I sat at one end of the bed and Zirdra at the other. 'Very well then,' she said. 'Tonight you'll sleep in your uniform.' She folded back the bedcover and blankets and patted the sheet, indicating where I should climb in. I did so and she covered me. She took my face in her hands and gave me a good-night kiss on my forehead. 'Soon you'll get used to our ways,' she told me. I closed my eyes and pretended to drop off to sleep. Soon after that I heard her turn off the light and close the door gently.

"I was overexcited and my head was spinning with all my new experiences. There was no way I could sleep. I lay on my side with my head still resting on the pillow. My eyes moved around the room.

"I was just about to get up and examine the room more closely when I heard footsteps approach my door and then stop. The door latch clicked open. I pretended to be asleep for a second time, but through my half-closed eyelids I could just make out Mr. Dzenis peering into the room to make sure that I was fast asleep. I heard him close the door gently. Then there was the click of the key as it was turned quietly in the lock.

"I'd been shut in like a prisoner. Perhaps Mr. Dzenis was still worried that I was going to escape and go in search of my real family.

"I sat on the edge of the bed for several minutes just staring into the darkened space. I couldn't resist the thought of the pajamas, and I decided that it would be safe enough for me to put them on. I told myself that I would have to wake up early the next morning, before the rest of the household, and change back into my uniform. I quietly slipped into them and folded my uniform neatly beside my pillow, within easy reach.

"I was still restless. My eyes scanned the room again. This time I noticed a sliver of light at the far end. It was coming from a tiny window. I went over and drew back the curtains.

"I don't know how long I stood there, mesmerized by the bright moonlight, but a scraping noise broke the spell. It was coming from the street below. I looked down and made out two figures cleaning the road. Their coats were tatty, even worse than mine from the forest. 'If only I'd kept the dead soldier's coat,' I thought to myself, 'I could have tossed it down to them. It'd be better than what they've got now.'

"Then something else caught my attention. It was like a jewel on the sleeves of their coats. A yellow star visible even at night and from this distance. 'What are street cleaners doing with such pretty stars?' I asked myself. In truth I was envious because it was much more attractive than the red badge of Latvia that'd been sewn onto the arm of my uniform."

My father gave an ironic, almost bitter laugh. "Uncanny. My instinct was to prefer the yellow star to the symbol of Latvia. Soon enough I learned the significance of that star. It wasn't remotely like a jewel. It was a curse on a people I knew I belonged with."

My father gave a deep sigh. After a few moments he spoke again.

"I climbed back into the bed and drew the covers up so that even my face was hidden, and that was that," my father said with finality. "My first night with my new family."

"Do you think any of them knew the truth about the fate of your family?" I asked.

"I can't see how they could have."

"Did Uncle know you were Jewish?" I asked, referring to Mr. Dzenis by the name I had used to address him when I was growing up.

"I'm sure he didn't . . ."

"Judging by his harsh reaction to Ausma, it's a possibility," I suggested. "He might have heard it from Kulis? Or perhaps Kulis had confided in Lobe, who then told Dzenis?"

My father was clearly perplexed. "Why would the sergeant have said anything when he'd warned me to be silent under threat of death? Besides, it would have been dangerous for him, too, if it'd been discovered that he was harboring a Jew."

My father shrugged. "In any case I'm sure that Ausma didn't know about me. How on earth could she?" he asked. "I think she was just using the worst insult of those times against me."

"Or perhaps Ausma had overheard a comment made in a private conversation between Uncle and Auntie," I said, "or Uncle and Lobe. Who knows? It's all possible, Dad."

I crossed to the sink and refilled the kettle for more tea. "How about later in life?" I asked, resting against the row of cupboards, waiting for the kettle to boil. "Did any of them ever give any indication that they knew you were Jewish?"

My father rose and joined me, leaning lightly against the refrigerator opposite, his hands behind his back. "Never," he said vehemently but the thought of it seemed to unsettle him. His eyes darted apprehensively, as if he still feared discovery.

After the war the Dzenis family had come to Melbourne, taking my father with them. Even after he had gone his own way and joined a traveling circus as an elephant boy, my father had kept in contact with them. In a sense, they were the only family that he had.

He had lost touch with Ausma, who had remained in Latvia with her mother after the war. Even when he was living on Valdemara Street, he only had sporadic contact with her when she came to the apartment to visit. According to my father, it was obvious that Ausma, like her sister Mirdza, resented his presence among them and the attention Uncle showered on him.

Auntie had passed away in 1970 and Uncle in 1979 in Melbourne, but my father had continued to see Uncle's other two daughters, Zirdra and Mirdza, who had also made it to Australia. It was natural that my father gravitated toward Zirdra: she had been the only one who hadn't seemed to resent him. He had spoken on several occasions of how he instinctively liked and trusted her. After divorcing her husband in Adelaide, she'd moved to Melbourne, where my father got to see her more regularly.

"Only once," my father now explained to me, "when I dropped by to say hello on the spur of the moment, did Zirdra mention the past. Uncannily, she reminisced about the pajamas incident. 'Why were you so terrified?' she asked me. I simply shrugged my shoulders noncommittally. 'You know what boys are like,' I said. She held my gaze for several moments; there was a shrewd expression in her eyes. But then she let the matter drop.

"We never mentioned the past again—everything remained unstated between us—as if we'd agreed to be silent forever. I was relieved. My secret had remained buried for many years, and I was content for it to continue that way."

My father seemed genuinely sad as he recalled her death many years ago. "Later in life, long after she'd died," he reflected, "it occurred to me that Zirdra understood my situation—what I felt inside—more than the others, perhaps even more than myself, without knowing that I was Jewish or any of the details of my story. Perhaps she even sensed that I had a history that might in some way shame Latvians if it ever became public.

"And then there is Mirdza," my father said. Mirdza was the only one of the sisters still living. With her husband, Edgars, she had also settled in Melbourne and raised three children. Now they lived only a few miles from my parents and saw each other occasionally when my father was in Mirdza's good books.

There had always been tension between my father and Mirdza. "She'd always been the center of attention, and then I was thrust into the limelight. I learned later that Uncle had always wanted a son, and it was clear from the outset that he loved having me there."

My father stood cupping his hands around the mug of tea I offered him. Then he sat back in his chair.

"Will you tell Mirdza any of your story?" I asked, joining him at the table.

"God forbid! Could you imagine?" He looked daunted by the prospect. "I'll have to. Just let me get over the shock I've brought on myself with all this . . ."

"What do you mean?" I asked. "Do you regret speaking to me?"

"No," my father said, "but to be truthful, I don't want to remember anything of what happened to me. Who in his right mind would? But the bigger truth is that I am more terrified to forget. I am trapped."

CHAPTER SEVEN
THE VOLHOV SWAMPS

I just couldn't settle at the Dzenises'," my father said. "First, Uncle and Auntie wanted me to give up my soldier's uniform, which I refused to do point-blank.

"Then there was the matter of school. I'd never attended school before, even in my village. I didn't want to go; I didn't see the point of it, especially when I could've been out on patrol with the soldiers. While Uncle was willing to compromise on my uniform, he wouldn't tolerate any resistance to school.

"From the outset school was disastrous. I was disruptive. I couldn't and wouldn't sit still at my desk like the other girls and boys, whom I looked down upon as silly and spoiled. Worst of all was that I wouldn't obey my teacher—I still recall her name, Miss Eglits. As the days passed I became more unruly and more than once drove her to tears of exasperation.

"I'd been at school for just over a fortnight when Auntie and Uncle were called in by the headmaster. He made it clear that I was beyond redemption as a student, if not as a child as well. The headmaster told Uncle that it might be better if I had a private tutor or was even returned to the soldiers. I'd been sitting there in his office perched between Auntie and Uncle, bored and staring down at my boots. But that suggestion brought a smile to my face. I was going to be free of books and ink pens and the sour-milky smell of the schoolroom. I looked up to share my pleasure with Auntie and Uncle, but when I caught a glimpse of Uncle's reddened and angry face I quickly bowed my head again. Auntie must have sensed my sudden fear of Uncle because she secretly took my hand and gave it a gentle and reassuring squeeze.

"In all the time that I knew him, Uncle never once laid a hand on me, but that day he must have come close to doing so. As we left the schoolyard he said to me in a very hard voice that I'd brought shame on his name.

"Auntie and Uncle talked intently about my situation as our limousine made its way back to Valdemara Street. I knew better than to show how pleased I was at my escape from school, so I sat quietly, staring out at the passing sights, trying to look contrite.

"At one point in the journey, I heard Uncle say the name of Commander Lobe. From the tone of her voice I could tell that Auntie disagreed with whatever Uncle had said and was trying to reason with him. I sensed that she was springing to my defense. But by the time we reached Valdemara Street, Auntie and Uncle had come to a decision. Once we were inside the apartment, Uncle sent me to my room, telling me that I would have to eat my lunch there alone as punishment.

"After lunch, Auntie came to collect me from my room. She peeked around the door. 'Uncle has returned to Laima,' she said in an exaggerated whisper. 'You can come out now.'

"That afternoon we went into the center of Riga. Auntie took me to my favorite café, where she let me eat as much strawberry ice cream as I desired. I didn't get it—I'd been expelled from school, and I was being rewarded with ice cream.

"It became even more baffling because after I'd quaffed down a second mountain of ice cream Auntie took me to the cinema. It was a German film—a silly romance of some sort that didn't interest me at all, although I could understand the gist of what was going on because by then I'd picked up some German. You see, out on patrol we'd cooperated with German soldiers, and quite a few of our commanding officers were German."

Suddenly my father stopped speaking. His face bore a startled expression, as if he'd just been slapped. "Wait!" he exclaimed, raising his hand. "It's on the tip of my tongue."

His eyes darted about. "Acun?" he said. "No! Not Acun but something like that."

"What on earth—" I began to say, but my father raised his hand again to silence me.

"Aizum!" my father said excitedly. He repeated the name. "Aizum."

"Aizum?"

"It's just come to me out of nowhere," my father said. "He was one of the German officers. Aizum. He was with us on patrol. I remember being photographed with him."

"On that day? The day of the massacre?"

My father shook his head. "I can't say for sure. It might've been. He was standing next to me. I was waist-high to him. He may have even had his arm around me. I remember staring at the pistol he had in his belt. He noticed me admiring it. He took it out and tucked it into my belt. But for the life of me I can't remember when and where this was."

My father gripped his head in both hands and stared down at the floor. Then he looked up. "It may come to me later," he said. His frustration was palpable.

My father returned to events in the Dzenis household. "Although the day had started out badly, the afternoon with Auntie had been wonderful, and at dinner that evening Uncle seemed to be in a better mood.

"I awoke the following morning to find the maid in my room. The small khaki rucksack that Sergeant Kulis had given me was open in front of her and she was stuffing my meager belongings into it. Uncle appeared and sat down beside me on the bed. He told me that Commander Lobe had been put in charge of a new brigade called the Second Latvian Division. Uncle explained to me that my old battalion, the Eighteenth Kurzeme, had been incorporated with another battalion that had in turn been divided to form two new divisions.

"Then came the piece of news I'd dreamed of. Commander Lobe wanted me to join the brigade and accompany them on a new mission. I was overjoyed and relieved, too, that my time as a 'normal' child was over. I was going to be a soldier again.

"It occurred to me then that Uncle had had enough of me after just two weeks and didn't want responsibility for me anymore. For a second I felt regretful about my unruly behavior. Auntie and Uncle and Zirdra, too, had been kind to me. For a second I even had a change of heart. While I'd been happy to put on a show of bravado about being a soldier, now that the reality was upon me I wasn't quite so sure I wanted to give up the comfort of life in Riga.

" 'All your old comrades will be with you,' Uncle said, 'so you'll be better off there. Of course, you shall still come and stay with us when you're not on duty. Now hurry up and get dressed. It's time for breakfast and then we'll be on our way. We don't want to keep the commander waiting.' That convinced me. The decision had been made, and I was capable of recognizing that it was the best possible solution. I was getting into such trouble in Riga, and it was better that I went back to a situation that I was used to, no matter how horrible it was."

"What year was this?" I asked.

"Around the summer of 1943."

"So you must have been seven, nearly eight years old by then."

"That's right."

My father returned to his story. "When we arrived at Laima Chocolates, Commander Lobe was already waiting in Uncle's office. I gave him a formal salute, but he waved at me quite casually, the way he did with Uncle, who was an old friend.

"The commander was in a good mood. He patted the spot next to him on the sofa so I sat down. He gave me a slap on my knee as if we were longtime friends, too. Then he reached into the inner pocket of his jacket and pulled out a piece of paper. He unfolded it and spread it out on the low table in front of him. It was a military map.

" 'See, here is Riga,' he said, pointing, 'and here is Leningrad. And this is where we'll be going—it's called Velikiye Luki. What do you think about that?' I grinned to show the commander that I was pleased, but in reality I didn't have any particular opinion about it. I'd heard of Leningrad, which I'd been told was in Russia. But I had no idea where it actually was.

"When I heard the next piece of news I was overjoyed. 'I've decided to promote you from private to corporal. You are now Corporal Kurzemnieks.' I was so proud of myself. I thought, 'Imagine! You are only a boy yet you are a corporal.'"

My father beamed with pleasure as he recalled this moment.

"But I could sense that Uncle had had a change of heart and like Auntie and Zirdra was not entirely happy about my fate. 'The boy is too young for this, Kārlis,' he said, but the commander was dismissive. 'The boy won't be in any danger,' he countered. 'We'll keep him behind the front line. His job will be to boost the morale of the troops. Like a puppy, that's all.'

"The commander rose, telling Uncle that he was taking me to SS headquarters for the fitting of a new uniform—an SS one. I was to be SS Sturmann Kurzemnieks."

I was appalled to hear what they had done to my father, and my face must have betrayed my sense of horror. But my father must have misread its source, and he sprang to his own defense.

"I did not volunteer or choose that," he insisted. "A decision was made to assign me to the brigade. There was no choice involved. I had no say in it."

Yet even as he spoke his voice lost its usual melodic vigor, as if with my reaction I had accused him of complicity. He sighed deeply. I watched as he struggled to take up where he had left off with his recollections.

"Uncle accompanied the commander and me as far as the foyer of Laima. As we were on the point of leaving, he pulled out a small parcel from his pocket. 'Chocolate bars,' he said, passing the package to me. 'A gift from Laima. Don't eat them all at once. Ration them.' Then he added, 'And don't let your comrades steal it from you. They have their own supply of Laima chocolates.'

"I shook Uncle's hand firmly. He told Commander Lobe to take good care of me. The commander reassured him casually and then looked at his watch. 'We have to be off, Jekabs,' he said. Taking me by the hand he ushered me briskly out onto the street so that I barely had time to turn and give Uncle a wave."

"The headquarters of the SS turned out to be quite close to the factory, so we walked there. En route Lobe put his arm around my shoulder and smiled at me, saying, 'One more thing, Corporal, you'll be with your comrade Sergeant Kulis in the Sapira Troop.' *Sapira* means pioneer.

"When I heard this, I forgot my anger toward Sergeant Kulis. I pictured myself alongside him on patrol as in the old days.

"When we reached Lobe's headquarters, the commander took me directly to a small office where his secretary was waiting. He passed me over to her care. She took me to a neighboring room where I noticed a box on a low table. It held my new SS uniform. Immediately she tried to remove my jacket. I adopted a no-nonsense, haughty attitude: I turned my back on the secretary, dismissing her with the words, 'You may go now.'

" 'Very well,' she said and then left me alone to put on the uniform.

"Several minutes later I returned to the office in my new uniform. The lady gave me a flirtatious pout and told me to wait for the commander, who would be back shortly. When he returned, Commander Lobe was carrying a full-length black leather overcoat that had been tailored especially for me. He held it open and I slipped my arms into the sleeves so that I was reminded for an instant of my dead soldier's overcoat: it was so heavy that I could barely move, and its hem dragged slightly on the floor. But it felt so much more elegant.

"The uniform was light khaki, but the design wasn't much different to the other ones I'd worn. And, of course, I still had my long riding boots, which I wore over my jodhpurs."

My father squinted. It was as if he were staring into his past, at an image of himself in Lobe's office. Then he nodded his head. "There were these—What do you call them? 'Insignia,' is it?—sewn onto the jacket, on its upper arm and sleeve and collar." My father raised his left arm slightly to show me.

"Here," he said, pointing first at his upper arm close to the shoulder, "was one identical to the one on the Wehrmacht uniform. It was shaped like a shield and was red-colored with a white band going across it at an angle. On it was written 'Latvijas,' which meant Latvia."

"And the sleeve?"

"The insignia of the SS. You must be familiar with the two esses shaped to look like lightning. On the other cuff was an eagle with its wings spread wide open, which was pretty—"

"Pretty?" I cut in. I was dismayed by my father's choice of word. For just a moment I had forgotten again that my father was remembering through not only a child's eyes but also the emotions he had felt at the time.

"Yes," my father answered; fortunately he seemed oblivious to my tone.

"But my favorite was the emblem on the collar of the jacket. There was a little black patch on either side of the neck. One had a stripe for my rank as Sturmann, and the other one had a symbol on it—an outline of the sun with three stars inside it, the symbol of the Latvian SS. I loved that one.

"Best of all, though, was the one Commander Lobe had. He'd been awarded one of the highest military medals of the German army: the German Medal—Gold Standard, which he wore around his neck on a ribbon. He would let me play with that, too, for hours on end. It kept me entertained whenever I got bored.

"In fact, Uncle told me that Commander Lobe had traveled to Berlin and received the medal from Hitler himself," my father added, both ashamed of and visibly impressed by Lobe's achievement.

I was aghast at the predicament of the innocent boy-soldier oblivious to the significance of the medal. The boy had treated as a toy a medal awarded to Lobe for his horrendous crimes.

"It was sometime in the midsummer of 1943 when we left Riga for the Russian front. Our first port of call in occupied Russia was Velikiye Luki.

I traveled with the commander up until that point, but immediately after we reached Velikiye Luki, the commander was taken up with serious military business, and I was handed back to Sergeant Kulis.

"I'd become a bit of a celebrity by that stage—I think that an article about me had been published in a newspaper in Riga, where I was pictured with Commander Lobe. So many of the soldiers knew about me. They were always wanting to play with me or simply have me around. Sometimes I'd get overwhelmed by it all. I'd be tired and grizzly and then Sergeant Kulis would keep the soldiers at bay.

"We must have stayed in Velikiye Luki for about a month. It was a base camp for our brigade, and the troop spent time doing extra training for the front line. During the day the sergeant was often involved in military activities away from base camp. When he returned in the evening, we'd sit together on the steps outside the barracks entrance. He would quietly smoke a cigarette, and I'd be by his side, scraping dried mud off his boots.

"I had my regular duties as well. The main one was to tidy our barracks once the soldiers had left for the day's training. But for most of the day I was left to my own devices. I'd chat with the soldiers who were off duty, and on rare occasions, if Commander Lobe allowed it, I would visit him in his makeshift office. He was always pleased to see me, and he'd sit me on his knee and ask me if I was being a good corporal. But when he was very busy and preoccupied I'd be told to sit quietly in the corner.

"There were so many visitors coming and going all day long. Some of them were clearly very important, German officers, for example, who arrived with entourages of assistants. But I can't remember any of their names. The commander didn't usually introduce me to them. I would simply salute them and after that he would dismiss me, telling me to return to my barracks."

"Eventually we were ordered to move farther north into Novgorod. We stopped briefly in the occupied city, where we then changed trains before heading north toward Volhov. In a matter of days we reached the Volhov area. There was no town or village that I can recall. Simply a train junction that was the end of the line. We had to change over to funny little trains, more like toy trains, on narrow-gauge tracks. There were no carriages as such, only open wagons that we had to crouch in. These took us as far as possible into the swamps of Volhov and then we had to dismount again. From there we made our way deeper into the swamps on foot along narrow wooden planks elevated off the ground.

"It was eerie. We were surrounded by trees that had no branches or leaves. Just trunks standing upright, like skeletons stretching up into the sky. I remember one of the soldiers joked that we were on patrol for ghosts.

"The heart of the swamps was like nothing I'd ever experienced even during my time alone in the forest. It was hellish. Everywhere was covered in mud and the stifling humidity was unbearable. It didn't seem to drop at all, day or night.

"On top of this, the air was thick with clouds of mosquitoes and other bugs so that within hours of arriving every part of our bodies that were exposed to air were covered in bright red bites and swollen lumps, even on our faces. They itched like hell.

"By night we slept in dugouts in small groups of about four men. This was terrible, too—the bottom of the dugouts often contained a few inches of water, which we had to scoop out. But the bottom always remained muddy.

"And then there were the rats that loved the dugouts. We could see their red eyes glowing up at us as we prepared to climb in for the night. We'd shoot at them, or if there were too many of them we'd simply toss down a hand grenade to kill them in one go. Then we'd have to fish them out before we could climb down to get some sleep. All this on top of the humidity and the mosquitoes. Sometimes the soldiers were too exhausted to care and just dropped down on the ground wherever they could and slept." My father shook his head in disbelief.

"In our crude camp there was an open kitchen that was equipped with an enormous cauldron for cooking. Three times a day, day in and day out, the same meal—a kind of soupy gruel—was cooked in it. It simmered away all day long. Before meals it was poured into a large trough at which the soldiers would line up, as if they were farm animals waiting for their turn at the watering hole. It tasted rancid, and the soldiers would constantly complain about it in low voices.

"The soldiers always put me at the head of the queue. 'Watch out,' they would shout. 'Let the little mascot through.' After my bowl had been filled I'd find a place to sit with the sergeant if he was around.

"The soldiers always passed me extra pieces of food from their kits. Our troop had received a small supply of Laima chocolate, and the soldiers would always slip me a chunk from their rations, which they received from Laima, the official sponsor of the Eighteenth and the Second Division that kept them supplied with chocolate.

"Unlike in Velikiye Luki things were now much less regulated and orderly. I would remain behind in the camp, but there wasn't much to do apart from my few duties. I'd try to be of use fetching things for the soldiers or helping them with their laundry. Not that any of us were ever very clean. It was hard to keep your dignity.

"More often than not the soldiers wanted me to simply sit and talk with them. They'd tell me stories about the villages they came from, or they'd talk endlessly about their families or girlfriends or school. To tell the truth, behind their camaraderie many of them seemed very lonely and frightened by their situation. And some of them seemed almost as young and childish as me. I couldn't equate these young men who were my friends with their savagery as soldiers.

"Sometimes I would be left alone for hours. Nobody watched me, and I'd venture outside the camp and often stray some distance away. But I always kept within earshot of the sound of gunfire and used that as a bearing to find my way back to camp.

"I often came across dead bodies as I had done in the forest. Some of the corpses were badly decomposed—they must have been there for months—and judging from the scraps of uniform that clung to their remains, some of them were soldiers. They'd been left where they had died, without even a burial in an unmarked grave. I'd become bigger and stronger by then, so I had no difficulty in turning them faceup in order to check their pockets.

"Then I'd sometimes come across a photograph of a loved one or an ID card, which I'd gently place back on them. It felt wrong to take anything from them now that I was being cared for.

"I'd put a twig or two over the body just to pretend that it was buried. I thought of it as my special secret duty. 'Nobody in my battalion needs to know about this,' I thought. I performed this ritual on every single corpse I came across regardless of whether they were soldiers or not. I guessed that some of them might even have been the enemy *partizani*, but I did the same for them.

"I always made my way back to camp before the light faded. I didn't want any trouble."

"One day when I'd ventured away from the camp, I was taken over by a sort of madness. 'Here's your chance,' I thought. 'Nobody will miss you. Just keep heading into the swamp and away from the brigade.' I was sure that I could survive, since I'd done so before in the forest.

"The afternoon wore on and I trudged deeper and deeper into the swamps. It was hard going. I kept falling down in the mud and struggled to get myself up again. The sun was behind me, so I knew that I was heading east. Gradually the sunlight grew thinner, but I didn't stop nor did I look back one single time.

"When I'd been alone in the forest before, I had grown used to it, despite my fear and desperation. But this was different and somehow unnerving, with the strange skeletons of trees that rose out of the swirling mist and noises of a sort I'd not heard before—creaking and whooshing sounds. There wasn't even the noise of birds. Perhaps the war had frightened them away. I started to think that my attempt to escape had not been such a good idea.

"I panicked. I turned and ran back in the direction of the setting sun, hoping that I would eventually reach the soldiers. I scrambled on and on through the swamp and the broken trees with their withered arms.

"It was almost twilight when I stopped for breath. There was still no sign of the camp, nor the sound of gunfire, and I hadn't been able to locate any of the markers that usually pointed me in the right direction. I realized then that I was completely lost.

"There was nothing to do but to keep on walking. To calm myself and keep myself company I chatted to myself in Latvian and sang songs that came to me."

My father hummed a few words in a soft voice. The lyrics were in a language I did not recognize. Nor could I identify the melody.

"Where did you learn that?" I asked.

"I don't know. I just know it."

I was intrigued by my father's recollection. Had it been something he had picked up from his mother? But my curiosity went unsatisfied as my father dived abruptly back into his story.

"Then I noticed something in the distance," he said. "At first I thought I was imagining it. In that gray wasteland of dead wood I saw what seemed to be a clump of green trees." My father gave a small laugh.

"As I made my way closer to it, I realized that I hadn't gone mad after all. It was real. I was relieved. I knew how to take refuge safely in a forest.

"I plunged into the rich undergrowth, then I stopped. Once again I panicked. 'What if this forest is ruled by those ghostly trees outside? What if this is a trap,' I thought, 'to catch me and devour me?'

"By the time night had fallen I'd reverted to my old strategy. I'd climbed a tree and tied myself into a fork in the branches, this time with the leather belt from my uniform. Nothing came that night to frighten me—the trees did not come to life, nor were there any sounds of wolves or bears or other predators.

"In the morning I remained where I was, perched high up in the tree, and looked all around, trying to get my bearings. I was surprised because through the tops of the trees I could see the outline of a city in the far distance. I thought that it must've been Leningrad because Sergeant Kulis had spoken of how close we were to 'the greatest of Russian cities.'

"I decided to make my way out of the forest and head in the direction of Leningrad. 'If I can see it,' I thought, 'then it cannot be too far away.' I unbuckled my belt and clambered down the tree. I wanted to reach Leningrad as quickly as possible. I took my bearings from the rising sun and headed off in what I estimated was a northerly direction.

"I'd taken no more than a dozen steps when I heard voices and footsteps nearby. Whoever they were, they were almost upon me. I scrambled back up the tree and held my breath. Then almost directly below me I saw about six people come to a halt. They were carrying guns. There were men and women, all quite young and speaking in a language I recognized—Russian."

"You knew that you were Russian?" I asked.

"I didn't think of myself as being any nationality, but I recognized some of the words that Kulis had tested on me and that he'd told me were Russian. And the other soldiers had kept insisting that I was Russian."

"How did you feel about your false identity?"

My father shrugged. "What could I do? Even though I knew it wasn't the truth, part of me accepted it as such. In any case, I had no clear idea who I really was, so what was the point of protesting against the identity they'd given me?"

"But you knew at least what had happened to your family. You realized that you were Jewish. Wasn't there anybody you felt you could confide in?"

"Not a soul. That would've meant certain death. It was clear Kulis didn't want to talk about it. I was an enemy of the Nazis and the Latvian people."

After several moments my father returned to his story. "I sensed that these people standing below my tree were the *partizani* that the soldiers were always cursing. One tiny move and they might discover me; if they saw my SS uniform, I would be shot on the spot. But then suddenly it also occurred to me that if they were the enemies of the Latvians, then perhaps I should be on their side.

"I sat there high up in the tree, both petrified and wondering what would be the right thing to do, when something very strange happened. I caught a glimpse of the face of one of the women. I recognized her. At first I didn't know who she was or where she was from, but then it dawned on me that she was from my village. I had this vivid impression that she'd been in our house when I was playing in the yard, and that she'd smiled at me. I nearly fell out of the tree. I had an overwhelming urge to spring down from my hiding spot and ask her outright, 'Do you remember me?'

"But I didn't. I cannot describe clearly what happened to me. I must have become transfixed by my thought of home because the next thing I recall was coming to and realizing that the group had picked up their packs and moved quietly away. I felt defeated by their departure. But still I couldn't make up my mind what to do. Try to find them or stay hidden in the tree? I was tormented.

"If only I'd made myself known to them . . ." my father said. Even now he appeared to be devastated by this lost chance.

"The forest was deadly silent. I rubbed my eyes. I must still have been half in a dream. 'Did this happen?' I asked myself. Or was it as I had suspected all along—that the forest held some kind of evil magic? Had they been ghosts? Had the woman I recognized from my village come back to punish me for deserting my family?

"Suddenly I didn't care whether that group of people was real or imagined. I scrambled down the tree and fled in the opposite direction. I ran without any concern about where I was going, and within moments I landed directly in the arms of two soldiers from the division who'd been sent out to search for me. I was hysterical and one soldier had to slap me hard to bring me to my senses.

"I learned that I'd been gone for nearly two days and how worried everybody had been. Many believed that I must have perished somewhere.

"The soldiers told me how ungrateful I was for all that had been done for me. But I was too overwhelmed by my experience to respond. They dragged me roughly back to camp. I feared what was in store for me.

"They took me directly to Sergeant Kulis, who was furious with me. One of the commanding German officers had ordered that I be sent back to Velikiye Luki immediately as punishment. The sergeant packed my stuff there and then, and that evening I left in the company of a platoon that was being relieved from frontline duty. I didn't even say farewell to Sergeant Kulis.

"The platoon reached Velikiye Luki a few days later. Even though I was famished, I wasn't permitted to stop at the mess for breakfast. I was ordered directly to Commander Lobe's quarters.

"The soldier who took me there pushed me forward, telling me to knock on the door. I heard the commander call out, 'Enter.' He was in his bathroom standing bare-chested at the sink, shaving. The commander stared at my reflection in his mirror. 'You,' he said, looking down at me disdainfully. Then he went on shaving in silence. I remained standing at attention, and he did not bother to put me at ease. I watched as he washed and dried himself off. He turned and brushed past me as he went into the main room. It was as if I'd become invisible.

"I remained standing where I was but felt drowsy because of lack of food and sleep. Suddenly his face was inches from mine. His eyes were bulbous and bloodshot, and his face was purple. He was like a vicious dog snarling and barking words at me, most of which I didn't hear because I was scared out of my wits, trembling and shaking uncontrollably.

"Then he stood upright and glared down at me with steely eyes. 'I know what you were trying to do,' he said. He realized that I had been trying to run away from the army. He brought his face close to mine again and raised his hand. I braced myself. But he didn't hit me—instead he tore off the corporal's insignia from the collar of my jacket. 'You're no longer a corporal,' he said sharply. 'You are a private again. You're no longer on active duty. You're going back to Riga, to the Dzenis family.'

"Then he dismissed me. As I left he called after me so that I had to stop and turn. 'You try this again,' he said, 'and I'll kill you.'

"I had been disgraced. I didn't feel like a soldier at all. I felt small, like a child, and was too ashamed of myself to be worried by his threat.

"I was sent back to Riga by train that same day in the company of a guard. All the way back to Riga he didn't utter a single word to me, as if he distrusted me as a traitor.

"Uncle was waiting for me at Riga station, but there was no celebration this time. He, too, had been made aware of my conduct." My father paused, seemingly exhausted by his recollection.

"I never saw Sergeant Kulis again," he said reflectively. "He never came for me as I thought he would, and I never asked about him. I didn't want to be reminded of my failure. Or remind anybody about it."

"Do you know what became of him?" I asked.

"For many years I assumed that he had died during the war. But then in the late fifties, long after the Dzenises took me with them to Australia, a letter arrived out of the blue. It was from Sergeant Kulis and had been sent from a suburb in New York City. He'd traced me through a network of Latvian soldiers—Daugavas Vanagi—he'd kept in touch with after the war.

"The envelope contained a short note and a photograph of Sergeant Kulis in the living room of his home with a boy of seven or eight sitting on his knee. I have the note here."

My father reached into his case and immediately produced a yellowed envelope. He perched his reading glasses on the end of his nose and began to read.

"'The seventh of June, 1958. Dear Uldis. It's been years since I last saw you. But I have often thought about you. Many times my wife Wilma and I have talked about you and wondered if you would remember us.

"'We spent some nice days in Riga, do you remember? Then came the day you were sent back to Riga. It's been fifteen long years since then. God gave me luck and I survived the war. Now I live in America and work in the building industry. I have a son who is the same age as you when we parted. It would make me very happy if you were interested to be in contact with me.

" 'I want to hear about you and your life in Australia. I still think of you as my son. I always regret that I never adopted you. With kind regards, Jekabs Kulis.' "

"Amazing. Did you reply to the letter, Dad?"

"No."

"Did you ever try to make contact with him?"

"Never."

"Why?"

"I wanted to look to the future. Not rake up the past. I locked the letter away in my case and for a very long time, decades in fact, I forgot that I'd ever received it or that Kulis existed. That case is a bit of a curse, isn't it? I never know what I might find in it."

I needed to clear my head. I rose and without thinking went to the back door. I opened it a fraction and was assaulted by a gust of icy wind.

"For God's sake!" my father exclaimed. I immediately slammed the door shut. I was disturbed, perhaps even slightly annoyed, that my father had kept so many things from me—more facts about Lobe, his initiation into the Latvian SS, the letter from Kulis, a fuller picture of his life in the Volhov swamps—and the truth was that I needed also to take stock of my father. I was baffled by the fact that my father had remained silent for more than fifty years. What almost superhuman strength had this required? What toll had silence taken on his inner life? My father seemed to inhabit two separate worlds. In one, he was my father with an "official" history, an authorized and edited version of the past. But in the other world he was still largely a stranger to me: a boy-soldier, origins unknown, who was shunted about, wide-eyed, in one of the worst bloodbaths in recent history.

One world was inexorably unraveling while a new, unpredictable one emerged.

CHAPTER EIGHT
THE CHOCOLATE SOLDIER

I t was late October 1943 when I arrived back in Riga. By my calcu-
lation I'd been away at the front for about four months.

"Uncle was waiting for me at the main station. All the way
back to the apartment in Valdemara Street he remained silent next to me
in the limousine.

"The atmosphere in the apartment was subdued when we went in. In
the entrance hall I heard only the ticking of the ornate grandfather clock
in the corner. Then I heard Auntie's footsteps in the hallway. She came
into the foyer and greeted me much more formally than she had ever
done before—she shook my hand. It dawned on me that the commander's suspicions about my attempted escape had been passed on to Uncle
and Auntie and that they, too, felt betrayed by me.

"That afternoon Uncle had to go back to work at Laima and he left
Auntie and me alone. No sooner had he closed the door behind him than
Auntie swept me up into her arms and planted kisses on both my cheeks.
She told me how much she'd missed me. I was overjoyed: Auntie had
been pleased to see me after all, and she still cared for me.

"She scrutinized my face and a look of concern crossed her features.
She told me that I had gotten much too frail and that I needed fattening
up, and lots of fresh air.

"That night I overheard her discussing a holiday with Uncle, and
shortly after that Auntie took me to a country house the family kept in a

place called Carnikava on the Riga coast, some miles northeast of the city. We stayed there for about a week." My father's face beamed at the memory so that I could almost see the little boy in him.

"I'd never laid eyes upon the sea before and, that first time, I was shocked. I stood on the shoreline for ages, entranced by the waves as they flowed to shore. Even though it was the Baltic and had nothing of the wildness I later saw in the Australian oceans, I remember how impressed I was by its immensity and power. For a moment I recollected when I was a child in the village and I'd pretend to be the ship's captain scanning the sea for pirates. Now here was the real sea before me, but I had no interest in playing pirates. I had become a real soldier.

"Auntie prepared delicacies for me every evening, especially my favorites, lamprey and smoked eel. At night together we'd build a fire to ward off the damp early autumn chill in the air. I'd lie on the sofa with my head on her lap, and she would read to me from a book of Latvian fairy tales. It was full of stories about ogres and mischievous spirits and other evil beings in the forests. I'd experienced enough of that already, but I didn't mind listening as it gave me an excuse to nestle close to Auntie. The sound of her gentle voice would lull me into a light slumber so that later Auntie would have to rouse me, take me upstairs, and tuck me in bed.

"I always dropped off to sleep easily, but later I'd wake up screaming, haunted by nightmares I couldn't remember. Auntie would rush to my room and, to calm me down, sing Latvian folk songs I'd never heard before or tell me another fairy tale until I eventually nodded off again."

When I was a child, my father had spoken of his time at Carnikava as one of happy and peaceful days spent in a rural idyll. He had even shown us photographs taken there. However, something unsettled me about these ostensibly innocent photographs in which my father seemed withdrawn and somehow damaged. His arms were folded guardedly across his chest. It was the expression on his face that had most disturbed me. He looked as if he had just woken from a nightmare at the moment the photograph was taken.

This impression hadn't made sense to me as a child because he'd

My father with Auntie in Carnikava, 1943.

never given us the slightest intimation of the violent and bloody world he had belonged to before Carnikava. Hearing his words now, I understood that expression on his face—truly he had just woken from the nightmare of his experiences with the soldiers.

At that moment, I felt an inexpressible gratitude to Auntie. I was moved to know that my father had had someone to comfort him and look out for him. In fact, my childhood memories of Auntie were of a kindly person who, although capable of little English, communicated to us through her warmth, often planting kisses on our foreheads unexpectedly, much as I imagine she'd done to my father as a boy.

But I couldn't escape the thought that my father did not wake up from his nightmares into the love of his own family; he was an orphan thrust among strangers. There had not been a soul who could reassure him that the world was as it should be, because he knew instinctively and through experience that it was not.

I turned my attention back to my father's words.

"In the week following our return from Carnikava, I overheard a conversation between Auntie and Uncle about whether I should return to school. Uncle's opinion was that it wouldn't be possible, because I'd become even more unruly after being at the front. He'd decided that, instead, I should go to Laima Chocolates with him every day and be tutored there.

"I was confused. 'Lessons in a chocolate factory?' I thought to myself. 'What could they teach me there?' But I also looked forward to it—I pictured myself gobbling chocolate all day long, as much as I desired. But I'd gotten it all wrong. Uncle had my day, particularly the mornings, mapped out for me.

"Our limousine would pull up outside the factory at seven forty-five. I still wore my uniform—I refused to wear civilian clothes—and I would give a curt salute to the receptionist. Then I'd trail into the factory behind Uncle as he went about his daily inspection of the workers, who stood to attention by their machines and packing tables.

"The workers would greet Uncle and then me. 'Good morning, Private Kurzemnieks,' they'd say, and I'd salute in response.

"When we reached his office, Uncle always gave me the same order: 'To your duty, young soldier!' he'd say, and I'd head over to a child's desk—stacked with books that he'd organized for me—by the window.

"Then we would both settle down to our work. Obviously, Uncle was very busy with the running of the factory. People would be coming and going all morning—his secretary, section managers, and others. He'd arranged for me to have a tutor—Miss Novackis, she was called—to teach me how to read and write in Latvian, as well as give me lessons in Latvian history. We'd always begin the day's classes with Latvian language. I'd read in halting Latvian from books. I was never any good at reading. I was never any good with books, for that matter. I couldn't even handle them properly—I'd fumble with them.

"I was a quick learner, but I couldn't settle. I'd get bored and easily distracted. I couldn't concentrate. It was hard going for a boy of my age, with all I'd been through, to sit diligently at my desk all morning long.

"As soon as Uncle was out of the office on some business, I'd jump out of my chair and head for the window. I'd gaze down at the street below. I longed to be outside and free, especially if I saw somebody in uniform passing by. It reminded me of my comrades who were still at the front.

"The afternoons were best of all." My father smiled nostalgically. "I was the king of Laima. I had the run of the factory and was free to do as I wished, as long as I stayed out of trouble.

"I'd become a popular figure among the workers on the factory floor and would wander among them, chatting. I was a greedy little thing as well, and I'd stuff both pockets of my jacket with chocolates. Later, I'd find a deserted corner of the storeroom, where I'd devour them until I was nearly sick.

"I loved to watch the engineer, too, as he maintained the factory's machinery. I'd question him endlessly and absorb every detail of how he fixed the plant equipment. Sometimes he'd pass me a small piece of equipment that I'd spend hours on, dismantling it and then putting it together again. I had an aptitude, it seemed, for mending things, which kept me out of mischief," my father joked, "but not away from the chocolates."

I was curious about Uncle and tried to steer our discussion in that direction.

"Tell me, Dad, did Uncle ever wear a uniform?" I interrupted my father.

"No. I never saw him in a uniform. He was a civilian."

"Did he mix with soldiers and officers?"

My father nodded. "Occasionally officers would appear at Laima."

"I wonder what they were doing in a chocolate factory?"

"To be honest, I never thought about it."

"Did you recognize any of them?"

"Only Commander Lobe. Quite a number of weeks had elapsed since my return to Riga, when one day, without any notice, he reappeared in Uncle's office. After that he turned up regularly at Laima so that I started to see more of him. His headquarters were just around the corner from Laima and from the window near my desk I could see him striding toward the factory."

"Why was Lobe there so frequently?"

"The commander and Uncle were old friends. They'd been in the Bolshevik revolution together years before. They fought against the Bolsheviks for Latvian independence. They belonged to a group called Lacplesis."

"Lacplesis?"

"That's right," my father said. "The Society of the Bear. It was the association of freedom fighters for Latvia. On the rare occasions the commander and Uncle spoke about Lacplesis, it was only in glowing terms of the bravery of Lacplesis members and its noble cause. In fact, I believe Uncle had been given the house in Carnikava as a reward for bravery and services to Lacplesis."

I made a mental note to try to discover more about this group. (Later I was to learn that Lacplesis was closer to an organization of Latvian Fascists.)

"Uncle also told me many years later that Commander Lobe had worked for him in Laima for a while, early on during the war. Uncle had helped him out with a job and a place to stay. According to Uncle, the commander had been on duty in Ventspils on the northwest coast of Latvia, but for some unknown reason, he'd been relieved of his command and had left the army. All I know is that it had something to do with not obeying a German order."

My father looked ill at ease and shifted in his seat. "But the commander's visits often had something to do with me as well. I hadn't seen him since he'd ordered me back from the front. At first things were uneasy between us: inside I was rigid with fear as I couldn't forget the threat that he'd made to kill me, but he was determined to break the ice.

"He'd sit down next to me as I studied at my desk and draw in his chair close to mine—so close that I could smell his uniform and the soap he used to wash himself—and check my work over my shoulder. He was less formal than Uncle, very hearty and cheerful, but he had sharp eyes. He watched everything like a hawk.

"One day, he and Uncle had a conversation in which my name was mentioned several times. I kept my head down, but in fact I was eavesdropping. It seemed that he was keen to organize something to do with me. Uncle appeared resistant to whatever it was, but Commander Lobe spoke forcefully back to him. After that Uncle seemed to give in to the commander. In reality, I suppose that Uncle didn't have much choice. Being a member of the SS, the commander usually got his way.

"The following morning, the commander reappeared. He took me away from Miss Novackis. He stood me in the center of the room and announced that I was reinstated as a corporal. He presented me with a new military jacket displaying the rank of corporal on the lower sleeve and the collar.

"I was over the moon. I'd no sooner put the jacket on—it fit perfectly—than he ordered me to make ready. I was to go out to lunch with him immediately, even though it was still early. I had a feast of lampreys and strawberry ice cream, while he sat back in his chair and examined me as if I were under a microscope. Then finally he spoke. 'Do you want to be a good patriot?' he asked. I didn't know what patriot meant, but I nodded my head gravely, my mouth still full of ice cream.

"'Do you want to help Latvia?' he went on. I nodded my head again, this time more enthusiastically. I would have done anything to redeem myself in his eyes. He tousled my hair. 'Good soldier,' he said.

"That day changed everything. I spent more time with Commander Lobe, several times a week, in fact.

"There was another incident in particular that changed the nature of our relationship. The commander had taken me to a park, and while he sat on a bench, smoking, I wandered off to a merry-go-round to play. At one point an elderly gentleman approached me, curious about how I'd become a soldier. I was lost for an answer—nobody had asked me this before. I ran back to the commander and asked him. I thought the commander would give me an answer. Instead he rose abruptly and, taking me by the hand, hurried back to headquarters.

"The commander was on edge. He sat me down in an armchair and stood towering above me. Then he started talking to himself in a low, agitated voice about how the soldiers had found me those many months ago. Kulis had told him that I had appeared from behind a tree on the outskirts of a deserted village. He was obsessed with the story and repeated it slowly as he paced up and down. Then he stopped and turned to look at me. He began to repeat the story again, but this time he'd embellished it so that it became different from the one Kulis had made up.

"In the commander's version, I was a Russian pigherd who'd been found wandering through a deserted village with a herd that I was tending. I appeared from behind a tree and told the soldiers that I'd become separated from my father and mother and asked if I could join them.

"It was not the last version to appear, either. From time to time in newspaper articles, the story was printed with variations. I remember one time Uncle read aloud an article that said that the soldiers had found me in a village where I was being looked after by two elderly peasant women who'd found me wandering alone in the forest."

My father laughed. "It was confusing, to say the least," he said. "I myself would occasionally get the details messed up."

"Why did Lobe change the details?" I asked.

My father shrugged.

"You don't think it was to make the soldiers look more heroic?"

My father shrugged again.

"What did you think about this story?"

"Nothing really," my father replied. "I told you before. I let people say what they wanted to. I wasn't going to make any trouble about it. Only one thing was certain: these stories were very far removed from the truth that I have told you.

"The afternoon wore on and I remained seated in the armchair. The commander was reading through documents at his desk. Suddenly he shouted my name, and I jumped to attention.

"He leaned back and pushed his chair away from his desk and called me over to sit on his knee. Yet again he went over the story, only this time he made me repeat it after him, word for word. He made it clear that I was to keep to it as much as possible. For the next few days, he didn't take me out in public.

"Then one day I was sitting quietly in his office, coloring in my book, when he suddenly quizzed me on his version of events to make sure I'd remembered it. I recited it verbatim. 'Perfect,' he exclaimed, clapping his hands together.

"After that, he began to take me out to cafés again to see how well I performed in public. Unsurprisingly, a child in an SS uniform attracted a lot of attention, and people would approach us, curious to know more about me. I'd ignore them and go on eating my ice cream or eels, until the commander gave me a nudge or a pinch under the table, and I'd swing into action like a puppet.

"I'd put my spoon down and stand and recite as naturally as I could what I'd been taught. If I was in the mood, I'd sing a few notes of one of the songs the soldiers had taught me."

"Do you think Lobe knew the true story of your capture?"

"I don't think so. I know that when he brought me to base camp for the first time, Sergeant Kulis told the commander that the soldiers had found me wandering alone in a forest on the perimeter of a village. Kulis had made up this story when he first took me out of the firing line and decided to let me live. If he'd told the commander the truth, then the commander would have suspected I was Jewish, and my fate would've been sealed. Even though none of the other soldiers knew I was Jewish or had any reason to want to protect me from Lobe, inexplicably, they all stuck to Kulis's story as well."

"This story covered up their deeds," I said contemptuously. "They portrayed themselves as kindly rescuers instead of the barbaric murderers of innocent people they truly were."

These last words shocked my father. His face reddened.

"But Sergeant Kulis wasn't like that," he offered. "Despite everything he'd done that I despised, there can't be any doubt that he tried to protect me. He warned me to hide my Jewishness or I would be killed. If he hadn't wanted to protect me, he could've returned me to face the firing squad. And I believe that he never told a soul about my true identity. And the other soldiers, though they didn't know I was Jewish, were kind to me. They protected me because I was a child."

"The question is, Dad, would they have been quite so kind if they knew you were a Jewish child?"

My father was grim-faced.

After several moments I pressed on. "You must have had a very strong and determined character to have kept it hidden from Uncle and Auntie while you were living under their roof."

"I don't think strength had anything to do with it," my father answered. "It was fear, son—pure fear! Fear of discovery. Fear of saying the wrong thing. I'd made that mistake once; after the party at the Dzenises' on my first night with them, when I said that I wanted my own brother and sister. I had to be certain never to do that again."

I immediately regretted the way I had cross-examined my father. He had suffered awfully under this conspiracy of silence about his identity. "Terrible," I said in a sympathetic tone.

Perhaps buoyed by this, my father appeared to relax and was suddenly eager to continue.

"Where was I?" he said, thinking aloud. "That's right. Commander Lobe was satisfied that I had mastered my routine. He then started to take me on visits to hospitals and clinics to boost the morale of sick and wounded soldiers. I'd tour the wards with him. He trained me to commend the patients, saying, 'Father Latvia thanks you for your courage and wishes you a speedy recovery.'"

My father gave an ironic laugh. "I was a child, but even I could see how empty those words were. I remember one time saying that nonsense to a soldier who was bandaged from head to toe. I could only see his eyes staring out at me. He wasn't going to recover, and even if he did, I wondered what condition he'd be in for the remainder of his life. There were many sad cases like him. I felt ashamed of my words."

My father rummaged in his case again. He passed me a small scrap of tattered paper.

I drew it close to my eyes. It was an article that had been torn roughly from a newspaper. The print was too faded to read, but the photograph above it was distinct enough for me to discern an image of my father in full military uniform, sitting on Lobe's knee and posing among bandaged soldiers and other dignitaries and officials. Standing to one side was the figure of Uncle, who seemed to be watching over the boy.

"Amazing," I said. "Where did you get this?"

"The commander tore it out of the newspaper for me. You can see, it says 1943 at the bottom of it."

"You've had it all this time?"

"Yes. Here in my case."

My father patted the lid of the case tenderly, as if stroking a pet. But the case's persona had irrevocably changed for me by this stage. So magical to me when I was a child, it now seemed malign. I had a sudden and almost uncontrollable urge to snatch it from my father and bury it. But the impulse to dispose of the case died away as quickly as it had come and, in its place, I found a question forming in my mind. Why hadn't he told us this story before?

"Worse was to come. One particular day when we had no tours planned, the commander sent me back to Uncle's office at Laima. I was glad to be back with Uncle. I was tired of being the commander's little

My father on a hospital tour, sitting on the knee of Commander Lobe. Mr. Dzenis stands to the right in a black suit.

windup doll. With Uncle, it was exactly as it had been before: I sat quietly at my desk.

"Suddenly the door flew open and in marched the commander. He never bothered to knock. He saluted quite casually and flopped himself down on the edge of Uncle's desk. Then he helped himself to a cigarette from Uncle's tobacco box.

"The commander was in an excited state, telling Uncle that a group of military officers would be arriving shortly that same day and that arrangements needed to be made for an experiment. Uncle seemed flabbergasted.

"Then the commander began to explain, and I could tell that Uncle was not pleased with what he was hearing. But the commander's voice conveyed that he would not harbor any objections.

"Their exchange was interrupted when a group of officers strode confidently into the room, about four of them Latvian, as well as a German in command. One of the Latvians was called Osis and the German had a name that sounded something like Jackal or Jekyll. They had a strong air of authority about them in their fine uniforms decorated with colorful medals.

"These men were only in Uncle's office for a short time before they headed off into the factory. I must have had some curiosity because I decided to tail them. They went into one of the storerooms upstairs at the rear of the factory.

"I managed to get close and see through the crack in the doorway. One of the officers was pointing at a diagram of what seemed to be a truck or tank. I soon grew bored of spying on them. I had no idea what was up.

"A few days later, the same officers reappeared with Commander Lobe. They were immersed in serious conversation and didn't even bother to greet me.

"All of a sudden the commander had stopped speaking midsentence. The room went quiet. I went on pretending to study, but I couldn't resist my curiosity and raised my head a fraction to see what had happened.

"The commander was standing, as if frozen to the spot, in the center of the room, staring intently at me. In the next instant he became animated. He clapped his hands together and gave a little jump, like an excited child. He sprang across the room and, in a single movement, he lifted me up out of my chair and high into the air, shaking me like a trophy he'd just won. He planted me on top of Uncle's desk and began to speak excitedly to the other soldiers.

"Almost immediately, upon hearing what the commander had said, the others began to nod their heads enthusiastically. All except Uncle, who became angry, almost apoplectic! I'd never seen him like that before.

"The commander simply raised his hand to silence Uncle. Then he turned to me again and, with his face only inches from mine, said, 'Do you want to help me on a very special project?' His tone was dramatic and heavy, so of course I nodded vigorously, eager to make myself useful. I hesitated to look directly at Uncle since I was going against his wish. Suddenly, the commander grabbed me by the waist and lifted me off the desk. Then he turned and strode toward the door with the officers following behind. I managed a brief and furtive glance back at Uncle, who looked deeply troubled.

"When we reached the rear steps of the factory that overlooked the yard, Commander Lobe put me down. I had a good view of the entire space. I was surprised because the courtyard was overflowing with people of all ages—old people, babies, women, children, anybody you could imagine. They stood quietly with their bags and cases as if waiting for a bus to take them on a journey. Only the babies were restless and crying.

"I tugged at the commander's jacket. I wondered what they were here for. I didn't like the atmosphere. I wanted to go back to Uncle.

"He glanced down at me and gave me a broad smile. He put his arm around my shoulder and led me down the steps. We joined the other officers, who'd dispersed among the crowd, inspecting them. Once we were in the thick of it, I was too tiny to see much at all, so I simply followed the commander, imitating the sharp and stern look on his face.

"Suddenly the gates into the yard clanked open with a screeching sound, and two gigantic transport trucks rumbled in and came to a halt.

"Soldiers guarding the crowd started to bark orders for everybody to get into the trucks as quickly as possible. Chaos broke out. People pushed and shoved to climb on, while trying to drag their belongings with them.

"I was disoriented and a little frightened by the mayhem and I drew away to the perimeter of the crowd. It was then that I noticed a little boy—he must have been only a year or two younger than me—standing nearby. He was crying. He must have become separated from his mother or whoever he was with. I wanted to do something for him, so I reached into my pocket and pulled out one of my chocolates from the secret stash.

"I held it out to the boy. He seemed very surprised, and his crying faded to a whimper. Then I could see how thin he was; his eyes protruded desperately from his gaunt face. Tentatively he put out his hand and then he snatched the chocolate greedily like a starving animal. 'He's just like me,' I thought, 'when Sergeant Kulis offered me a scrap of bread in the schoolroom.'

"I felt so sorry for him. I knew what it was like, the pit in your belly that gnawed away at you. I passed him another chocolate, which he accepted more graciously this time. Then I passed him another chocolate and yet another one, pacing them, so that his stomach would accept the chocolates and he didn't become sick. Then I noticed something that had escaped my attention up until then—the boy was wearing a yellow star on his jacket. By then I knew what that meant: he was Jewish. He was even more like me than I had imagined. He could have been my little brother. I was tormented. 'Should I feed him more?' I said to myself. 'Or should I ignore him?' If I showed him any kindness, the soldiers might become suspicious of me.

"'Or should I help him to escape?' I turned away from him in anguish. Instinctively, I looked toward the fence to see if there was a gap in it. For a moment, I imagined that we could both escape together, through the gap in the fence, as I had done by myself, in my village. But I knew that this time it would be impossible. I remained with my back to the boy.

"That moment has overshadowed my entire life," my father said in a low voice. "I don't want to sound dramatic, but I carry his image with me, like it's been imprinted on my retina. Frequently I wonder if he survived, if he grew into a man. I wonder if he remembers that day when I turned my back on him. It was as if I had turned my back on my own reflection at that moment. The questions always come down to that in the end."

My father was subdued. I felt helpless to console him.

"I noticed that one of the German officers was looking at me. He'd observed what had gone on between the boy and me. He flashed a big smile at me, and at the same time he began to speak with the other officers, who all nodded.

"They, too, stared across at me, confronting me with their smiles. At that moment I noticed Uncle standing at the rear door of the factory. He looked worried and disapproving.

"Then I heard the German officer call out my name loudly above the din. Snapping his fingers at me, he ordered me to join him. I pretended that I couldn't hear him and stayed where I was. Instead, I glanced across at Uncle. He, too, had seen the officer summon me. I hoped that he would rescue me from this situation, but he only indicated with his eyes that I shouldn't resist the soldiers.

"I went over to the German officer. I still had no idea what he wanted. He snapped his fingers yet again, and this time one of the soldiers stepped forward with a big paper bag. The chief officer thrust it into my hand. It was full of Laima chocolates. I was surprised. I thought that I'd been mistaken about his intentions and that the chocolates were a gift for me. I began to bite into one of them, but he gave me such a slap that it shot out of my mouth.

" 'Not for you, idiot,' he said harshly. Then he led me over to the rear of one of the trucks and had me stand at attention there. He gave an order for the crowd to form a line leading to the truck. Immediately I grasped what was required of me: I was to hand out a chocolate to each person in the queue as they climbed onto the truck.

"Commander Lobe joined us, and he told me that I should make sure to give every person a big smile as I presented their chocolate. It seemed that my job was to pacify them before their journey, especially the children, who loved the chocolates.

"So that's what I did—on and on throughout the afternoon. My jaw ached from smiling.

"I didn't notice Uncle's presence again until the end of the afternoon when he reappeared on the steps. He still seemed very disturbed, not only by what was happening generally but at what I was doing. He signaled angrily for me to join him and took my hand firmly. Without a word to anybody, we walked back into the factory.

"However, as we climbed the stairs to Uncle's office, the commander's voice boomed out from behind us, ordering us to stop. He was seething with anger and told Uncle to release me. Uncle refused, and I felt his grip tighten on my hand.

"Commander Lobe tried to break Uncle's grip, but Uncle pushed me behind him. Both men were keyed up, and there was a tense exchange of words. It was a terrifying standoff. Then Uncle uttered something—I didn't hear what—to the commander, who drew back, visibly shocked. The commander retreated down the stairs, and Uncle strode to his office, dragging me in his wake. For the moment at least, Uncle had won.

"When we reached his office, he told me sharply to get back to my books and to keep my head down, even if the officers and Commander Lobe returned.

"Before long, the sound of the trucks leaving reached my ears, and shortly after that Commander Lobe and the other officers came in. They made themselves comfortable wherever they could find a place. The commander ordered Uncle to get beer and schnapps for everybody. Uncle ordered it but refused to join them in their celebrations. As the men became drunk, their attitude toward Uncle harshened. They criticized him for protecting me. The German officer warned Uncle in no uncertain terms that his behavior wouldn't be tolerated a second time. With that, the party came to an abrupt end. As he was about to leave, the German officer turned to me and said, 'Morgens'—tomorrow. I realized that my job was not yet over.

"Uncle was subdued that evening as we headed home. He remained silent and preoccupied over dinner, too. Later, I lay awake all night, worried about my terrible duty, although I hadn't any idea of what lay in store for those people.

"The next morning I was bleary-eyed. My senses were dull from lack of sleep. It was probably better that way. One of the officers came to collect me from Uncle's office. But I had no choice. I knew what was in store for me, and I wanted nothing at all to do with it."

"How many times did this take place?" I asked.

"Three times, perhaps. There were no more trucks after that." My father paused. He appeared relieved to have finally spoken of the incident. The tightness around his mouth loosened slightly.

"That must have been the idea that Lobe hit upon in Uncle's office—the presence of a child would calm the crowd—and then the chocolates became an added touch after I'd been noticed with the boy." My father looked guilt-ridden. "At least the chocolates seemed to make it easier for them." My father was speaking through the eyes of the boy he had once been.

In the next breath he suddenly turned against himself. "A chocolate for their journey!" he exclaimed. "What idiocy am I talking? I did sense that something dark was going on, but Commander Lobe had told me that they were being relocated to another part of the country. But they killed them, didn't they?" He struggled to control his hysteria.

"Little children. Younger even than me or my brother and sister. They took them away to concentration camps or to forests—to isolated forests—to be massacred—to be robbed of their lives—their dignity—that was their final destination!"

My father flinched involuntarily, as if trying to dodge a blow. He took several deep breaths, trying to calm himself.

"The women and children and old people at Laima were innocent. Their only crime was to be born Jewish. Somewhere inside me I must have registered what their fate, as Jews, would be. After all, Sergeant Kulis had warned me to hide my Jewishness because it meant death. That was my only crime, too."

My father was ashen-faced and drawn. "Or am I guilty?" he asked. "Am I responsible, like the soldiers, for what went on? I don't know what to think. Those people in the yard at Laima were murdered, and I eased them on their way, not with a gun but with those damned chocolates."

My father withdrew further into himself. He seemed beaten: not a shred of his usual animation remained. "Even though I was only a child, I should have known. I must have blocked it out. It was only later that I understood what I had been party to." My father bowed his head so that I could no longer see his face.

"But at that time I didn't understand," my father pleaded meekly in his own defense. "I was shell-shocked. Frozen," he said in a weak voice. "I didn't understand the adults around me, or the world I was living in. I just went from moment to moment—what child doesn't?—grateful for food and shelter and warmth. Even more than that, I was so terrified that my true identity would be discovered. I just kept my antennae up and my head down."

After several moments of silence, a gasp of grief came from him as he struggled to gain control of his emotions. He looked up at me.

"Let's stop, son," he pleaded.

I was thankful to do so. I didn't know how much more I could endure.

But I was more worried about my father's emotional state. It seemed as if he were driving himself to the gallows to be hanged by his past. I was overwhelmed at the thought of the toll—the inner terror—his silence must have taken on him. It was not only his physical survival that had been at stake.

I sighed, suddenly exhausted by all I had just learned and all that was still likely to come.

"It's almost five o'clock," my father said. "You get some sleep, son."

"What about you, Dad?" I asked. I found myself fretting also about my father's physical state. He suffered at times from high blood pressure, and I prayed that it would remain stable under the burden of this night.

"I'll be fine," he replied. "I'll just wash the teacups and then get some rest myself."

I left him to it, suddenly embarrassed by our intimacy. I sensed my father felt the same way, as he rose without another word, crossed to the sink, and turned his back on me.

I dropped off to sleep just before dawn but not before scrawling a few notes on a scrap of paper. The rest I had was fitful, and in the few moments that I was able to doze off I had disturbing dreams: at one point I was standing knee-deep in a swamp, paralyzed by blood-red, glutinous mud. I struggled to raise myself out of it but was hopelessly trapped in the quagmire.

My inner life had been churned up in ways that I was not yet able to fully understand. Soon wide awake again, I lay in bed feeling drained. Outside I could hear the dawn chorus and the sound of my mother rising and moving through the house to the kitchen.

CHAPTER NINE

JUDGMENT

The sound of the front door slamming woke me. I must have drifted off into a light sleep again. I drew my arm out from under the blankets and looked at my watch. It was nearly 11:00 a.m. I'd slept about five hours, but I was instantly alert. I sprang out of bed and drew back the curtain. Immediately the light blinded me: it was a bright winter's day in Melbourne. The sky was a thin cloudless blue.

The house seemed deserted as I headed for the kitchen. There was no sign of life. Then I remembered that it was Friday. This time every week my mother met her close friend Maria in town for lunch, a film, and some window-shopping, returning at about six in the evening.

Just as I went to the kitchen window to get a view of my father's workshop, I heard the sound of his car pulling up in the drive. A few moments later the rear gate clicked open, and I saw him cross to his bolt-hole. I opened the window slightly and called out to him: "Dad! Coffee?" He gave a slight start and turned to face me.

I'd expected him to be tired and subdued. I was mistaken. He seemed to have regained his composure completely. There was no sign of what had taken place only hours ago. He looked positively robust. He headed toward the house, warning me in advance not to forget his three sugars.

I took his coffee over to the table where he'd just sat down.

"It's after eleven," he teased me. "You should've been up hours ago. I've been working since nine."

"You're superhuman, aren't you," I tossed back, before it occurred to me that my choice of words might have been an unconscious response to what I had learned about him earlier that morning. I joined my father at the table. In the harsh light of day the kitchen no longer seemed like the confessional from the night before.

My father sipped his coffee in silence. Then I heard him clear his throat nervously, and unexpectedly he began to speak in a lively and confident voice.

"I never finished telling you what happened," he said, searching my face for a response. "Are you still interested?"

His naïveté stunned me.

"I've thought of nothing else," I answered. His face registered relief and shyness in equal measures.

"After the incident with the chocolates at Laima," he began, "Commander Lobe partly surrendered me back to Uncle. I've no idea why this happened. On occasion I still visited hospitals and other institutions with the commander, but these were interspersed with days in Uncle's office when I simply got on with my old routine of study.

"Until one particular day," my father said, "when the commander arrived in an exuberant mood. He didn't bother to greet Uncle, and before I could even stand to attention, he'd snatched me up and then sat down on the sofa with his arms around my waist so I couldn't escape him. 'How is my little corporal today?' he asked. 'Have you been working hard at your lessons?' I nodded, and he looked at Uncle. 'Has he, Mr. Dzenis?' It was no longer Jekabs, as he used to call Uncle. Uncle nodded but remained silent.

"'In that case I think you deserve a treat,' Commander Lobe said, squeezing me so tightly I could barely breathe. My ears pricked up at the mention of 'treat.' I thought that with a bit of luck he might take me out to a fancy café for ice cream the way he used to do.

"But it was even better than I'd hoped for. He offered me a break in Carnikava. 'It's a special holiday, only for important children of the Reich,' he said. 'You'll have a wonderful time. A whole week there with boys and girls of your own age. Playing on the beach, dancing, exercises every day.'

"I nodded, excited by the prospect.

"Commander Lobe explained that I'd have to leave almost immediately, and Uncle insisted that he and Auntie accompany me. Uncle had been wary of the commander's attitude toward me ever since the chocolates affair.

"The commander shrugged as if he didn't care either way. Then he sprang an even bigger surprise on me. 'And you, Corporal,' he said slowly and with gravity, 'will have a special part to play at Carnikava. Berlin is sending a crew to film you.'

"He lifted me off his knee and began to pace up and down, smoking his cigar. 'Every single person throughout the German empire, even the Führer himself, will learn about the life of Latvia's great mascot,' he said, waving his hand in the air extravagantly. 'It is a great honor for you to be chosen. You must make all Latvians proud of you.'"

My father went on to recount his patchy memories of the filming. It had actually taken place in two locations—sections were filmed both at Carnikava and Dzintari, a town on the Riga coast, whose scenery was more appealing than that at Carnikava.

He remembered clearly one scene in which he was filmed doing handstands and running on the beach with the other children. In a second scene, he recalled what may have been a kind of maypole dancing with a few of the young girls, who were dressed in traditional Latvian folk costumes. His other memories, he said, were too vague. "They are like shadows moving across a screen," he complained, screwing up his face in frustration.

One thing he knew for certain was that the material had been included in a German newsreel, which the commander later told him had been shown in movie theaters across the German Reich. He himself had seen it play in a cinema in Riga.

I was intrigued by talk of the newsreel. Even these scant memories were more than I'd heard during my childhood when my father had mentioned the film. He would boast that he'd become such a celebrity in Latvia that they'd—we never asked who "they" were—made a film about him. But whenever my brothers and I would pester him about the film's content, he'd always claim to be unable to recall any details.

My father told me now that he didn't know what had become of the film. It had occurred to him when he was younger to find it, but he'd had no idea how to locate it. As time passed, and he'd gone on to raise a family, he'd put it at the back of his mind. "I decided that the film belonged to a previous life," he said. In any case, he suspected that the footage hadn't survived the war.

I suggested that we contact various film archives in Russia, Latvia, and Germany. My father seemed genuinely excited by this. His mood was buoyant, and he perched on the edge of his seat, apparently eager to talk more.

Before he began, however, I was compelled to ask him something we had not yet touched on directly. My father and I had never discussed our emotions with each other, but I decided to take the plunge.

"How did you feel about all of this, Dad?" I asked. Mere mention of the word "feel" made me awkward and self-conscious.

My father was taken aback by my question and seemed perplexed. "What do you mean, *feel*?" He put stress on the word.

"Well . . . did you feel close to the Latvians?" I blustered, not quite able to say what I meant after all. "Did you feel like one of them when you made this film?"

The vehemence of his response surprised me. "Don't be absurd," he said. "I never felt part of them. I had to cooperate, that's all."

My father shrank back into his seat. He seemed both annoyed and dismayed by my question and began to shake his head. "You don't understand the way it was," he murmured. "I just made the best of my situation. I stayed as silent as possible, all my time with them. I was never one of them. Ever! Deep down I knew they were not my people. They were strangers to me. All the time, strangers. They loved me, cared for me, treated me as one of their own. But I always knew what I was, even if I didn't know who I was. I was a Jewish boy. That meant I had to be on guard every moment I was with them. I couldn't risk being discovered. I would have been killed. I feared for my life all the time. The fear was ingrained in me. Can you imagine how it would be for a child to live like that every waking moment? And even when sleeping—I never slept well—I had nightmares about it. I always worried that I would talk in my sleep and somehow someone would overhear me."

My father's features tensed and he stared bleakly in front of him. "I realize now, speaking for the first time," he said, "that I have been frightened all my life."

This seemed to be an explanation for my father's silence: his persistent fear of discovery.

"It's not like I could've run away or something. Besides, where would I have run to? Back to my village? I didn't know where my village was. I couldn't even remember its name. I still can't. And even if I had, what would I have found there? The pit where my family was buried?

"There was nobody else to care for me," my father said with grim finality. "This was the card that fate had dealt me."

My father seemed lost for words. Then he leaned forward in his seat, staring intently at me. "Absurd!" he muttered under his breath. It was the first time in my life that my father had reacted so intensely to something I said.

I tried to steer him onto another topic. "Why didn't you speak of your experiences when the war had ended?" I asked.

My father shrugged evasively. "I wasn't protecting the Latvians, if that's what you're getting at," he said defensively.

Our discussion had taken a turn for the worse, and I worried my father felt trusting me had been a mistake.

My father took a deep breath. "Who wanted to hear about the horrors I witnessed? In those days everybody in Australia just wanted to get on with their life, forget their past, and I learned to want the same thing. I just focused on Mum and you boys and the future. I wanted to protect you from my past. Just think of the shadow that would have cast over your lives."

I let that go. "Do you think Mum even suspected anything?" I asked.

My father shook his head.

"I hope not. And that's how I wanted it to be. I didn't want to burden your mother. You know how she is. She'd grown up here shielded from the war and things like that. She has a kind nature, and she doesn't understand cruelty at all. To expose her to what I'd been through—I feared that it would be too much for her."

"That's terrible, Dad," I said. "To live alone with this. Nobody you could confide in."

My father gave a nervous cough. Then he spoke again.

"I did tell somebody once," he said, "completely on the spur of the moment, in early 1960. I was in the center of Melbourne. I saw a nameplate on the door of a lawyer's office. I could tell the name was Jewish. I thought to myself, 'This man might be able to steer me in the right direction.' I don't know what came over me—I went in. It was a small office—a one-man show. The lawyer himself was sitting there behind a desk.

"I asked if I could talk to him. He invited me to sit down, I began to tell him what had happened to me. He was spellbound. He let me talk on and on. When I'd finished, he asked what I wanted to do, and I told him then what I have told you now—I want to know who I am, who my family was, and where I come from.

"The lawyer was silent for some time. Finally, he spoke: 'Forget it, young man!' he said. 'If what you say is true, there is nobody left for you. And even if someone did survive, then they would believe that you had died with your family. Nobody would come looking for you, and in any case, how would they know where to find you?' He said that the best thing was to look to the future. 'You have a family, build a life with them. Your past is a lost cause!' I was dejected, but there was nothing else for it. I resolved to follow his advice. 'He's an educated man,' I said to myself. 'He knows about these things.' I thanked him and left. That was that—I buried my past."

"Do you regret that, Dad?" I ventured.

My father seemed momentarily thrown by the question. He moved uncomfortably in his seat. "To be honest," he replied, "I feel guilty now about keeping my secret from all of you. Perhaps it seems to you that I didn't trust any of you. That I betrayed you somehow."

My father's words struck a raw nerve in me. As I had sat with him through the early hours of that morning, I had occasionally felt toward him an anger that I'd only gradually been able to acknowledge. He was correct: I'd felt that he'd betrayed me and the entire family. Though he may have protected us from the horrors of his secret, I could not escape my growing sense that his secretiveness would, in the long term, make him a stranger to us all.

My father shook his head, ashamed of himself. There was a momentary silence between us.

"I've lied to you all, haven't I?" my father said. "People outside the family assumed that I was Latvian, and I didn't bother to correct them." His regret was palpable, and I wanted to spare him any further self-accusation.

"No you didn't," I replied. "You didn't lie." I hesitated, struggling to find the right way to describe what had gone on. "You simply didn't tell us everything," I said. "It was a sort of half-truth."

"A half-truth?" my father observed wryly. "How can anything be a half-truth?" He understood all too well what I was trying to do. I was trying to make excuses for what he'd done.

"It's like a truth not fully revealed," I offered.

"There's no such thing," he challenged me perversely.

But he was wrong. An image of his brown case, firmly locked, came to mind. I recalled the control he had exercised over whatever was removed from it, in order to maintain the carefully constructed narrative of his life.

I reflected on all those years growing up under the same roof as my father, and how we, his family, had let him get away with this narrative. None of us had ever stopped to reflect seriously on the mystery of his origins and existence, and we were content to let him deflect any mild curiosity we did show.

What if we had pushed him harder? Would he have given in and told us more? I wondered whether it was us—our family—who had failed our father by not asking questions, and that his decision not to offer us anything was a terrible indictment of us all. Had he seen something in us that disappointed him? I was left with a sense that somehow he had not deemed any of us worthy of his secret.

I had been so absorbed in my reflections that it was only the sound of my father's voice that brought me back to the present.

"Marky?" he said.

"Sorry," I said. "I drifted off for a moment." I met my father's eyes. "You will tell Mum and the boys, won't you?" I said gently.

My father nodded, grim-faced. "I don't know how I'll go about it," he said, "but I know that I must speak now." In an unself-conscious gesture, he raised the brown case, which had been on the floor beside him, and hugged it to his chest, as if it were both his protector and his most precious possession.

I looked at my watch. "I'd better get dressed. Mum will be back before too long. She'll be wondering what's up if she finds me like this."

My father took the cups over to the sink. "I've got some repairs to do," he said and headed back out to his workshop.

CHAPTER TEN

THE GROUND SHIFTS

I remained in Melbourne for another fortnight. My father went about his business, spending more and more of the day tinkering in his workshop, and, I suspect, deliberately avoiding me. In a way I was relieved. Already overwhelmed by what I had learned about my father's childhood, I was struggling to come to terms with it.

When I woke early one morning feeling unwell, I made a decision: rather than remain in Melbourne any longer, growing impatient with my father, I would head to Tokyo as soon as possible to begin my research. My departure might give my father the time and space he clearly needed to talk to the family.

Three days later my father backed the car out of the driveway on the start of our journey to the airport. From the backseat I kept my eye out for traffic. At one end of our street, I caught sight of the oil refinery. As it came into view this time any nostalgic sentiments evaporated. The corporate signs affixed to the refinery fence were those of powerful German industrial conglomerates. Though these signs had been there all my life, I now began to see them in an entirely new light: Germany, with one of its most forbidding emblems—the belching chimney—surrounded our neighborhood.

This was how I had grown up—with the inextinguishable German flame at one end of the street and a slaughterhouse owned, as it happened to be, by a Jewish family at the other. I'd never given much thought to either, but now there seemed to have been a coded message buried in the landscape of my childhood that I had failed to detect.

The flight to Tokyo went smoothly enough, punctuated only by mild turbulence. The same could not be said of my mood. While I felt a deepened sense of companionship with my father, there was also an odd sense of foreboding. I felt dislocated, cast adrift to face an open, possibly hostile sea.

The heat and humidity of Tokyo in the summer was so stifling that it was always a relief to get back to my *manshon*, as the Japanese called the tiny studios in downtown Tokyo. It was a lighthearted linguistic play on the English word "mansion," since most of them, mine included, were no more than three hundred square feet. Yet as I opened the front door a wall of heat hit me. The room was suffocating, like an oven or a sauna. Before I had even closed the door behind me, it and the windowpanes began to rattle, almost imperceptibly at first. I held my breath, waiting to see if the gentle shaking developed into an earth tremor, turning mere inconvenience into real danger. My *manshon* and my nerves continued to rattle, until abruptly, with one slight jolt, the room settled. I switched on the air conditioner and waited for it to kick in.

There was a loud knock on my door. For an instant I thought it was my father.

"*Moshi moshi, yubin desu!*" a voice called out. It was the postman with a special delivery.

The book-sized package he handed me bore few details on its exterior, apart from a customs declaration and my address inscribed in my father's unusually thick black lettering, as if this would somehow guarantee its delivery. I tore off the outer wrapping and found an unlabeled videocassette encased in Bubble Wrap.

I headed back across the darkened room, slipped the cassette into the VCR, and pushed Play. After several moments the screen came to life: a head-and-shoulders close-up of my father suddenly appeared. Below his image, as if imprinted on his upper chest like a prison ID number, a running time code and the date of the recording had been super-imposed. It appeared to have been made three weeks earlier, in fact on the very day I had departed Australia.

But what shocked me was my father's appearance. I pressed the pause button immediately to take a closer look at him.

I recognized the features of the person on screen as my father's, of course, but they were gray and washed out; his eyes were drawn and without any of their usual curiosity. His face was quite immobile, so different from his usually animated expression.

After several moments I pressed the play button and my father's image came to life again.

He stared directly into the camera. Suddenly from offscreen a man's voice addressed him. "Would you state your full name, please?" The voice had a northern European accent, clipped and precise, and was politely solicitous.

My father's head turned toward it. "Alex Kurzem," he mumbled in response.

I sat on my futon, spellbound, as my father repeated the story of his wartime childhood to what was apparently a Jewish Holocaust organization. Only this time he did not speak in any great detail, as he had with me in Melbourne. Rather he skimmed across incidents as the interviewer, unnamed and unseen, tried to get a broad picture of what had happened to my father. My father answered the interviewer's questions as best he could, but the harsh lighting and unforgiving angle of the camera, positioned slightly above him and off to the left, seemed to have made him shy. The scene had none of the intimacy afforded him by the darkened kitchen at home. It was a disconcerting experience for me to observe my father clinically, in this mediated format, rather than sit close to him at home.

At one point the voice of an unidentified woman with a heavy northern European accent joined the interview. When my father mentioned Commander Lobe as a person who took an extraordinary and somewhat sinister interest in creating his identity as a mascot, she came to life. I shifted my position onto the tatami floor closer to the television so that I could hear their exchange more clearly.

She was shocked that my father had been acquainted with the commander and seemed to know a great deal about his wartime activities. She spoke of Lobe's reputation as a war criminal: according to many historians, he was responsible for the murder of tens of thousands of Jews. She told my father that he had unwittingly kept company with the highest echelons of the Latvian Nazi elite. Even though my father must've been aware of Lobe's wartime actions, he appeared genuinely horrified by this the extent of these revelations, so much so that he was left speechless for several moments.

Even this brief reference to the commander suggested that there was still much more not only to him, but to the other men who had controlled my father's life. While there was little I could do in Tokyo, I resolved to move forward in my investigations once I was back in Oxford.

Shortly after that the interview came to a close. An instant before the camera was turned off I caught a final glimpse of my father rising from his chair and noticed that he had been nursing his case the whole time. Then the screen turned to static.

I looked at my watch. It was after 11:00 p.m. I'd been watching the tape for almost two hours. I calculated that it must have been midnight in Melbourne. I considered calling my father, who was likely awake with insomnia, but not wanting to rouse and alarm my mother, I decided to wait until the next morning.

The usual drop in temperature overnight—a welcome relief in a Tokyo summer—had not come, and there didn't seem to be much point in trying to sleep. Instead I prepared some strong black coffee and opened the window.

I was anxious to call my father, even though I was unsure how to broach the topic of the tape with him. He'd told me that he didn't feel particularly Jewish. Why had he given his testimony to a Jewish Holocaust organization? He'd clearly been hoping for information they might have about Koidanov and Panok, but they hadn't heard of these words. Or was there a deeper purpose to his visit? Was he looking to know more about his Jewishness? If so, there were no answers in the tape, which focused mainly on his time with the Latvians. Was he simply hoping to find a community who shared his earliest history? Or was he searching for some sort of absolution from these people simply because they were Jewish? It was impossible to know.

It was now 7:00 a.m. I dialed my parents' number and almost immediately my father answered. If I'd imagined that he'd want to discuss his past, I couldn't have been more wrong. I was pleased to hear him in high spirits: I imagined that the pressure of the horrific memories that had been building up inside him for more than five decades was for the moment alleviated. Perhaps he even felt safe. I couldn't help but wonder how long this Indian summer would last.

He told me excitedly about a trip he was planning with my mother. They were going to drive from Melbourne to Rockhampton, in the subtropical north of Australia, to visit some old friends who had retired there. I could picture them as they sped silently across the dry, inhospitable terrain. They had grown so comfortable with each other in more than forty years of marriage and seemed often to communicate almost by telepathy.

"Then," my father said, waking me from my thoughts, "your mum and I will continue along Highway One, all the way to Rockie." He used the shorthand commonplace among Australians, "Rockie" or "The Rock," as I had also heard Rockhampton called.

"You should drop in and see Ilse," I suggested. Ilse was Mirdza's only daughter. She lived just north of Brisbane on Queensland's coast. I hoped that the mention of Ilse would provide a pretext for discussing the videotape.

But my father shut this down. "No," he said, "can't see Ilse this time. Have to get to Dirk's as quickly as possible."

"What's the rush?" I asked.

"No rush," he replied. "I just don't want to dally-dilly."

"You mean dilly-dally, Dad," I corrected him and again made ready to ask him about the tape.

I should have known better. My father had finely tuned antennae and must have sensed what was coming. He seized the opportunity provided by his linguistic blunder.

"Why not dally-dilly?" he said, exaggerating his Russian accent to dramatize the fact that English was not his native tongue. "It sounds as good as dilly-dally. Even dilly-dilly sounds good. Dally-dally does, too, for that matter."

I couldn't help but laugh. My father knew how to disarm me. But it was also a laugh of nervous relief: I had resurfaced to a familiar reality. To hear him be as quick-witted as usual reassured me that he was fine, even if he was keeping the demons at bay.

In the weeks that followed I made regular telephone calls to Melbourne but never successfully broached the subject of the videotape with my father. Whenever he answered the phone and heard my voice, he would tell me that he could speak for only a moment, that he was busy.

"Too busy to speak with your son?" I responded testily on more than one occasion. But he would brush aside my accusation and tell me that he was doing a favor for a neighbor, or collecting spare parts for his beloved VCRs and broken televisions, or even, preposterously, feeding his cat, Princess, who couldn't be kept waiting. Then he would hand the phone over to my mother.

Eventually I became vexed. Why on earth had he chosen to speak of his past and then been so reluctant to discuss it further?

As the weeks passed, I lost the urge to socialize with friends and colleagues in Tokyo. Perhaps as a way of filling my father's silence, I became increasingly preoccupied with the contents of the videotape. In truth, I had time for little else.

I would play the tape repeatedly and pause at moments that struck me as somehow critical to his story. I found I was able to observe my father in a way I would never have been able to do in real life. I became an expert at decoding his body language and facial expressions, so that eventually the image on the screen became more real to me than my father himself. I clung to his words, too, and jotted them down in a notebook I'd begun in Melbourne. It was a macabre obsession. If anybody had called upon me to recite the words on the tape, I am convinced that I would have been able to parrot them without difficulty.

Then one night, while I was replaying the video, the nightmarish spell was broken unexpectedly. Though I would have been incapable of making such a gesture in real life, I reached out to the image of my father on the screen and, as if it would allay his troubles, touched his cheek.

Two floors below my *manshon* tremors began deep below the earth's crust, and it seemed that Tokyo was still waiting to see if the vibrations aboveground would end in a jolt or develop into something much more terrible. My own foundations were already irretrievably shaken. My center of gravity was shifting.

I decided it was time to make the journey back to Oxford.

CHAPTER ELEVEN
CAST ADRIFT

My flight was the last in a long queue waiting at Narita airport on the outskirts of Tokyo. I closed the shade and curled up in my seat, covering myself in a blanket. Almost immediately I began to feel anxious, as if everything I had gone through in Tokyo had been lying in wait.

I wanted to know more about the triumvirate of men—Commander Lobe, Jekabs Dzenis, and Sergeant Kulis—who had played a critical role in my father's fate during the war years, and whose influence had extended into his new life in Australia. The shadow that loomed most heavily over me at that moment was that of Commander Lobe. I'd grown up believing him to be a kind and heroic person who had figured strongly in what I now knew to be the false version of my father's rescue. The female interviewer on the tape had stated with absolute certainty that Lobe had been not only a high-ranking Latvian Nazi but also a war criminal notorious for his cruelty. He had never been punished for his crimes. She had made particular mention of two mass exterminations at places called Slonim and Rumbula. I had never heard of them, and, of course, my father had made no mention of either of these locations, or exterminations of any kind, in his fictionalized version of life with Lobe.

It was still not clear to me why my father hadn't come clean about

Commander Lobe after the war had ended, when he was free to do so. Why had my father maintained the fiction that he was a pigherd boy discovered by soldiers? I wondered whether the intimidation my father had suffered in Australia had been more pervasive than he'd suggested. Clearly, there was much more to discover.

I had, in fact, gone in search of Lobe in Stockholm, in the early 1980s, to thank him for his kindness to my father. From London, I'd excitedly phoned my father in Melbourne to tell him of my plan. He'd been hesitant rather than pleased, claiming that I'd disrupt the peaceful life of an elderly couple who did not enjoy good health. As I continued to express my determination to visit the Lobes, he protested more vehemently against my plan. I chose to ignore what I saw as an irrational objection.

It was my first visit to northern Europe in the winter.

Stockholm was blanketed in snow and, even though it was the middle of the day, it was almost pitch-dark on the streets. As a student, I didn't have much money, but I managed to find a room in a fleabag hotel near the main station. That first night I had to sleep in my overcoat, and when I woke in the morning, my blankets had a thin layer of ice on them.

When I left the hotel the next morning, I found a public telephone in the park opposite. I dialed Lobe's number, but there was no reply. During that day, in between sightseeing, I must have dialed the number at least a dozen times.

The following morning I tried again, but again nobody picked up. I wondered if Lobe had moved or, even worse, recently died. I was very disappointed because I wanted to express my gratitude to the hero who'd rescued my father from the terrors of the forest. Therefore, I resolved to make my way to Lobe's address on the off chance that he might still be there.

I got directions from the receptionist at the hotel and boarded a tram that would take me directly to the suburb known as Handen, where he lived. I got off the tram and headed in the direction of what turned out to be public housing.

I located Lobe's building and finally found my way to the right floor in a dingy, barely lit elevator. The smell of human urine in the rear corner was so overpowering that I had to cover my nose and mouth with my hand.

I knocked on the front door of what I thought was the right apartment. There was no answer. I waited several moments and then knocked again, more loudly.

There was still no answer, but this time I was convinced that I'd heard a shuffling sound inside. I placed my ear to the door and just at that moment it sprang open violently, still on its chain. I got the shock of my life. Through the gap I could see part of an elderly man's face. His rheumy eye examined me.

"Yes?" he asked me in Swedish.

"*Herr Lobe?*" I replied in German.

At first he didn't answer me. His one eye continued to evaluate me. Then he spoke. "What do you want?" he asked me in perfect, formal German.

"You are Mr. Lobe, aren't you?" I asked.

"Who are you?" he said.

"I am Mark, the son of Uldis Kurzemnieks," I replied, using my father's Latvian name. I'd expected the expression in his eye to change upon hearing this, and for him to welcome me with open arms.

Instead the eye looked startled and darted about. "Go away!" he hissed.

I was greatly shocked.

"Sir," I said. "You remember Uldis Kurzemnieks, don't you?"

"I told you, go away from here." He spat out the words.

"The little corporal!" I pleaded with him. "Remember?"

"Go away or I will call the police!" he warned me. Then he slammed the door shut in my face.

I was completely mystified by his attitude. "Surely he couldn't have forgotten," I thought. I rapped loudly on the door, calling out "Commander Lobe" and pleading with him to open up, when suddenly, still on its chain, the door flew open again. The long blade of a carving knife came violently through the opening, waving about.

I jumped backward. Without uttering a word, Lobe continued to brandish the knife. I backed farther away, totally bewildered.

Why hadn't the mention of my father's name allayed his fears? I wondered. Was he sick? Suffering from some sort of dementia? I could only conjecture. I left.

As I boarded the elevator, I was shaking from head to toe. When it stopped during its descent and the doors opened to two elderly women, they took an abrupt step backward, eyeing me suspiciously: I must have looked shattered. One of them waved her hand at me, indicating that they'd wait for the next ride.

I hurried out of the building without looking back. There was nothing else to do but return to the hotel. And on the way back I hatched a plan.

When I got up the next morning, I wrote a note. In it I apologized to Lobe for frightening him and explained again who I was. I wrote that I knew he had saved my father's life and that I wanted to thank him for that. I folded the letter, put it in an envelope, and sealed it.

I headed back to Handens. I slipped the envelope under Lobe's door and stepped away to wait at a safe distance. From where I stood, I could hear movement inside. Several moments passed.

Then I heard the lock click. The door opened, this time more gently, although still on its chain. Lobe's partly hidden face again appeared in the gap. His eye still appraised me, but it was less wary. He must have been satisfied by my submissive demeanor because when the door closed for a moment, I heard the sound of the chain being removed. Finally the door opened to reveal the full figure of Commander Lobe.

He was short and fairly rotund, no longer the fit and dashing commandant he'd once been. He looked like any other man in his seventies, apart from the fiery expression etched into his face over the years. "Please come in," he said, shaking my hand rather formally.

I stepped inside.

The interior was cozy, what the Germans call "gemütlich," but also quite shabby. It was clear that he was not well-off. An elderly woman was standing rather awkwardly behind him. He introduced her as Mrs. Lobe. She seemed kindly, smiling warmly at me, and then, as Auntie used to do, she stepped forward, took my face in her hands, and kissed me on both cheeks.

"Little Uldis!" she exclaimed. "A perfect angel."

Lobe gave a chuckle. "A little rascal, that's what I remember," he said.

"He looks like his father, doesn't he, Kārlis?" Mrs. Lobe continued.

I felt Lobe appraising me more closely. Then he grunted in response to his wife's words.

Mrs. Lobe ushered me further into the room. "You must be freezing," she said. "Come and sit by the heater."

I sat down on the shabby sofa and Lobe sat down next to me. Suddenly he was full of bonhomie.

"May I offer you coffee?" he said. "Or something stronger? Schnapps! That'll warm us. Dearest! Glasses!"

Mrs. Lobe brought the drinks, and the commander proposed a toast to my father. After that we chatted about him. The curious thing was that Lobe seemed to know so much about my father's life in Australia: his job, that he had three sons, that I was the oldest.

What followed was mystifying at the time and has stayed with me all these years.

"My father has spoken of how you found him," I told Lobe. Immediately he went on the alert; I could sense his tension.

"Did he?" Lobe said. "What did the corporal say?"

I told him only what I knew at that time: that soldiers on patrol had found a small boy in the woods, dressed in rags. And so on.

You could almost see the tension leave Lobe's body. He laughed loudly at what I'd recounted and poured himself another schnapps. But there was one tiny part of him that was still on guard, and coolly observing my movements.

Then Lobe started to add to what I'd just told him, describing how my father couldn't remember his name, not even his first name, or where he was from. All the boy knew was that he was a pigherd who'd lost his animals. He told me how his soldiers chose the boy's name and birthday.

"What was I to do?" he said. "I couldn't let this child wander alone in the forest. He would surely have died: if he didn't starve to death, the wolves would have devoured him, and if not that, then the partisans would have captured him. They were ruthless—they would have cut his throat on the spot, the partisans. Make no mistake about it!"

By that stage, Lobe was drunk, and he became slightly aggressive for a moment. "Nowadays," he grumbled, "those partisans are looked back upon as heroes. Not us, though! After the war the Soviets portrayed us as devils." He paused for another swig of schnapps.

"Tell me," he said, "if we were villains, then why did we worry about a little boy in the forest? Who cared whether he lived or died? We did! Nobody else! We, the devils, took him with us." Lobe laughed harshly.

He rambled on incoherently about the war so that I thought he'd forgotten that I was sitting beside him. I let him talk. I'd begun to nod off in the stultifying heat of the room when suddenly he gripped my forearm tightly. I snapped awake. For a second I wondered where I was and what he was talking about, when I heard him say, "He was a brave little boy and what a soldier!"

I laughed because I'd never thought of my father as a soldier. He'd always made it sound as if he were a Boy Scout. I was a little unnerved by the description.

"No!" Lobe exclaimed. "He was! He looked magnificent in his uniform. We called him our mascot."

The heat and the alcohol must have gotten to him, because then he, too, drifted off to sleep. I sat silently on the sofa listening to his snores and waiting for him to come round. Finally, his wife, who'd been quietly listening to our conversation, left and returned with coffee. She woke him. The doze seemed to have reinvigorated him, and he picked up another thread.

"I am still considered a hero in Latvia," he said. "There were so many requests from patriotic Latvians all over the world, even old members of the Eighteenth Battalion—'Why don't you write about your life?' 'We want to hear of your feats in the struggle for independence,' those sorts of things—that I decided to write my memoirs." At that, he rose heavily from the sofa and disappeared into another room.

He returned moments later with a box. I noticed his labored breathing as he sat down beside me and gently placed the box on the coffee table in front of us. It appeared to be nothing more than an old cardboard grocery container.

"My box of memories," he said, patting it lovingly, as if it were a loyal old dog. He lifted off its lid and delicately removed a book. Then he passed it across to me. It was a copy of the memoirs he'd just spoken of. I opened it, and the frontispiece carried a photograph of him, taken perhaps when he was in his fifties. I wouldn't have said that he was a handsome man—his expression was far too austere—but he did have a commanding presence, even on the page.

He reached across for the book and flicked through it until he found what he was searching for. He cleared his throat in between his ponderous intake of air and began to read a passage aloud, translating into German, about how my father was found by the soldiers.

When he'd finished, Lobe poured himself yet another schnapps. "That's what we did for your father," he said proudly. Lobe had had so much to drink that I worried he'd drop off to sleep again.

But instead the schnapps fueled his ire, and he began to rail a second time against those who had tarnished his reputation. As he gesticulated somewhat wildly with one hand, he pulled a folded sheet of paper from his box with the other. He gripped the paper tightly and rubbed it repeatedly, almost neurotically, with his thumb. It struck me as a rather childish gesture.

"After the war they called us Nazis," he said, outraged. "They said that we Latvians welcomed the Nazis when they entered our country. Absurd! We didn't follow their philosophy. We hoped the Germans would be a means to an end: to free us from Soviet oppression. That's all!

They said that we turned on our own people. But they were not our people! They were partisans. Bolsheviks! Traitors!"

I remember thinking to myself "and Jews as well."

Lobe claimed to me that he'd had one wish his entire life—to see Latvia free, and that was not a crime. At the time I knew little about Latvia's role in the war, but I recalled enough to see that he was trying to justify Latvia's past. There was little I could do to stem the tide of his mounting hysteria as he began to rave, running his words together into an indecipherable mixture of Latvian, Swedish, and German.

His rant was reaching a crescendo and he'd become quite disturbed, almost apoplectic. Mrs. Lobe must have been listening from the kitchen because suddenly she rushed in with a tablet and a glass of water, anxiously reminding him about his high blood pressure. He swallowed it and then sank back on the sofa. I waited beside him in silence, until he had calmed himself, and after several minutes his wheezing subsided.

All through his tirade, and even now, as he rested, Lobe had continued to wave the paper around in his fist. When I asked him what it was, he was startled. He appeared to have forgotten that it was still in his hand and looked at it curiously, but ignored my question. He returned the paper to the box. Then, shifting awkwardly in his seat so that he was almost facing me, he said with finality, "War is a nasty business. And I have paid the price."

I was young, with no experience of war. I didn't know how to respond, so I nodded, putting on a grave expression that I hoped was appropriate. And the truth was that I did sincerely feel for him and was indignant on his behalf.

By this time it was getting late, and I thought it best that I should leave. Besides, I'd grown increasingly uncomfortable. Intuitively, I knew something was amiss, but I couldn't put my finger on it.

Before I departed, I took a photograph of the commander and his wife together on the sofa. For an instant, they both seemed so vulnerable as they sat there, looking up into the camera lens as I focused. Poor Mrs. Lobe gave a weak, tired smile, while beside her, Mr. Lobe's face regained

Mr. and Mrs. Lobe at home in Stockholm, early 1980s.

its sharp, bullish expression. The abruptness of the transformation unnerved me.

But still he wasn't well enough to see me to the door. He couldn't
even rise to shake my hand. Instead he gave me a salute from where he
was seated and told me that he was sad to see me go; he promised to stay
in touch.

Mrs. Lobe unbolted the door to let me out, and when she shut it
behind me, I heard her refasten the locks. It struck me as quite pathetic,
and I had to pause outside for a moment; I felt quite moved by their
circumstances. I sensed that I would never meet them again.

I departed Stockholm, aware that much lay beneath the bonhomie of
my father's relationship with the Lobes but perplexed as to what it could
be. I never told my father the truth about what had taken place in Sweden. I'd merely described it as pleasant and said it was good to have met
Lobe. He'd never asked me more about it. Now I was certain that it was
the key to something very significant.

I also had questions about the other men in my father's life. Uncle—
Jekabs Dzenis—had been a central part of my own life as I grew up in
Melbourne. To me he was an austere and formidable figure, but I had
never sensed any malevolence in his character; rather I thought of him

and of his wife, Emily, as my adoptive grandparents. I fondly remembered driving with him to his holiday cottage in the countryside outside Melbourne. En route, to try to engage him, I'd recited poetry by Goethe, Schiller, and Heine in German. As the car wove its way through the narrow, hilly lanes, he gently corrected my mistakes in memorization and pronunciation.

As a child I had felt sorry for the Dzenises, whom I saw as being buffeted by fate, pawns in the theater of war. Now my sympathy had evaporated: Uncle had deceived me about who he was—and their exodus from the fatherland seemed less a cruelty and more an attempt to cover their tracks.

Jekabs and Emily Dzenis were dead, but I hoped that I could turn to surviving relatives for more information about the role they had played in my father's past. I knew I'd have to tread cautiously while ferreting out their wartime sympathies and associations.

Then there was Jekabs Kulis, the soldier who had actually saved my father from the firing squad. He would be in his late seventies or early eighties by now. Was he still living near New York City? If not, where?

I drifted into a light doze, only to wake with a start as heavy turbulence hit the plane, causing it to shudder violently. I gave up on trying to sleep.

During the seemingly interminable hours that followed, I couldn't help but reflect on my father, even though I had tried deliberately to avoid doing so. My image of him had been turned upside down.

On one hand, he was still my father, the person I thought I knew. We would banter and joke easily with each other, and had what many would see as a good relationship. But as is common with fathers and sons, there was also a suffocating silence between us whenever our emotions were exposed. We never confronted each other, and as I matured into adulthood I understood that we could both live comfortably with that tacit agreement.

But it was also true that my father had lived a double life, and I didn't really know who he was.

Why had my father kept the truth from us? While I could accept what he had said to me about protecting his family from the shadows of his past, I didn't believe that this was the full story. Were there threats from other sources that he was yet still unwilling to discuss?

Was he frightened of himself and of his own memories? To never speak of one's memories did not mean that one had escaped them. I could not imagine what it would be like to live in the imminent danger of the revelation one's self.

When my father looked at my brothers and me, did he see what had been cruelly taken from him? Did he long to utter the words "my brother" or "my sister," words that my brothers and I used without a second thought?

Above all, I wondered how my father had managed to keep his past "unspoken" all these years. Had his enduring silence been a form of survival he was as unwilling to relinquish as his life?

Questions like these plagued me during the flight, and I realized I would have to let my father fill in the details of his story at his own pace. I decided to walk to the rear of the plane to stretch my limbs.

I had paid little attention to the other passengers, so I was surprised when I entered the rear cabin and found myself in the midst of what appeared to be a religious jamboree. On the side of the plane where I stood, four Orthodox Jews draped in their traditional prayer shawls and wearing yarmulke had gathered in the space around the emergency exit. In low voices they were chanting in unison while davening toward the wall of the cabin. I felt inexplicably confronted by their behavior and turned away, only to notice that on the far side of the cabin a much larger prayer meeting was going on. It seemed that most of the rear cabin had been occupied by a group of Japanese Christians, perhaps en route to a pilgrimage in Europe. Standing at the front of the group, a man in a priest's collar was leading row upon row of followers in slightly fevered prayer.

I moved unsteadily back toward my seat, feeling lightheaded and disconcerted.

Half an hour later the plane entered its holding pattern, circling to the west of the airport and waiting for permission to land. But I felt anchorless and directionless, cast adrift on a sea between past and present. Filled with an inchoate fear that the mysteries of my father's past would be the harbinger of a dangerous squall for our whole family, I had no idea when and where I would reach safe harbor again.

CHAPTER TWELVE

OXFORD

Eventually I settled back into my routine in Oxford, but my academic research quickly took a backseat to my father's story, which now dominated my thoughts.

In the weeks that followed my return, I made numerous phone calls to my father; the little dance that had begun over the telephone in Tokyo continued. Whenever I tried to broach what had happened to him, let alone the mere existence of the tape and its contents, my father would lapse into an unshakable silence before either abruptly changing the topic or, more often, rapidly handing the telephone to my unsuspecting mother.

I soon grew tired of pursuing my elusive father. In the meantime, I would gather what scraps of his past were available to me and see where they would lead. I retrieved the videotape from where I'd hidden it in the bottom drawer of the desk in my study, perhaps in an unconscious emulation of the way my father had secreted his case. Then I found myself repeating the ritual I'd developed in my studio in Tokyo. I spent an entire weekend with the curtains drawn, playing the tape repeatedly. Only this time, I coolly jotted down further details of his story. By Sunday evening, I had filled a small notebook with observations and queries and, after I had returned the video to its hiding place, I settled into an armchair and began to review my notes.

Ultimately, my father's recollections were impressionistic. With few exceptions, they lacked objective markers that could pinpoint a precise moment or place. I had a handful of names of places and people from which to begin my research—Laima chocolate factory, Valdemara Street, Riga, Carnikava, the Volhov swamps, Lobe, Dzenis, and Kulis—and the mysterious words "Koidanov" and "Panok." It wasn't much to go on. My father's vivid account of the burning of people in a synagogue was unaccompanied by a place or a time.

While I did not hold my father responsible for the nature of his memories—one would expect little more from a terrified child's point of view—I felt thwarted by them. By the time I'd reached the last page of my notes, I realized that my frustration had boiled over unconsciously. In the margin, I had jotted down words such as "silence," "memory," and "truth," which I had then underlined once or twice for further emphasis.

I lay on my bed, mulling over the information that I did have. Foremost in my mind were "Koidanov" and "Panok," the words my father had revealed to me at the Café Daquise in London. Where did they come from? Were they the names of people or places? Did they have any connection with his family? My father claimed that he'd held these names inside him for as long as he could remember. Had the extermination itself imprinted them on his soul?

I was intrigued, too, by my father's cryptic recollections of his early family life. He had said that he had a younger brother and a baby sister. What were their names? How old were they when they were killed? His memories of his own father were baffling: sometime after being told that his father was dead, Alex saw him. His father lowered himself from a hole in the ceiling of the family home to gently whisper good-bye to Alex.

Finally, my father was adamant that on the night prior to the extermination of his village his mother had taken him onto her lap and told him that they were all to die in the morning.

Without the name of my father's family or a village to go on, how would I ever uncover the truth of these memories or give him back his original identity?

I lived in a university town populated with some of the world's finest scholars. It was only natural, then, that I begin my search for the meaning of Koidanov and Panok in Oxford. Through academic contacts, I was put in touch with a number of Holocaust historians.

Their responses disappointed me: most of the experts were unwilling to listen to my father's story with an open mind—their reservations stemmed from the fact that his recollections were too vague and anecdotal. I was surprised by this: I thought my father's recollections had been quite sharp for a young child. And I considered anecdotes important to our understanding of the Holocaust. Because most survivors had been significantly older than my father at the time of the Holocaust, their stories contained more objective signposts, most notably the central symbol of the Holocaust: the concentration camp. My father's story had no such icon. I didn't think this would matter, but I was to realize soon enough my naïveté would be evident.

Three professors were intrigued enough to fit me into their busy schedules, and I set up appointments to meet one of them in London and the other two in Oxford. In advance of our meetings, I sent each one an outline of my father's story. As it turned out, all three took a depressingly skeptical stance toward my father's story. Professor M., a distinguished historian at Oxford, delivered the most vehement critique.

Our meeting took place in his office in one of Oxford's most prestigious colleges. He welcomed me warmly. Within moments of shaking my hand, he told me that he had conducted more than three decades of extensive research into the Holocaust, adding that he was a man who had heard many incredible stories of survival. My father's story, he said, was the most incredible.

I noted some reticence in his voice, but I put it out of my mind as he ushered me graciously into his room. He poured me a cup of coffee and offered me a comfortable armchair, while he sat behind his desk.

I began to describe my father's story in closer detail. He did not interrupt me, but occasionally nodded his head or smiled thinly in response to something I said. When I had finished speaking, he began to cross-examine me about details of the story. At the end of our lengthy exchange, he took a gulp of his cold coffee and then offered me his opinion.

He had heard of neither Koidanov nor Panok and was unable to place them as the names of persons or locations.

I was prepared at that moment to let the matter rest. He had not been able to help me. However, before I could even thank him, he raised a finger to interrupt me.

"I cannot deny the story outright," he said. "The broad canvas of your father's story may be true, but not in all of its details. Some of them are so fantastic as to be improbable."

I was flabbergasted.

"Which ones exactly?" I asked.

It seemed that he had prepared for our discussion. He rested his elbows on the desk and began to tap his fingertips gently together. He consulted a sheet of paper. As I waited for him to speak, I found myself distracted by the sight of his delicately manicured fingernails.

"What bothers me most of all," he said, "is your father's claims about the manner in which he survived. No child of five could have survived under such conditions—alone in a forest during a northern Europe winter. Even soldiers and partisans found it hard to withstand the freezing conditions and depredations of the situation.

"And over and above that," he continued, "why would these Nazis—any Nazis—keep a Jewish boy alive? What possible advantage would it have had for them?"

I explained to him again that as far as I knew only Jekabs Kulis, and nobody else, had known my father was Jewish, and he alone had instructed my father to keep his Jewish identity hidden. It had involved no great conspiracy of silence among a number of men. But the professor found this explanation hard to accept.

"There was no way that your father would've been able to keep it secret," he said irritably. "Somebody would have caught your father out at some stage. And apart from that, no child of that age could be capable of such vigilance in protecting himself. It would have required a superhuman effort, not only physically: the mental strain would've been unbearable.

"What also creates doubt in my mind is your father's account of his escape from his village. To be frank with you, it would have been absolutely impossible for his mother to have known what was going to happen to her family the following morning," he said. "From the chronology you have conveyed to me, I am certain that the extermination must have happened sometime in perhaps autumn or early winter 1941. Given my knowledge of history, it is likely to have taken place somewhere in Russia.

"Now here is the difficulty I have with the incident. You have heard of the Wannsee Conference, I take it?"

I nodded.

"The Wannsee Conference took place in January 1942 and is held to be the time when the program and methods for the mass extermination of the Jews became systematized.

"Prior to that was a period that I call the proto-Holocaust, when the Nazis experimented with a variety of methods of extermination. At that time they began to clear out the Jewish communities in the villages of eastern Europe. They did this to make way for the deportation and temporary resettlement of western European Jews there. The Nazis moved swiftly from village to village in units known as Einsatzgruppen, or extermination squads, German-led but manned mainly by Baltic volunteer forces, police brigades and the like, carrying out *Aktionen*, as they called their ruthless work.

"The Jewish population in the villages would have been largely unsuspecting about their imminent fate. There are two key things here. Firstly, the communication between villages for the most part would have been poor, so it was highly unlikely that the Jews in these villages knew about presence of the Einsatzgruppen until they were literally upon them. The second thing is that the Jews from these villages had a long history of being subject to pogroms, in which the men and boys may have been killed, but not the women and children. There was no way they, including your father's mother—a simple peasant woman, according to your father—would have any inkling that a new imperative for extermination that required the liquidation of all the Jewish men, women, and children in her village had come into existence."

I didn't know how to respond to his assertion. Professor M. was a world-renowned expert in the field. Yet I could not believe that my father was lying about what he remembered. Certainly my father was a great storyteller. The tales of his adventures in the Australian outback and elsewhere had always been slightly embellished—even as a child I'd sensed this—but the raw pain and grief I had witnessed on my father's face were another matter. Unlike the voluble and masterful raconteur I knew, he had struggled with every syllable as he endeavored to give life to his experiences.

I'd been absorbed in my reflections and was brought back to the present by a tapping sound. The professor was impatiently drumming his fingers on his blotter. It occurred to me that he'd grown bored with the discussion—or worse, he didn't believe entirely my father's version of events at all. He looked at his watch.

"I am sorry to have to say this to you, young man," he said, waving his hand in a dismissive gesture, "but it's altogether too implausible."

My suspicions had been correct. "Are you saying that my father is lying?" I blurted out. For a moment, he was taken aback and looked worried. Then he regained his composure.

Perhaps he thought better of what he'd just said, because suddenly he adopted a more conciliatory tone and suggested that we move to one of the college's common rooms. I agreed readily. I wanted to be on more neutral ground.

It was late afternoon and the darkened common room was deserted. The professor discreetly closed the heavy wooden door behind us as we entered, thereby softening the sounds of the outside world. We made ourselves comfortable in deep leather armchairs that faced each other. A mood of calmness and civility prevailed. I waited for the professor to speak.

"Please let me give you some advice," he said. This time there was a note of sympathy in his tone. "I do not necessarily deny that an extermination took place," the professor continued from where he had left off. "But I cannot accept that events unfolded as your father has described them. In essence, that is my problem with the entire story. He must have embellished it."

"It's not clear to me why he, or anybody, would embellish such a litany of horror," I said, trying to remain even-tempered. "What purpose would it serve? What do you think actually happened, then?"

"Only your father knows. It is highly likely that somewhere inside himself, your father feels guilty about his own survival, however it may have occurred, so he has dramatized it to make it seem more out of his own control. For example, what child would have the wherewithal to escape in the way that he claims he did—and the personal resources to survive in the forest for such a long time? The wolves at night, the corpses in the forest, tying himself in the trees, caught by the woodsman! It has all the trappings of a fairy tale told to exaggerate his own innocence."

"You're not serious!" I said angrily.

The professor held up his hand to indicate that he had not finished what he wanted to say. "And this question of how he was found," he said. "Perhaps he volunteered to go with the soldiers in order to save himself . . ."

My sense of outrage was almost palpable. My heart was beating so loudly in my ears that I could barely hear my own response.

"Of course he wanted to live. Who wouldn't?" I raised my voice. "But that didn't mean that he made a conscious free choice to join the soldiers. What child of five volunteers for anything?"

The professor indicated with both hands that I should quiet down. I looked around me and noticed a member of the staff tidying newspapers in the far corner of the room.

"Yes, perhaps 'volunteer' is too strong a word," the professor said, trying to sound reasonable, but I had no time for his semantics.

"You are wrong," I said. "Nobody in their right mind could concoct even a single moment of what my father has been through."

The professor remained silent for several moments, perhaps to let my anger settle. "Perhaps you've hit the nail on the head," he said slowly, as if testing the water.

I gave him a look of incomprehension.

"Perhaps your father is not in his right mind," he said, choosing his words carefully. "I believe that your father may be suffering from a form of false-memory syndrome that causes him to exaggerate the story that he has thus far told.

"I'm not saying that he's lying intentionally. It's more complicated than that. Your father has chosen to speak for whatever reason, and he is driven by an urge to make sense of the story as he tells anybody who will listen. I've seen this with other survivors. They have to find a way to describe the indescribable.

"Especially child survivors have to make sense of an arbitrary adult world in which they had no grasp of why they survived. And, as I said before, because they feel guilt about their survival, they believe there is an incriminating truth about themselves that they cannot see, but which, nonetheless, they feel that they must hide. They exaggerate the details of their story, because they cannot face the truth about themselves even when no such truth exists. So it is with your father.

"Have you noticed," the professor continued, "how your father describes himself in the story? He is the cute mascot at the center of the Latvians' world—"

"I don't think he has concocted that," I cut in. "They protected him and showered him with love and attention. And I assume you have looked at the photographs and newspaper articles I sent you in which he was featured. And what about the film he remembers starring in? He was a hero to them. My father did not overestimate his importance to the Latvians."

"True," the professor agreed. "But guilt causes complex contradictions in the survivor. Your father also portrays himself, and wants others to see him, as the hapless victim of all the attention showered on him in that crazed adult world. He wants us all to believe that everything that happened to him was fate and beyond his control. Nothing of his survival was due to his own cunning or wits."

"No!" I protested. "My father would be the very first to admit that he used all his cunning to survive—in the forest and to conceal his Jewishness from his captors and adopted family. He had to, in order to survive!"

And then, dishearteningly, the discussion changed direction.

"It's a complicated matter, this survivor business," the professor reiterated. "It's rife with contradictions. This denial of involvement in one's own fate is a retrospective survival tactic by the survivor, not to save his body but rather his moral conscience. The fantastical elements of his story distract us from the most important question . . ." The professor paused midsentence. His eyes would not meet mine. Then he spoke. "Complicity," he said in a matter-of-fact voice.

"My father was complicit in nothing," I responded firmly. "What on earth can a child of that age be complicit in?"

The professor pursed his lips but remained silent, staring at me intently.

The implication was that a young boy was capable of conscious moral decisions, and my father had somehow been a willing participant in his terrible fate. Now he was trying to cover up his part in the war by manipulating the truth about his role. He was refusing to face up to his complicity.

I needed time to digest this. In a half-absent state, I repeated to the professor that he was wrong.

In response he removed a piece of paper from the pocket of his jacket and offered it to me. He had jotted down a number.

I raised an eyebrow.

"Don't be offended," he said. "It's the telephone number of a friend of mine. Your father should speak with her. She's a psychiatrist, an expert in victims of war crimes and violence."

"And how might she help him?" I asked with some sarcasm. "Therapy? Analysis?"

"You must not blame your father, Mark," he insisted, misreading the look of irritation on my face. "Your father is sick, and he's not responsible for that," he said with deliberation. "He was made sick, traumatized by what happened to him, and is now trapped by the workings of the subconscious of a terrified child. This has been the only way for him to handle what happened to him."

He paused briefly to gather momentum. "Ultimately, your father is trying to distract us from the most important question," he said gravely.

I didn't believe that there was much point in continuing the discussion. I had come in search of basic information and had been subjected to a barrage of criticism and doubt about my father's story. I knew that I would not be able to convince him otherwise. I'd had enough, so I rose to leave, hoping that he would take the hint, but the professor was determined to have the final word.

"Did your father," he said from his comfortable armchair, "kill Jews?" For just a moment, an almost indiscernible smile of satisfaction crossed his face.

I froze to the spot, not because of the professor's smugness, but because the same question had crossed my mind.

"No," I answered firmly.

Our good-byes were terse. I thanked the professor, and he told me to take care of myself, as if warning me further against my father. I made my way along a maze of passageways until I finally reached the main quadrangle of the college. From there, I easily found my way out through the gates and onto Oxford's bustling High Street.

Stunned, I hunched my shoulders, feeling diminished somehow by the buildings towering above me as I began to weave my way back to my digs on the other side of town. As I walked I thought about Benjamin Wilkomirski, the key figure in a recent literary scandal.

I was only vaguely aware of the Wilkomirski fraud. When *Fragments*, the memoir of his childhood during the Holocaust, had first been published, one couldn't help but notice the lavish praise heaped upon it from all quarters. It was considered nothing short of a masterpiece of Holocaust literature. Many had proclaimed Wilkomirski the iconic survivor—the innocent child who had miraculously survived the concentration camps.

When the memoir was exposed as a fraud—Wilkomirski was not Jewish, and, having grown up in Switzerland, he had no experience of the Holocaust—the establishment conceded that they had been deceived by the unsignposted memories and impressions described unanchored by historical fact in *Fragments*. It had made them wary of future impostors.

In our discussion, the professor had stated that my father suffered from a surfeit of unsignposted memories. "Your father's story is highly dramatic and fantastical in nature," he had said, "but we cannot verify it. Children's memories are unreliable. They often distort things." He went on to draw a connection between Wilkomirski and my father: "With Wilkomirski, the world has made the error of accepting his story without any anchors, and Wilkomirski has turned out to be an impostor. You should be wary . . ."

He had not bothered to complete his sentence, but his insinuation was clear: he had put my father in the same boat as Wilkomirski. But this was unjust. Despite what he'd endured, my father did have verifiable memories, especially after he was taken to Riga by Sergeant Kulis: in particular there were the newspaper clippings and other documents that he had removed from their hiding place inside his case. And my father had mentioned a propaganda film about himself made by the Nazis.

The professor's words challenged me to verify my father's story. I knew that I would have to find this film, even a scrap of its footage, if it still existed. Its discovery would put the veracity of my father's story on firmer ground.

Eventually I came to my front door. But I didn't reach for my key. I decided instead to head for Port Meadow, an expanse of commons near my home. As I made my way there along the narrow canal path, I sensed more than ever that my father and I were on our own. Another door had closed in our faces.

I walked across the meadow toward the river Thames, feeling even more dispirited since meeting with the professor. Despite my earlier objections, I had to be honest with myself and admit that the professor's words had planted in me seeds of confusion and doubt. Were my father's revelations too fantastical or, even worse, a Wilkomirski-like deception? However, my father had not spent most of his lifetime telling people "embellished" stories about his wartime past; rather, he'd spent his adult years trying to prevent them from being discovered.

And then there was my father's behavior when giving evidence on the videotape. Surely this was proof, I thought, that he had not softened his story to protect himself: although I knew my father to be a resilient man, I had seen how painful it had been for him to speak for the first time of his terrible past.

Though he had risked condemnation from the interviewers, he hadn't skirted around their questions or compromised his story in any way. He'd stated what he could remember and what he could not; in particular, much to the annoyance of the interviewers, he had refused to condemn his Latvian "kidnappers" out of hand. It seemed to me that having begun the painful task of dragging his wartime past into the open my father would remain adamant about the truth, even when I suspected that this would not be the last time he would face pressure to tailor it to the agenda of his audience.

Doubtless there would be other individuals who would question my father's integrity, especially in the light of his fifty-year silence. He told me that he'd maintained his silence to protect his wife and sons from the trauma of his past. I'd accepted that but also suspected that he may have faced pressure from Dzenis and Lobe. Did he feel shy or even ashamed about his original identity?

The question that loomed largest was how my father had maintained his silence all this time. I began to reflect on a childhood spent in his company, wondering whether there was anything, in retrospect, that might provide a clue.

I reached the riverbank and sat down opposite the wooden footbridge that traversed the river. I started to nod off in the warm afternoon sun, and as I did, I remembered a favorite family anecdote.

My father loved two-up, the illegal game of chance and mateship that he'd first learned to play while on the road in the Australian outback. Two or three times a year he would suddenly announce that he was gripped by the urge to "play the pennies." My mother would never let us wait up for him because he rarely returned before midnight. However, one night my father failed to return at the expected hour. At around 2:00 a.m. I was roused by the sound of my parents' voices in the kitchen. My father had only just come in, and my mother was making him a cup of tea. As I tiptoed past my brothers to the kitchen, they fell in behind me. I put my ear to the door.

"That was a close escape," I heard my mother say. "You were lucky this time."

Upon hearing those words, my youngest brother, Andrew, became overexcited. "What happened, Daddy?" he cried out. At the same moment, my brother Martin pushed me forward so that I stumbled into the kitchen and almost fell on the floor.

My parents jumped in surprise. "In God's name, what are you boys doing up at this hour?" my mother exclaimed. "Back to bed this instant. The lot of you."

"No!" Andrew protested loudly, ignoring our mother. "Tell us about your lucky escape, Daddy."

"Well, it was like this," he said, looking slowly at each of us in turn. "We were all gathered in a circle around the spinner. He had the coins on the paddle and was holding it in the air. The toss was about to begin, so we were all as quiet as mice. You could have heard a pin drop, when suddenly there was a noise, like the whistle of a bird. Only it was the middle of the night.

"It was the warning signal from Bert, the 'cockie,' or watch, who was on lookout upstairs. The police were on their way to raid us. Before we'd even fully taken that in, Bert called out, 'Crikey, the coppers are already at the door.'

"Everybody panicked. All hell broke loose! Mayhem. Somebody

gave the order 'out through the back door,' so all of us made a charge in that direction. There must've been more than a hundred of us, and we were all desperately trying to squeeze through the door at the same time. Somehow I made it through and into the backyard. It was almost pitch-black so that I could just make out the figures of men hoisting each other up over the fence. You see, we're all mates there and we look after each other.

"Behind us," my father whispered excitedly, "we could hear the police breaking down the doors of the warehouse, and I thought, 'This is it. My number's up,' when somebody yelled out: 'Over here. There's a loose plank. We can get through the fence here.' With that we all charged over like a swarm of ants."

My father's eyes moved slowly across each of our faces with such dramatic intensity that we all held our breath.

"But it was just my luck," he said, his voice unexpectedly dropping a register. "Just as I reached the gap, a fat man jumped in ahead of me. And you wouldn't believe it, boys: Fatty was stuck."

We all squealed with pleasure.

"Alex," my mother interrupted him, "don't talk about the poor chap like that. He can't help it if he's overweight."

My brothers and I shifted irritably on our stools. Our mother had broken the spell.

"But that was his nickname," my father protested. "We all called him that. He didn't mind in the least. Anyway, where was I?"

"Fatty's stuck, Dad," I said.

"That's right. His head and shoulders were on one side of the fence and his enormous bottom and legs were on our side. We were trapped."

"What did you do?" Martin asked solemnly.

"What could we do?" my father answered. "We pushed! We got a good grip on his cheeks and shoved him as hard as we could. But he didn't budge. He was wedged in so tightly that he began to squeal like a little piggy.

"By this time, I could hear the cops making their way across the warehouse and heading toward the yard. In the next moment they were at the back door."

We were all wide-eyed with terror.

"I called out one final desperate time," my father said. "'Everyone together . . . one . . . two . . . three,' and we gave Fatty one last big push. Lo and behold, we heard a pop, like a bottle of champagne being opened, and Fatty was flat on his face on the other side of the fence.

"With that I jumped through. I was free."

We all sprang to our feet, cheering. I recalled with clarity how my father then switched to the present tense, heightening the drama of the moment.

"I make my way in the darkness along the back lane, careful to avoid being caught by the police. There is nobody else around, not a soul. I am totally alone. I have no idea where the other men have gone.

"Then suddenly I come to a clearing and beyond that is a small park. I am sure that my car is in the street on the other side of the park. It is deadly quiet, and through the trees I can see my car, its surface glistening in the rain.

"I make a dash for the park. I sneak through the trees. I only have to cross the street and put the key in the lock. It's now or never. I take a deep breath and run for the car. I do it. I escape . . .

"Hey, presto! Here I am!" My father snapped his fingers and smiled.

My brothers and I leaned back in our chairs, exhausted and relieved.

The room was silent, and it took several seconds before any of us could rouse ourselves. Finally, it was my mother who made a move.

"Come on, Alex," she said. "Let's get the littlies back to bed."

The sound of a jogger crossing the rickety bridge brought me back to the present and I suddenly had a revelation. I was certain that my father's silence had some connection with his storytelling.

Everyone who heard my father tell a story appreciated his talents. He had embellished his various tales, usually about his early years in Australia, transforming them into wondrous adventures. If my mother was around at the time, she would castigate my father, playfully saying, "You've put the enlarger on again, luv."

I sat bolt upright. I'd had a flash of clarity about my father's two-up story: as he told us about his getaway, he might have been reliving another event whose memory exerted itself so powerfully in him that he spoke of it as if it had only just happened.

Even though the surface details were different, my father had been reliving the extremity of his escape from his village: his climb through the fence at the back of his house and his journey past the open graves of his neighbors. I shuddered.

He had found a way to tell us what had happened to him without telling us. Somehow, incredibly, he'd woven a cataclysmic event of his childhood—the separation from his family—into a recent humorous incident. Perhaps the story had denatured his terror and alleviated the pressure of keeping his secret.

I could see already that without the safety valve of his stories, my father was having more trouble repressing the truth of his childhood than he had perhaps imagined. But this did not in any way compromise the veracity of his words now that he had finally found the courage to speak. To tell his most amazing story, the consummate storyteller would have to abandon the tools of his trade. Although I could not as yet say unequivocally that I was relieved the truth was coming out.

The flurry and squawking of ducks on the river snapped me back to the current time in a flash. It was twilight, and the meadow was now nearly deserted apart from the occasional solitary cyclist taking a shortcut across the field. I got up and dusted myself off.

CHAPTER THIRTEEN

ELLI

I could no longer keep my father's story to myself. When I was a student I'd become friendly with an Israeli woman at my college. We first met one evening when she was seated across from me in the dining hall.

She overheard a conversation I was having with a colleague and detected my slight Aussie accent. Later she approached me and introduced herself over coffee in the common room. Her name was Elli. She was a historian keenly interested in issues related to Judaism.

She mimicked my Australian accent while telling me that she'd spent some of her teenage years in Sydney—her father had been posted there as an executive for an Israeli import/export business. She told me no more than that, and even as our acquaintanceship grew, I could not get her to open up about her time in Australia.

I sought out Elli now, thinking that she might understand my predicament. Although the new academic term had not yet begun, I called her on the off chance that she'd already returned from her home in Jerusalem.

She answered the telephone immediately. "Dearie, you're back!"

We exchanged news about our respective travels and then I suggested that we meet for coffee later in the week. Elli must have sensed something in the tone of my voice.

"You sound worried," she said, becoming serious. "Is everything okay?"

"I'll tell you more when we meet," I said.

"As you wish," she replied.

We made arrangements to meet at a tearoom on the High.

Two days later, I waited for her at the appointed time at the rear of the shop. I heard the bell above the door ring and looked up to see Elli struggle into the shop with a carryall full of, I was sure, academic books and journals. She was something of a cross between a bag lady and the stereotypical absentminded professor, but one with a shrewdly appraising expression.

I spent the rest of the afternoon with Elli doing my best to describe in a coherent manner what my father told me and all that had followed: the question of who Lobe really was, my father's memories of exterminations, and my inability to unearth the significance of Koidanov and Panok.

I was impressed and grateful for the extraordinary care Elli took to understand the details of my father's case. When I had exhausted myself, she was silent for some time. She was clearly mulling something over. Then she reached across the table and took my hand in both of hers. Her grip was firm.

"Don't worry, dearie," she said. I could sense the compassion in her voice. "We'll get this sorted out. First of all, if your father is Jewish, then these names that he's held inside him probably have Jewish or perhaps even eastern European Yiddish associations. And I know just the person to help you with that," she declared decisively. "Frank. A genealogist who specializes in Judaic culture."

I jumped at the opportunity to meet Frank, and there and then Elli called him and arranged for me to meet with him the following morning.

I waited for Frank at the Jericho Café. I'd barely had time to seat myself at an empty table by the window when I saw a motor scooter pull up outside and, somewhat incongruously, a man in his late forties dismount. He was perilously thin and sparrowlike, but his dark hair, dark brooding eyes, and dark beard gave him a rabbinical aura.

Somehow he must have surmised that I was the individual he was to meet. He waved from the other side of the window, giving me a broad and intelligent smile, and entered with a vital nervous energy. Over coffee I described my father's story, and it was clear that Frank observed the effect it was having on me.

"Both my parents lost their families in the war," he said. "It had a terrible effect on me as well, but you've got to learn to live in the light, Mark. Not be consumed by the darkness of the past as some of them have."

Frank told me more about his interests in the genealogy and dialects of eastern European Jewry, and I learned of his especial interest in life in the shtetlach before the war. We eventually got down to the question of Panok and Koidanov. Frank was immediately dismissive of my suggestion that either of these words might be my father's family name. He must have noticed how disheartened I was by his opinion, because he quickly promised that he would investigate them further and get back to me.

Early the next morning I was woken up by the telephone. Groggy at first, I didn't recognize the man's voice at the other end of the line.

"I was wrong! There was a family of Panoks!" It was Frank. He was so excited that he hadn't bothered with the formality of a greeting. I was instantly alert.

"It's a very uncommon name for Jews," he continued, without pausing for breath, "but there was one extended family of Jews who went by that name. They lived mainly on the outskirts of Minsk, the capital of Belarus."

I started to shiver uncontrollably. I was shocked and greedy for more good news.

"Anything on Koidanov?" I asked, my teeth slightly chattering.

"Not a scrap," he replied, "but I'm working on it. I'll get back to you as soon as I know more."

I thanked Frank profusely and hung up.

I lay back on my bed. For the first time in quite a while I felt optimistic. "Was my father a Panok?" I asked aloud. Perhaps he was from Minsk. A Belarusian. I knew nothing about the country. But what was Koidanov?

My thoughts were racing. I was far too restless to return to sleep, so I decided that I would head to the Bodleian Library in town, where I would look for a detailed map of Belarus. I was climbing the stairs to the bathroom to take a shower when suddenly the telephone rang again. It was just eight o'clock, far too early for a regular caller. "It must be Frank again," I told myself, "already back with another clue."

I picked up the receiver and held it to my ear. At first I thought that there was nobody at the other end of the line. Then I heard a familiar voice.

It was my mother.

Immediately I knew that something was wrong. It was the first time that she had ever telephoned me in Oxford.

"Is that you, Mark?" I heard her ask for a second time.

"Mum?"

"It's your father, luv," she whispered, sounding worried.

"What's up?" I snapped, fearing the worst from a call such as this.

She hesitated. I could hear the sound of her breathing as she struggled to say something. "He won't stop crying." She choked on her words for a moment. "Your father's been crying for two days. Every time I ask him what's wrong he just shakes his head and says, 'All the memories are coming back to me now. I can't stop them.' That's all he says, over and over. Nothing else.

"He's been unsettled for months now. But it's gotten worse recently."

My mother began to sob gently. "I don't understand what's going on," she murmured. Then she regained her composure. "You don't know what this is about, do you, luv?"

"No, Mum," I said quietly, "I don't."

It was clear that my father had still not told my mother anything. I wanted to tell her what I knew, if only to allay her fears, but I worried that the truth would devastate her. My father had put me in an untenable position.

My mother spoke again: "Your father said he wants to talk to you in person. You should be here."

I didn't go to the Bodleian that day. Maps would have to wait. Instead I headed back to Heathrow airport that evening to begin my long journey home.

PART II

CHAPTER FOURTEEN
HOME, AGAIN

My father was waiting for me in the arrivals terminal at Melbourne airport, as he had some months ago. He was less buoyant than he'd been and was silent during the entire journey home. This time it was the tape that had become the lodestone of our relationship, and until it was broached we wouldn't have much to say to each other.

I had a strong sense of déjà vu as the car turned into the driveway. My mother waited on the porch and ushered me into the kitchen to give me breakfast. It was as if I'd never been away, as if nothing had changed. In one respect at least, this turned out to be true: my father had still not revealed his past either to my mother or to anyone else we knew. Instead, he had videotaped a testimony at a Holocaust center.

I'd slept well on the flight and didn't feel the slightest bit jet-lagged. Indeed, the bright sunshine of the Australian September spring morning energized me. I chatted with my mother before heading outside to my father's workshop with a cup of tea. I crossed the yard, calling out in advance, "Tea's up!"

My father turned to face me, about to say something.

"Yes," I said, anticipating his words, "it's got three sugars in it."

"As if I'm not sweet enough," he joked in response.

I leaned on the doorjamb and watched him as he tinkered inside the open back of a television set. Occasionally he surfaced to sip at his tea and at one such moment I caught his eye. "So what's going on, Dad?" I asked.

"What do you mean?" he replied, not looking at me.

"Mum's worried about you. She called me . . ."

"I'll be fine," he said and buried his head in the television.

"Dad," I insisted, "talk to me. You avoid me over the phone. I came all the way back here because Mum said you wanted to talk to me. What's bothering you?"

My father raised his head. He shrugged and I could now see how tense and coiled up inside he was. "That videotape I sent you . . ." he murmured.

I nodded.

"I wish I'd never made it."

"Why?"

"It just didn't work out . . ."

"Why did you go there, Dad?" I challenged him.

My father scratched the back of his head. "To be honest, I'm not quite sure. I don't know what I was thinking."

"You *must* have some idea," I said edgily.

He grimaced. "I was looking for answers." He gave a deep sigh.

"To what?"

"To questions that I don't even know." He laughed bitterly before continuing. "What happened to me is part of what is called the Holocaust, isn't it?" He stared at me intently. "So I thought that Jewish people, more than anyone else, would understand what had happened to me. More than that, I thought that somebody at the center might recognize the words 'Koidanov' and 'Panok.'"

"So did they come up with anything?" I asked.

He shook his head despondently. I considered telling him I had Frank on the case back in Oxford, but for the moment I wanted to stick to the topic of the interview.

"I thought they would, being Jewish," he said. "To be honest, I think they were more interested in how I felt about being Jewish. They asked me what I knew about being Jewish and if I considered myself to be Jewish."

My father shrugged and looked slightly bewildered. "You know how I feel," he said.

"Anyway, after the man there heard some of my story he told me I should give my whole testimony. He explained to me what that meant, and I agreed to do it."

"So how did it go?" I asked.

"I was frustrated by the vagueness of my memories at times. I have the feeling that the interviewers were as well. But I couldn't help that. I was only a child, after all. Some things were vivid, others weren't." My father was about to say something else but then stopped himself.

"What?" I asked.

"Recently things have changed," he said with some deliberation. He nestled his head in his folded arms atop the television set.

"It's as if there are two men inside me, and one of them has been asleep for more than fifty years. Now he's waking up, and the two are not getting on so well."

"How are they not getting on, Dad?"

"The one that is waking up, well, he won't be pacified. It's as if he's whispering in my ear over and over: 'Find out who you are. Now!' So I'm taking his advice. It's a simple wish—I want to know who I am. Doesn't every person have that right?"

I remained silent, staring at the floor, but felt the intensity of my father's eyes upon me.

Suddenly my father snapped. He stood bolt upright and rigid as he burst into a torrent of words while still keeping his voice low and controlled. "It's a cruel fate. Every day I ask myself why this happened to me. Why did I decide that I wanted to live? Sometimes I think that it would have been better if I hadn't woken up. That it would've been better to have gone to the grave with my family. What does it mean that I survived?"

There was no note of self-pity in my father's words, and his face conveyed only bewilderment as he continued. "My identity was snatched away as a child and now I feel I'm denied one as an adult. There must be someplace I belong. Am I Jewish? Am I Russian? Am I Latvian? Am I guilty or innocent for what happened to me? The more I talk about my past, the more confused I am."

The flow of words stopped as abruptly as they had begun, leaving my desolate father in their wake.

I understood better now what had driven my father toward the Jewish community. It was not simply his burning desire to find the meaning of Koidanov and Panok. These questions had worried him for most of his life. I sensed that my father had been clutching desperately at this old, Jewish identity in an effort to stay afloat amid the wreckage of long-manufactured self. He had gone seeking something from the Holocaust center, but for whatever reason had not found what he was looking for.

CHAPTER FIFTEEN
ESCAPE FROM RIGA

I resolved to put everything aside in order to help my father solve the riddle of his identity.

Later on that first night in the safety of the dark kitchen, he began to talk to me again.

"I'll tell you about the end of the war," he said, "when we fled Riga and took refuge in Germany." He began rummaging in his case.

During my childhood I had never heard my father use such words—"fled" and "refuge"—in relation to his time in Europe during the war. In fact, the period from the war's end until his arrival in Australia was another black hole for us all. He had offered us only the scantest of details about what had gone on, as if by magic he had, first, resurfaced after the war in a displaced-persons camp outside Hamburg and then, in a second sleight of hand, emerged into the bright Australian sunshine.

And, bizarre as it may sound, none of us ever pushed him to reveal more about that period of his life. We gratefully accepted whatever morsel he fed us, never pausing to digest what we'd been given.

"Here they are," he said brightly, pulling out a slip of paper.

"Why are you looking for them?" I asked.

"I wanted to check the date when I arrived in Germany. It should be printed here. Let me see . . ." My father adjusted his reading glasses, and I seized the moment.

"Here, let me do it," I said, snatching the piece of paper from him before he could protest or shove it back in the case.

I looked down at the yellowed document. It simply stated my father's name, his nationality (Latvian), his date of birth, and his place of birth, which was given as Riga. At the bottom of the sheet, there was the imprint of an official border-entry stamp dated October 21, 1944. My father would have been about nine years old by then.

My father stared at me intently. After a pause I asked, "Why did you flee Riga?"

"We had to escape the Russians before they entered Riga." He warmed to his story right away. "I tell you, it was chaos. Suitcases were piled up all over the place in Valdemara Street. Uncle was pacing up and down the room, staring at his watch. I sat quietly on the couch. I didn't want to get in anyone's way. You see, I was worried that if I did, one of them would stop and think to themselves, 'Why are we taking him with us? Why do we need another person to worry about, another mouth to feed?'

"So I sat there in my new navy suit and cap that Auntie had brought to my room the night before. She told me that I would no longer be a soldier, that it would be too dangerous to be one from then on. I loved being a corporal, so I was very annoyed. But I could sense the tension in the apartment and knew better than to create a fuss. Later I learned that Auntie had stoked the stove in the kitchen one last time for the purpose of burning every single one of my uniforms."

My father seemed wistful for a moment. "See this, my case," he said. "I had it with me as well. It was brand-new then—Uncle had presented it to me as a gift for my belongings—it looked much better than it does these days." He flashed a grin at me and said, "Like me, you could say."

"Where was Zirdra?" I asked my father.

"She wasn't coming with us," he answered. "I don't know the exact details, but I seem to recall that she had been sent to work with a Latvian medical brigade."

My father continued with his story.

"As we headed toward the main railway station in Riga, I noticed that the streets seemed to have changed dramatically: like people's faces, they looked grimmer and grubbier.

"Suddenly I remembered that I had not said good-bye to the sergeant nor to Commander Lobe. I turned to Uncle and begged him to take me to them. He said that it was impossible, but I would see them soon in Germany, which pacified me. 'Germany,' I thought, 'the place that everybody talked about all the time, as if it were heaven, or a pot of gold at the end of the rainbow.' It was only natural that the commander and Sergeant Kulis would be there, too. It seemed that all the Latvians around me were going there.

"It was a scramble at Riga station. People were milling about everywhere, and trying to find any vacant seats on the train was nightmarish. Although Uncle had reservations, people had occupied our seats and refused to budge, even when he waved our tickets authoritatively in front of them.

"Uncle and I moved further down the train toward the front carriages. We found free seats there, which I guarded until he came back with Auntie and Mirdza.

"I must have fallen asleep on Auntie's lap. At one point, I opened my eyes briefly and saw Uncle sitting opposite me. I could see his reflection in the carriage window as he stared into the darkness beyond it. His face was tired and worried—I'd never seen him like that before. Then I must have nodded off again.

"The next thing I remember was being gently shaken by Auntie trying to wake me. I sat up bleary-eyed and she began to smooth my hair.

" 'We're here,' she said.

" 'Germany!' I exclaimed.

" 'No, silly, the ship that will take us there.'

"I peered through the dirty train window and saw that we had indeed reached a port. The ship was more like a ferry. *Steuben*, it was called. It was going to take us to Gotenhafen, a German port on the Baltic.

"We made our way up the gangplank and onto the deck, which was loaded with cargo boxes and cases. There were people who'd boarded before us and were already sleeping in the corridors and even on the floor of the dining cabin, as we passed through it.

"Uncle must have been a person of some status, because a steward led us to a cabin that was spacious enough to accommodate us all. It was a lot more than most people seemed to get.

"I don't remember much after that. I'd been only half-awake, and I quickly nodded off to sleep in my narrow top bunk.

"Over breakfast, Uncle told us that we would be in Germany by that evening. I was excited by the news, but suddenly I began to worry about what would happen to me. 'Will my secret be discovered by these Germans?' I asked myself. I'd met quite a few German officers in Riga, and they'd always terrified me. They were arrogant and behaved as if they could do anything, even read your mind. They'd have no difficulty discovering that I was Jewish.

"I went back on deck and stayed there all day, staring at the murky waters through the swirls of mist. At one stage, I started to hatch a plan of escape for when we'd docked. But I felt muddle-headed and told myself to wait until I saw the lay of the land before trying anything.

"The fog thickened gradually during the afternoon. 'At least the Germans won't see me,' I reassured myself.

"By early evening the lights of a harbor pierced the mist. Uncle joined me on deck. He leaned over the rail, quietly contemplating the vista of the town that was slowly crystallizing before us. 'Gotenhafen,' he said."

My father smiled wryly. "Gotenhafen," he said to me. "God's harbor."

"In the months that followed, we took refuge wherever we could, as if we were on the run. Families, contacts of Uncle's, I guess, took us in for various periods. I don't know who arranged this for us or how. We slept wherever we could—on living room floors, huddled by brick ovens—sharing whatever food our hosts could provide.

"At one stage we stayed with a family I think were called Siegel, but my memories of names are confused because we moved so frequently. But we were there for perhaps a month or so, and for the first time we had a room to ourselves.

"I didn't see much of Uncle in that period. He was away from the house for days on end. I suspect that he may have been seeing officials, trying to get a place of our own or arranging passage farther on.

"When he wasn't away on business, he'd usually arrive home in time for dinner, when we'd all crowd around the table together. There'd be Mr. and Mrs. Siegel and their two sons about my age, who'd always want me to join in their games and other antics.

"But I wasn't interested in that sort of thing. I had more important things to do. I'd quickly figured out my way about town. I hung around the railway station. Nobody paid any attention to a kid. But I paid a lot of attention to what was going on and I soon worked out how the black market operated.

"Before long, the Dzenises and the Siegels had me out bartering for them on a regular basis. I traded clothes and valuables for food and medicine. One time, Uncle ordered me to barter the silk stockings that Mirdza had smuggled with her from Riga. Uncle had confiscated them when he'd discovered them. I remember the way he scolded her: 'God knows who you think you are or where you think you are going,' he'd said. 'To a fancy ball or something!'

"Seeing me roll the stockings into a ball and stuff them into my jacket was the last straw for Mirdza. She scowled at me viciously. I think she has hated me ever since—especially when I came back with horse-meat, bread, and pickled cucumbers in place of her precious stockings.

"Mr. Siegel was a hearty type who loved his food, and when he saw my booty, he slapped me on the back and tousled my hair. Everybody was pleased except for Mirdza, who glowered at me from the opposite side of the table, even though she, too, feasted on the gains from my black marketeering.

"It was crazy when you think of it—a child having the knowledge and skills to do this. They would've starved without me. I was more re-sourceful than all of them put together. They were like the children and I was the father."

For an instant I had an image of my father as an Oliver Twist–type character—a street urchin with a smeared face—not dressed in rags, admittedly, but in a sailor outfit, darting in and out among the crowds.

"Then one night over dinner, Uncle made an announcement that our departure from the Siegels was imminent. We would be leaving for an unknown destination where the authorities had promised us an apartment of our own.

"Two days later, we were told that we had an hour to gather our belongings, and by midmorning we found ourselves waiting in the freezing cold at the railway station. There were long queues of other refugees who were in the same situation as us.

"We ended up waiting there all day without food, wondering what was going to become of us. Finally, an official told us we were going to Essen.

"That night we departed for Essen, hoping that we would end up in our own quarters, no matter how tiny. We were in Essen for only a matter of hours before boarding another train headed for Dresden. We'd barely reached Dresden when it came under siege from intensive firebombing. That would make it February 1945. The authorities thought that we'd be safer elsewhere, so we were evacuated to the grounds of a castle in a place called Moritzburg, on the outskirts of Dresden.

"When we got there, the place was overflowing with people wrapped in blankets huddled together in groups. To my child's eyes, it seemed like there were thousands of people assembled there. We found a spot on the ground as well and wrapped ourselves as warmly as possible.

"Auntie warned me to stay by her side, but, of course, I didn't. I wandered among the throng. They were different nationalities, too—as well as Latvians there were Lithuanians, Estonians, and Germans. I heard other languages I didn't recognize being spoken. They must've all been on the run from the Allied forces.

"The bombing of Dresden intensified during the night. The noise was tremendous, even from where we were, and the sky was lit up almost as if it were daytime. Everybody was fearful—you could see it on their faces—and some appeared on the verge of panic."

My father stared intently at me.

"You know what I did next, son?" he said then, without waiting for a response, "I climbed up the steps overlooking the grounds and shouted for everybody to remain calm. I told them to trust me, that we would be safe.

"What's even more amazing is that they listened to me. They were like a frightened flock of sheep, but somehow the sight of me, a mere child, speaking confidently, calmed them."

My father shook his head in disbelief. "But the truth is that inside I hoped that they would all be bombed. I wanted us all to disappear into oblivion. That's what I really felt."

"Even you, Dad?"

He nodded. "I'd had enough. The war, the fighting, the crisscrossing of Germany without any idea where I was being taken . . ."

My father rummaged in his case again. "Look!" he exclaimed, removing another photograph. "Here I am at Moritzburg Castle."

He held the photo out for me to see. Although the image was slightly unclear, one could indeed tell that it was my father, now about nine years old, dressed in a cap, a sailor's jacket, and trousers. In it, he smiles shyly at the camera, just as he was doing at this moment, a man in his sixties, as he waited for my response. I could only stare at it in amazement.

"After another day, we were moved on again, this time to Schwerin, in the northern part of Germany, where finally we did get a place of our own. But it was a dump! There was no other word for it: a dark, damp single room, with a single gas ring in the corner for cooking, and heating that didn't work. There was no bathroom—we had to share with at least a half-dozen other refugees on the same floor. Still, Auntie did her best to make it cozy so that it felt like a home.

"I remember the night that the war ended. Everybody from our floor had crammed into the room of one family who had a radio set. We listened in silence to a broadcast from the American military, who announced that the town was now in the hands of Allied forces. The atmosphere was solemn. I glanced at Uncle, but his face was immobile. Everybody was like that—their expressions were frozen. God knows what was going on in their heads at that moment. I guess they thought that their number was up, as they say.

"Suddenly Uncle rose and left. Auntie told us to go back to our room and then followed Uncle out. We waited silently in the darkness of our room. Even Mirdza was quiet, for a change—but not for long!

"'Uldis,' she whispered, 'what will happen to us?'

"'We're all going to die!' I exclaimed in a terrifying voice. I wanted to frighten Mirdza as revenge for all the trouble she caused me.

"She jumped up in a panic. Then, suddenly, she weakened, because I saw her silhouette stumble and reach for the wall for support. I rushed to her, regretting what I had just said, and tried to comfort her. 'We will be fine,' I said. 'Uncle won't let anything happen to us.'

"Despite her fear, Mirdza dropped off to sleep. But I couldn't. I sat there in the darkness, listening to her breathing. I was petrified, and I worried about what would happen to me. After all, if we were captured by the Allies, then there was the chance that they'd find out the truth about my past and then see me as the worst traitor of all. This time it'd be the Allies who'd put me up against a wall and shoot me for what I was—a Jewish boy among Nazis.

My father on the steps of Moritzburg Castle, outside Dresden, during the firebombings of 1945.

"I didn't know where Auntie and Uncle had gone, but they didn't return till just before dawn. I suppose that they must've been with other Latvians, discussing what was going to happen in the immediate future.

"They woke us up. Uncle wanted to talk. It was as if he'd read my mind. He put his arm around my shoulders and sat me down on the side of my bed. Then he crouched down to my level and stared into my eyes.

"'From now on,' he said, 'if any person, no matter who they are, asks who you are, you say that you are the son of my cousin. You must remember this!'

"Then he turned to the others in the room and warned them, too. 'Young Uldis is the son of my cousin whom we care for because his parents died in the war. Remember that.'

"Uncle had heard that the Americans were going to hand Schwerin over to the Soviets. He said that this was the worst thing that could happen to us. No Latvian could live under the oppression of the Soviet Union again.

"Among the other Latvian refugees he'd met, it'd been agreed that we needed to head farther west to Hamburg, which was in the British zone. We'd be safer there. We had to leave immediately, before the sun came up, and to pack only the bare minimum.

"There was a truck waiting for us in a nearby alleyway. Families were crammed onto the back of it, so that we had to squash in as best we could. I was wedged into a corner, but at least I could get some air and see through the slats.

"The truck soon picked up speed, and we had got some way out of Schwerin, when it came to a sudden halt. We were transferred to an old bus, so quickly that it was all I could do to hold on to my case. Still it was wonderful, finally, to be able to sit down and breathe properly.

"I nodded off with my head on Auntie's shoulder and didn't wake until the bus came to a halt in the middle of nowhere. It had broken down, and nobody had any idea what we should do. We simply sat there quietly on the bus while the driver examined the engine.

"A short time later, two soldiers—American—appeared in a jeep and took over. They ordered everybody off the bus. It was quite warm, so everybody headed for the shade of some trees by the side of the road. They lounged there passively, making occasional complaints about their discomfort and the heat of the afternoon. I was embarrassed by their complaints and laziness.

"I returned to the bus, where the two soldiers and the driver were working on the engine. Soon another jeep pulled up. For a second, I froze to the spot when I noticed that there was a black soldier among them. I had never seen a black man before. Full of bravado, I resolved to tell him that it was about time for a wash. I walked over to the jeep, but when I got close enough, I got an enormous shock! I realized that he wasn't dirty—it was the color of his skin! I just stood there, transfixed.

"At a certain moment, he looked across and noticed me. I don't know what expression I had on my face, but he laughed out loud and flashed me a big smile. His teeth were brilliant white, not yellowed and decayed like the Europeans'. I imagined that he must've come from some sort of paradise. 'That's where I want to go, this place called America,' I said to myself.

"The soldier reached into his pocket and pulled something out, beckoning me over the way Sergeant Kulis had done all those years earlier in the schoolhouse. This time I was not tentative. I knew that I'd be safe. I went over to him. Then I saw that it was a chocolate bar. I was so pleased. In Riga, I'd almost lived on the stuff.

"He leaned back against the side of the jeep, watching me as I gulped down the chocolate. It was richer and creamier and so much better than Laima's.

"I could tell that he was a kind person, and I wanted to communicate with him, despite the—to me—still-disturbing color of his skin. I tried to say thank you, but he didn't understand a word of what I was saying. But something about me must have moved him because he tousled my hair and smiled warmly at me. He passed me more chocolate and some chewing gum as well. He even gave me a puff on his cigarette. I almost choked.

I'd never had one before: the Latvian soldiers had never let me smoke because it wasn't good for my lungs, they said."

My father raised his eyebrows. "I witnessed atrocities, but they wouldn't let me smoke."

"Then the soldier pulled out a scrap of paper and wrote something on it. He pointed at the words and at his chest. Then he kept repeating 'America!' and 'Illinois!'

I didn't get it. 'Illinois. What a strange sound!' I remember thinking to myself. 'American won't be easy to learn.'

"It's obvious now that he'd written down his name and address in America." My father's mood became somber. "In all the mayhem," he said, "I lost that scrap of paper." He shifted in his seat. "It's a deep regret to me," he murmured. "I'll go to my grave without meeting this man who showed me kindness. Who knows how life would have turned out for me if I'd gone to America and found him?"

I wondered the same thing. Australia was a land of refuge from the war in the 1950s, but it would be fair to say that it lacked then the entrepreneurial spirit that prevailed in the United States. Even though my father loved Australia, I believe that America would have better suited his temperament and sense of adventure.

"Where was I?" I heard my father say.

"The bus . . ." I prompted him.

"That's right," he said. "It was eventually repaired, and everybody climbed back on board. I hid behind the jeep. I didn't want to rejoin the Latvians. I wanted to stay with my new friend, the soldier. I decided that somehow I would be able to tell him what had happened to me, and that he wouldn't let the Allies punish me. 'Who knows,' I thought, 'he might even be able to find out who I had once been.'

"At that moment I heard Uncle calling out my name. He'd noticed that I hadn't taken my seat on the bus.

"The soldiers began a search for me, and in a matter of only moments they'd uncovered my hiding place. The black soldier nudged me out into the open. I tried to convey to him that I wanted to stay with him

and that I knew all about soldiering—I even marched about while miming shooting a rifle—but he only laughed out loud, thinking I was playing the fool.

"He offered me his hand to shake and then grabbed me around the
waist and carried me over to the bus. Uncle was waiting for me on its
steps, and I knew that he had witnessed my feeble effort to be rescued,
even this late in the game. He deposited me, roughly, I might add, on a
spare seat next to Mirdza, who gave me a disgusted look. I waved a final
good-bye to the soldier from where I was seated and then the bus took
off in the direction of Hamburg.

"The journey seemed to take forever. The roads were blocked with
cars and tanks and convoys of soldiers. People were fleeing in both directions. I even saw German soldiers in their Wehrmacht uniforms, standing with their hands in the air, having just surrendered.

"It was bittersweet. I was glad that the Germans had been defeated,
but I also tasted bitterness for the first time. I don't know whether it was
hate or not, but my anger for what they'd put me through suddenly overwhelmed me. I thought my head was going to burst. And all around me,
the Latvians were deadly quiet and staring straight ahead. They seemed
too frightened to even glance at what was happening outside the bus
windows. They must have feared being caught. Part of me hoped they
would be.

"The bus moved on slowly and was eventually stopped by British
soldiers on the outskirts of Hamburg. They directed us to Geesthacht.
There was a camp there, an officer told us. When they heard this, some
of the Latvians panicked and tried to scramble off the bus.

"The word 'camp' must've triggered the worst possible associations
in their minds. The soldiers had to draw their rifles to calm the potential
stampede. Then, through an interpreter, the officer explained that the
camp was administered by the British. We'd all be fed, clothed, given a
bed, and looked after by the Red Cross. What's more, the soldiers told
us that they had named the camp Saules—that was Latvian for sunshine—
and that stopped people in their tracks.

"Most remained standing in the aisle of the bus, and many turned to look at Uncle, who was still seated toward the rear. He'd already become a sort of de facto leader among us, having dealt with several difficult situations en route to Hamburg. He nodded without speaking. That calmed people's nerves, and they returned to their seats. Then the bus moved on toward Geesthacht. That's where we ended up finally. Our escape from Latvia was over."

CHAPTER SIXTEEN
TO FREEDOM

I t was now almost 3:00 a.m. The house was silent, apart from the ticking of the clock on the kitchen wall.

But my father showed no signs of flagging. Now that the floodgates had opened, it seemed that the flow of memories could not be stemmed.

"Over the next days more people arrived at the camp," he said. "It turned out that the camp had been designated especially for Latvian displaced persons, or DPs, as they called us. The camp must have held over a thousand people—and there were about seventy in our barracks, number forty-one.

"There was a long queue on the first day we arrived. Hundreds were milling about, waiting to be assigned to huts and receive their provisions.

"When we reached the head of the queue, we were met by a British officer and a Red Cross worker, who wanted to check our papers. The soldier looked down at me and asked Uncle if I was his son. Uncle hesitated and then thought better of it.

"'No, sir,' he said. 'His father was my cousin. Both his father and mother died in the war, and I am the boy's guardian, sir.'

"The soldier did not seem suspicious or even particularly interested in Uncle's explanation, but he did ask for my papers, and to my surprise, Uncle pulled out a wallet full of documentation. 'Here are documents from the Riga Orphan's Court in 1943,' he said, 'where I was awarded custody of the boy. His name is Uldis. My family wants to continue to look after him.' Uncle passed the papers over to the officer.

My father lifted the lid of his case and fished out a piece of paper. "Here is the certificate," he said, passing it across.

I looked down at the paper. It was dated 1943 and written in Latvian, so I could only make sense of a small portion of it. What stood out most sinisterly was the address of the court—Hermann Göring Street.

"I didn't know that Uncle had adopted you formally."

"He didn't. It's more like a guardian's certificate—though he did try to adopt me on a number of occasions. He really wanted me to be his son."

"Why didn't it happen, then?"

"I don't know, to be honest," my father said. "Uncle could have done it without my consent, but for some reason he was determined that I agree to it. But I wouldn't. He asked me at least three times and each time I refused. He was shocked and disgruntled, but he never insisted that I cooperate nor asked me my reasons. Eventually he let the matter drop. I wouldn't have been able to explain myself in any case."

"Do you understand now?" I asked.

My father grimaced. "They were not my people," he said, "and inside me I felt that if I let myself be adopted then, I would have surrendered completely to them."

"How long were you in the camp?"

"Over four years. We had to wait for a country to accept us. It wasn't so bad, except that they tried to get me to attend school. I did go on occasion, but mostly I played truant. I was still too restless after my life with the soldiers to sit at a desk."

I was not surprised to hear my father speak of his restlessness, since he had been that way for as long as I could remember. And he loved the little adventures he cooked up for us, sometimes enjoying them more than we did. Perhaps it was a way for him to create some of his missing childhood, or what he imagined a childhood should be.

He was great fun to be with, precisely because he sidestepped the difficult times of our childhood: he was rarely ill-tempered and not the type of father to scold, forbid, or punish us. He always put pleasure and enjoyment above the practicalities of money, and many people, including my brothers, understandably came to judge him harshly for what they saw as his financial profligacy.

One day, on trust, he handed over his life savings—our security—to a Frenchman known only as Michel, with whom he'd become acquainted. Michel had tempted my father with a business proposal and convinced him that it would be a surefire winner. The money had barely touched Michel's palm when he vanished. Incredibly, my father had demanded neither contract nor guarantees of any sort from the Frenchman. We lived hand to mouth for many years after that.

There was a time when I, too, found it difficult to forgive my father for this mistake. I worried especially on behalf of my mother, who found our financial insecurity extremely difficult. Living in a constant state of exasperation with my father, she made an almost saintly effort to cope with his recklessness and to protect us from its consequences. If we turned to our father for fun, we turned to our mother in times of trouble, looking for love and affection. This more than anything was a testament of her love both for him and for her sons.

Learning about my father's early life was akin to looking through a kaleidoscope: its shifting colors and shapes kept me enchanted for hours on end, but my eyes ached from searching for patterns. I now saw his attitude toward money, especially, as symptomatic of a "madness" that had infected him—money, like life itself, was a gamble that came and went easily.

But it was not the madness of a poor soul lost to himself: my father's madness somehow tempered the coexistence of child and man within one being. I realized now that part of my father was still a child of five, frozen in time at the split second before he had witnessed the extermination of his family.

He removed two photographs and laid them both on the table. I reached for the one nearest to me. It was a group photograph of the Latvians who lived in Barrack 41 at Saules. In the photograph, my father sits at the very end of the front row with all the other children, while the adults stand behind.

My immediate impression of the picture is that my father seems to be a stranger or an outsider among these people. It is not simply because he is positioned at the edge of the frame; rather, it is his demeanor, and, most notably, his clothes. By looking at the Latvians, dressed as they are in thick woolen overcoats with drawn, pallid features, it is easy to discern that it is winter.

My father wears short trousers, and his feet are bare. His body language indicates that he is freezing: he is hunched in on himself, trying to keep warm. Nonetheless, his small face grins determinedly out of the photograph.

I wanted to ask my father directly about how he saw himself in this photograph. But it seemed such an intimate question, and I was too shy. I returned the photograph to its resting place and picked up the other one.

This one, too, told a story different from the idyllic depiction of camp life my father had offered us as children. I'd seen the photograph just once before, during one of my father's storytelling sessions years earlier. It was stuck to the back of another picture he wished to show us, and he had inadvertently drawn it from his case. As it fluttered to the floor, I made a grab for it ahead of my father. I caught a glimpse of it for an instant, before he snatched it back from me with an unexpected force. Even though I was only a child, what I had seen in that moment filled me with unease.

Free to examine it at length now, I understood why the photograph had disturbed me. It is an ostensibly innocent-looking snap of my father: around ten or eleven years old, he is sitting alone at a table decorated with flowers. But if one looks closely, the boy appears deeply unhappy, as if, despite his own best efforts to maintain his composure, the mask has slipped from his small face to reveal terrible damage. His expression is so raw that it pained me to look.

I wanted to ask my father about this photograph as well, but again I held back, not wanting to further intrude upon his suffering.

I suddenly remembered that Auntie had told us that during his time at

My father at the kitchen table at Saules, 1943: "His expression is so raw that it pained me to look."

Saules my father would frequently wake up screaming in the middle of the night. It now occurred to me that in both the photographs I had just seen the aftereffects of his nightmares were still visible on his face.

Was he oblivious to his own suffering? Whatever effect he'd imagined these photographs would have upon me, I could only feel anger against all the Latvians in the camp, including Auntie and Uncle.

My father spoke again.

"The living conditions in the hut were cramped," he said. "All the families created their own space by hanging blankets to create rooms of sorts. In our place, we'd crammed in the bunk beds and a small table that we sat around for hours on end.

"Uncle worked in the camp's office, and sometimes Auntie would get me to take something over to him. He was never busy when I dropped by. He usually sat behind a large desk, chatting with other Latvian men who were also in the office."

My father paused and looked at me excitedly. "Do you know who one of them was?" he asked, and without waiting for an answer, went on. "Apparently it was Konrad Kalejs. The war criminal who's been in the news recently."

I had heard of Kalejs, who'd been a member of Latvia's notorious Arajs Kommando, an extermination squad that even unreconstructed Latvians had difficulty explaining away. Kalejs had lived freely in the United States and later in Australia before his true identity had been uncovered. Shamefully, the Australian government had vacillated over his prosecution for war crimes, and Kalejs had died before being brought to justice.

"Whenever I played hooky from school, I'd go out to deal on the black market. When I'd return home with the day's booty, I'd make a grand show of it. Uncle and Auntie would look up, smiling, as I flung down my forage bag—the same one Kulis had given me to collect wood—and laid out what I had bartered for that day: chocolates, tobacco, and the occasional note or coin.

"I'd sit on the edge of my bunk while Uncle counted the coins. He kept a small box hidden under the floorboards. He would get it out, untie it, and add the day's takings to the coins and notes that were already in it.

"Auntie would be responsible for the food. She had her own secret box and would store the chocolates and sugar in it. But before retying the box and hiding it, she always passed me a chocolate as a reward. Sometimes I'd forget that I was supposed to be civilized, as Uncle demanded, and I'd revert to my habits in the forest. I'd snatch the chocolate from Auntie's hand and retreat to my bunk, like an animal returning to the lair with its catch. Auntie would shake her head despondently. Those days in the forest have left their imprint on me.

"But they were always pleased with my work. Uncle would compliment me, saying such things as, 'You are truly—what do these English say?—a wheeler and dealer!'

"Once, when Mirdza was still living with us, and she heard Uncle praise me, she harrumphed indignantly, 'He must have a touch of the

Jew in him!' At the mention of that word, I headed for my bunk—I half-expected to hear the sound of Mirdza receiving a slap like the one Ausma had once gotten for making a similar accusation. But nothing happened. It was no longer a crime to be Jewish, though it was obviously still an insult."

"Did you ever think of telling the Dzenis family that you were Jewish?" I asked. "After all, as you said, it wasn't a crime to be Jewish by then."

"What would've been the point?" he answered.

"Would they have accepted you?" I pressed him.

My father didn't answer. His body language made it clear that he didn't wish to dwell on the issue of his Jewishness, which even now seemed to make him nervous. I wondered what made him want to skirt around the issue.

When he spoke again, it was to change the topic. "I spent four years in Geesthacht."

"You said that," I replied. "What other things did you get up to?"

"This and that," my father answered, shrugging and rubbing the back of his neck. His reluctance slightly annoyed me, though I assumed that it was due to the almost instinctive caution that he had lived with for so long.

"Weren't you ever tempted to tell anyone about the kind of people who were in the camp?" I asked.

"To be honest, it never crossed my mind." My father paused. "I was still in another world. Looking back, I know I had no idea what had happened to me and who these people really were. I was shell-shocked and vulnerable and disturbed by what I had gone through. I can tell you that I wasn't the only one like that. There were individuals in that camp who died under mysterious circumstances. In other words, they committed suicide.

"In the early years after the war, Europe was in chaos, and I clung to the Dzenis family, who'd promised to take me with them wherever they ended up. They were my anchor. How could I inform on their compatriots?

My father at Saules DP camp outside Hamburg, 1947.

"I should have been old enough to take care of myself. After all, I was nine."

"No way!" I exclaimed. "Think of children today at the age of nine."

"There was another reason I kept quiet about the past," my father said. "The British who ran the camp seemed to really like the Latvians. I didn't understand that: one minute we were at war with them, the next they were looking after us!"

"Do you think that they knew who these Latvians were?" I asked.

"They might've chosen simply to turn a blind eye to things. It was strange that there were no questions asked about these people, that they were given some sort of special status and priority, when the Allies knew that they'd not been occupied by the Nazis but had cooperated with them."

"It seems that the Latvians have done a good job of whitewashing their past, and many of them got away with it."

"They investigated Commander Lobe, you know. For war crimes."

"When was this?"

"The early 1960s."

"Who was it?"

"The Swedes. I think on request from the Soviets, who claimed that Lobe had ordered massacres. They were interested in what I had to say then about my memories. I signed a statement . . ."

"Against Lobe?"

"No, the opposite! For Lobe . . . in his defense."

"Is this what you meant that day in London when you said they made you do it? Uncle and Lobe?"

My father nodded.

"Did you lie?"

My father was taken aback by my directness.

"I don't know if I did or did not," he answered. The expression on his face tightened. "I have memories of exterminations—the ones I mentioned to you—but I don't remember specifically if Commander Lobe himself was there. I do know that he was in charge of the Eighteenth, along with another soldier, Captain Rubenis. I didn't have much to do with him, though."

"Do you want to tell me about this statement?" I asked my father, who gave a deep sigh and shifted in his seat. He nodded.

CHAPTER SEVENTEEN
THE AFFIDAVIT

While I did want to learn as much as I could about whatever my father volunteered about his past, at certain moments I found myself resisting his words. I had begun to sense that my father hoped for redemption or absolution in exchange for his confessions. I didn't know in what shape or form he hoped to find this, nor who he hoped would deliver it, but I prayed that it was not me—I felt that I had little wisdom regarding his situation and that I, too, was now struggling to keep from drowning in the horrors of his past.

"It must have been sometime late in 1963," my father began. "By then I was living in Melbourne." He shifted in his chair again, trying to make himself more comfortable.

"One day I heard from Uncle. He wanted to see me as soon as possible. I found my way to their home in Elsternwick. It was on an ordinary suburban street, in a row of small white cottages. Theirs was partly hidden behind a picket fence and a front garden dominated by a beautiful silver birch that always reminded me of the forests I'd patrolled with the soldiers in Latvia. Uncle and Auntie had created a little bit of their homeland.

"I went through the gate and started to make my way up to the front door, when suddenly I stopped and looked down at my crumpled suit and brown case. I was overcome with shame. I felt that I didn't have much to show for nearly fifteen years of life in Australia: I'd spent most of my life here as a vagabond, which suited me down to the ground at the time, but somehow I still couldn't shed that shabby aura.

"I tried to smooth out the creases in my suit and then went up to the front door. I had to knock only once before the door was opened by Auntie. It had been quite a while since I'd seen her, but the expression of kindness in her light blue eyes was always the same. Before I knew what was happening, she was hugging me and kissing both of my cheeks.

"'Come in, Uldis, come in,' she exclaimed warmly, ushering me into the living room. Inside I was reminded even more of the past. The furnishings and decorations were as if they'd been transported from the apartment in Riga. The curtains had been closed to keep out the strong Australian light so that the room was in semidarkness apart from the soft light coming from a lamp on a side table. One wall was covered with shelves of books. Only the muted ticking of a grandfather clock in one corner could be heard.

"What I most remembered was the sweet scent—a mixture of flowers, ripened apples, and furniture polish—identical to that in the apartment on Valdemara Street.

, "'Please sit, my boy,' Auntie said. 'I'll tell Uncle you're here.' She always referred to her husband as Uncle in my company.

"Auntie tapped lightly on a door on the opposite side of the room. It was then that I heard Uncle's voice, telling her to enter. She flashed me a nervous smile before disappearing inside and closing the door tightly behind her.

"After several moments the door opened again and when I looked up Uncle was standing in the doorway. From where I was seated, he towered above everything in the room. He'd not lost his aura of formality, even in Australia, the most easygoing of places. He stepped forward with his arm outstretched, and I rose to shake his hand. Then he told me to be seated again.

"Auntie hovered nervously behind him. She seemed concerned that Uncle and I should be pleased to see each other. I had no idea why, as there'd rarely been any tension between Uncle and me. He told Auntie to prepare coffee for us, and she disappeared into the kitchen.

"Uncle and I sat quietly for several minutes. He seemed to be coolly appraising me. I could sense his unease, but I hadn't the slightest idea what was bothering him.

" 'You look well!' he said finally. 'Strong! And you've put on some weight, too.'

" 'It's the good Australian food,' I answered.

"Uncle gave a little smile, before lapsing into silence again. I began to feel on edge, when suddenly he spoke.

" 'Why have you come here?' he asked.

"I was taken aback. 'Sir?' was all I could manage to say. I thought of this visit as my responding to his summons.

" 'What do you want?' he insisted.

" 'To see you and Auntie,' I blustered, feeling even more confused about why I was there.

" 'I have always believed that we would never see you again,' he said slowly. Then it must have registered with Uncle how startled I was. 'After all that happened . . .' he added, without completing the sentence.

" 'But you were kind to me, Uncle. You cared for me. Auntie loved me like I was her own,' I answered. Immediately I felt that I'd said too much, been too emotional, as I saw Uncle stiffen. 'Were we?' he said, somewhat distantly, while still sitting formally and staring straight ahead.

"Fortunately, Auntie returned just at that moment. 'It is so good to see Uldis, isn't it, Jekabs?' she said, while pouring coffee for the three of us. 'You do look well.'

" 'It's all the good tucker and hard yakka,' I replied.

" 'Yakka? Tucker?' Auntie laughed. 'What are these yakka and tucker?'

" 'Yakka is Aussie for work and tucker's food,' I declared, proud of my mastery of the Australian lingo.

" 'It's a strange place, this Australia!' she said, clapping her hands together in amusement.

" 'Fair dinkum!' I exclaimed, spurred on by her delight. I'd picked up this term as well and was keen to show off in front of them. They were at a loss and both stared at me as if I were mad.

" 'That's Aussie for "certainly"!' I explained this time.

"Auntie chuckled at my authoritative tone and repeated the term out loud, and we both burst into hysterics at her mispronunciation.

"Opposite us, Uncle remained stony silent. In fact, he seemed to be so uncomfortable with my presence that I decided there and then that I should leave, even if I'd only just arrived. But as soon as Auntie saw me make a move to depart, she jumped to her feet, insisting that I stay for dinner. I didn't want to cause any fuss, but she was adamant.

"That evening she prepared a feast of all the Latvian dishes that I loved as a boy, especially the eels and lampreys. Over the meal Auntie was very talkative, telling me about their life in Australia and how perplexing the customs were. They found it hard to adjust to the new world at their age. But despite that, Auntie obviously liked it here.

"Every time I visited, I'd regale her with one of my stories about my life in Australia. Her eyes lit up with pleasure and amazement at some of my tales: she loved especially the story of my escape from the job on the railways in the outback, when I'd climbed on board a passing trolley and headed off into the night, destination unknown.

"Later Uncle invited me to join him in the living room while Auntie cleared away the remains of the meal. He lit a thin cigar without offering me one and smoked it quietly. I felt like a naughty pupil before a headmaster, waiting for him to speak. I still had no idea what I had done wrong.

"After several minutes Auntie rejoined us. I thought that it was time to go and again reached for my jacket. Immediately she stopped me.

" 'You've had a lot to drink,' she said. 'Why don't you stay here tonight?'

"It was true. Uncle had been offering me vodka all evening. I muttered something about work the next day, but Auntie dismissed this, turning to Uncle. 'He must stay with us, mustn't he, Uncle?'

"Uncle merely grunted his assent. Auntie made up a bed on the sofa in the living room while Uncle and I sat in silence.

"Finally, it was Uncle and I, alone and without any risk of interruption. He poured us each a brandy, his favorite, and raised his glass. 'To the men of the Kurzeme Battalion!' he said. Then he looked me directly in the face and said, 'You must have many memories of your time with them.'

"I was surprised by his comment because after the war he'd given me the impression that he wanted never to speak of the past again.

" 'Yes,' I mumbled. 'A few.'

" 'They were better times for us, weren't they?' he said. 'How did we end up here, in this wasteland on the other side of the world?'

"I laughed out of politeness, but I didn't share his opinion at all. I loved the life here. Europe with its landscape of destruction was the wasteland as far as I was concerned. I never wanted to go back there.

" 'Good memories, are they?' Uncle probed. But before I could answer, he continued. 'Do you remember when you first came to Riga? What trouble you were. I took you to our apartment on Valdemara Street. Everyone was there to welcome you. But you didn't want to stay! "I am a soldier," you insisted. "I must stay with my troop." And the difficulty we had in getting you to sleep in a bed. The only place you really loved was in Carnikava.'

"I nodded and began to tell Uncle about my happy memories there, mostly with Auntie. However, he didn't want to dwell on my recollections and instead shifted the conversation, asking me if I remembered Commander Lobe.

"I thought it was a strange question because, apart from Uncle and Kulis, the commander was the man with whom I'd had the most contact. How on earth could I ever forget him?

" 'He was a good soldier,' Uncle said, 'and a good man!'

" 'He was kind to me,' I commented, wondering what else I could add.

" 'Not only to you,' he said. 'He was generous to all of us.'

"Then he fell silent for several moments before he spoke again. 'I am sure you haven't heard of his recent problem?'

" 'No,' I said. 'I haven't seen Commander Lobe since the war.'

Uncle knew this, so I wondered why he had raised the topic of the commander in this manner.

" 'All I know is that he went to Sweden.'

" 'Stockholm, in fact,' Uncle said. 'With his wife.'

" 'Are they well?' I asked.

"He ignored my question, saying instead, 'Like us, he was fortunate to have escaped the tyranny of the Soviet Union. We exchange letters now and then, and always on Latvian National Day. Your birthday, remember?'

"I nodded.

" 'However, some time ago the letters stopped coming. Only a matter of weeks ago I learned the reason. There has been a claim that the Eighteenth Kurzeme Battalion, when it was still in the form of a police brigade, was involved in a massacre of Jews in Belarus in the winter of 1941.

" 'The Slonim massacre, they call it. Some former members of the Eighteenth—the ones who didn't get out of Latvia—have already been arrested and tried by the Soviets. They were found guilty and have been executed. Have you heard of this catastrophe?'

"I was shocked. It was the first I'd heard of this and I told Uncle so."

"Did Uncle mention the names of any of the men executed, Dad?" I asked.

My father nodded grimly. "Tillers, Upe. I knew Upe better. He was with the band of soldiers that captured me." Even now my father seemed to be in a state of disbelief.

"Uncle said that the Soviets were liars. The whole thing had been a show trial and historical records could not place the Eighteenth anywhere near Slonim at that time. In fact, the Eighteenth did not arrive in Belarus until March 1942, so it was absurd to hold them accountable for an incident that had occurred months earlier.

"According to Uncle, the Soviets wanted to punish the Latvians, especially the high-ranking ones, for their collaboration with the Nazis. What they didn't understand, Uncle claimed, was that the Latvians were driven purely by patriotism. They didn't share the ideology of the Nazis. They hoped only for independence.

" 'Now the Swedish have become interested in Lobe's background,' Uncle said, 'because he'd been the commander of the Eighteenth. If there were even the slightest possibility that he could be extradited to Latvia, there is no doubt he would be executed.

" 'It doesn't seem to matter to the Soviets at all that Lobe was never permanently and totally in command of the Eighteenth. Throughout the battalion's tour of duty in Belarus, Lobe occasionally shared command with Captain Rubenis whenever he was recalled to Riga on other duties. You might not remember him.'

"I was surprised when I heard this," my father said, "but it also cleared something up in my mind. I've always been a bit confused about who was in command of the Eighteenth. I've nearly always recalled Commander Lobe in that position, but I also remember another officer, Rubenis, who occasionally appeared as top dog. I'd heard him addressed as Captain but that was all I knew about him. He showed no interest in me at all, so I rarely saw him.

" 'Perhaps they should be investigating Rubenis rather than Commander Lobe,' I heard Uncle say. I couldn't believe my ears. There seemed to be no loyalty among the desperate. Uncle was clutching at straws to defend the commander, and it struck me as odd that on the one hand Uncle denied that the Eighteenth was in Belarus, while at the same time claiming that another member of the same battalion could be responsible for the crime. Either the battalion was there, or it was not. I thought to myself then that Uncle knew more about the movements of the Eighteenth than he was prepared to let on. But I said nothing, allowing him to press on.

" 'How on earth could the Eighteenth have been responsible?' he repeated.

"I nodded absently because at that moment, while Uncle was speaking, something much more significant struck me: what if the Eighteenth had been in Belarus sooner than claimed? To me, Uncle's insistence that the Soviets were lying didn't seem entirely plausible. What if it was the Latvians who were lying about when the Eighteenth had arrived in Belarus? It was in their interest to cover their tracks since they'd participated in atrocities. It wouldn't take much to create false documents to support their claims. This led me to a new train of thought: what if I had been picked up sooner, before the Slonim massacre, by the Eighteenth? After all, if Commander Lobe had lied so easily about the circumstances in which I was saved, then surely he wouldn't have hesitated to alter the date the troops had found me. What if I had been with the troops at Slonim?"

My father paused.

"But what about official records of the Eighteenth?" I asked him.

"They may have been altered, too, in order to protect the reputation of the Eighteenth," my father conjectured. After several pensive moments, he continued, "Of course, I was only a child and had no sense of the passing of time, but what bothers me is even I find it hard to completely accept that I survived alone in the freezing forests for that length of time."

"The six to nine months before you were picked up?"

My father nodded. "A few weeks—that I can imagine—but six months? That would explain my impression that there was snow on the ground when Kulis took me out of the firing line, although I don't know why I remember butterflies. Perhaps they were around the dead bodies? It may have been in the winter of 1941, and not, as they said, in May of 1942. Thinking about it now, I wonder whether the murder of the people in the synagogue at the time I was with Sergeant Kulis—you remember, don't you, son?—the incident I told you about . . . What if that was Slonim?

"And there's one more thing," my father said, "the extermination in my village . . . would have been in the early winter in 1941."

"That sounds right," I agreed, recalling that the professor from Oxford had made a similar estimation.

"If only we knew the village's name," he said. "Then we could know for certain if any extermination did actually occur there in late 1941, before the Slonim massacre. That would at least make it possible that I could have witnessed Slonim."

"And we'd also be able to see if it was physically possible for the Eighteenth to be able to make it to Slonim from where they took you," I added.

"My village," my father said with finality, "is the starting point for unraveling my past."

Now animated and red-faced, my father continued to recount his meeting with Uncle.

"After what had occurred to me about the massacre at the synagogue and the presence there of the Eighteenth, including me," he said, "I knew that I had to be honest with Uncle and with myself. I was torn. I wondered how best to broach what I suspected. I began by telling Uncle that I did have memories of a massacre in a town. He was immediately alert."

" 'What do you remember?' he asked.

"I was straightforward with him, telling him that I was able only to recall some details. He listened intently to my description of events, and I'd barely uttered my final word when he waved his hand dismissively. 'Nothing more than impressions,' he said. 'Your memories have to be clearer than that, and you need to be sure that your memories are true.'

"I was surprised and confused by Uncle's comments. Even though my memories were incomplete, I knew that I had not imagined the incident." My father's voice rose as he insisted that he had not been lying. He put his head in his hands. "I did witness that atrocity," he said, "even if Sergeant Kulis usually tried to keep me from seeing the worst things.

"And I told Uncle what I later realized about those people—that they must have been Jewish. Much later, I also remembered one man with long strands of hair hanging down either side of his head. And also his large black hat. He must've been a rabbi.

"Uncle didn't seem to believe me. 'How could you tell such a thing about these people?' he asked, sounding outraged."

My father wiped his fists across his eyes, as if clearing his vision.

"I know I was right," he said to me. "You heard my description of people being killed in the building on fire: you were convinced that the building was a synagogue.

"Uncle glowered at me. 'Do you remember if Mr. Lobe was with you?' he snapped at me. 'Did you see him commit violence against these people, or not?'

"I had to be honest with Uncle. I didn't recall seeing the commander there.

"'So what do you know for certain?' Uncle said gravely. 'You don't know if you were in Slonim. You don't know if Lobe was there. What do you know?'

"In one respect Uncle was correct. I saw so much violence when I was with the brigade that there was sometimes a confusion of faces and locations. The only soldier I remembered for certain on the day of the killings was Sergeant Kulis because he shot at the burning people. So the Eighteenth was there that day, wherever *there* turns out to be.

"So, I felt compelled to answer no to Uncle's earlier question: I did not see Commander Lobe himself. Uncle jumped at the chance to warn me. 'If you're confused, then I would be very cautious about speaking about the past,' he said. 'After all, you were only a child. What can a child remember?' Uncle seemed to relax for the first time since I'd arrived. But I felt beaten down by him.

"You know, thinking about it now," my father said to me, "I wonder if Uncle, in fact, knew more than he'd let on about Slonim—that he knew Commander Lobe was implicated in Slonim."

"It's possible," I agreed, "that Uncle knew the true chronology of when you'd been captured—assuming there is another truth—and was testing the waters about what you actually remembered. He'd have to reassure both himself and the commander that you had no objective details to jeopardize the commander's defense."

My father nodded. "Perhaps he and the commander had wrongly assumed that I would have no memories, or at best only highly confused ones. The strength of some of my impressions did unnerve him.

"Talking with you about it now, it occurs to me that Uncle's behavior was intentional. He had been manipulating me, playing some sort of power game with me. His distant and unfriendly attitude had been a ploy to baffle me so that when he finally chose to relate properly to me, I would be eager to listen to him.

"I have to admit that his strategy worked. He knew my sense of obligation to the Latvians had been deeply ingrained in me."

My father was silent for a moment. "If only I'd stood up to Uncle," he said, anguished.

"But you couldn't remember, Dad," I replied. "You still can't."

"But why can't I, when I remember other faces, other details?" He began to castigate himself. "What if somehow I've chosen to forget? That I've blocked things out because deep down I am loyal to Lobe and the Latvians?"

"Dad," I argued, "you feared Lobe and the other soldiers. You may have blocked memories out of terror rather than loyalty."

My father nodded, but I could tell he was not convinced. He returned to the incident at Uncle's.

"'You know, young man,' Uncle said, 'you can do Mr. and Mrs. Lobe, as well as Auntie and me, a great favor.' Without waiting for a response from me, Uncle went on. 'You'd never want to harm them,' he said and then gave me a thin smile. I waited for him to continue.

"'Commander Lobe is preparing a written defense that he wants to present to the Swedish authorities. It would be a fine thing if you showed Mr. Lobe your support,' he said slowly. 'Let the authorities know Mr. Lobe didn't do anything.'

"I knew then where this talk was leading.

"'Some of us have already submitted statements testifying to Mr. Lobe's good character,' Uncle said. 'Mr. Lobe needs your help. A simple statement from you, nothing more than an innocent child at the time, would do much to support his defense.'

"I didn't want to anger Uncle again, but I tried to be frank. 'It's difficult for me to say anything either way,' I said.

"'Tell the investigators how good Mr. Lobe was to you, how he rescued you," Uncle insisted. 'That you cannot remember any wrong-doing on his part. That should suffice. Everybody will believe you in this situation because you were a child of only five or six years. Why would you lie?'

" 'Precisely because I was a child in your power, and still am,' I thought to myself. It seemed to me that Uncle had it all worked out in advance and was determined that I cooperate.

" 'Let me be direct,' he said, as if he were being perfectly reasonable. 'You owe Mr. Lobe your life. Now is your opportunity to pay him back. He didn't have to keep you alive.'

"I was shocked," my father said. "I was grateful to be alive, but I didn't ever imagine that a price tag would be put on my life. And I didn't think it would be put to me so bluntly.

" 'You just said Commander Lobe wasn't a violent man,' I blurted out without thinking, 'but now you say he could have killed me, a child, because I was an inconvenience?'

"Even though it made sense, it had been stupid to make such a comment. Uncle became irate, no doubt believing that I was trying to be clever.

" 'I know for a fact that the Lobes have very little,' he said sharply. 'Think of poor Mrs. Lobe. She's old now. How could she manage by herself if anything happened to her husband? It would be cruel to deny your help. And very dishonest to condemn a man based on a few vague impressions.'

"I faltered. The truth was that I'd witnessed other things when I was with the soldiers, and even though I knew no dates and places my impressions were not vague. They were so vivid. I will never escape them.

"But another part of me wanted to end this struggle. Uncle must have thought my silence was resistance because he rose impatiently and moved toward the window. He peered out into the darkness through a gap in the curtains as if he were expecting someone, then suddenly he turned back to me, his face contorted with barely suppressed anger.

" 'Do it for me!' he barked. 'You owe me your life!'

"I was dumbfounded by his vehemence.

" 'I wouldn't know what to write,' I tried to excuse myself.

" 'Let me take care of that,' he said firmly. 'We'll deal with this in the morning, before Auntie wakes.'

"Uncle was calmer by then. He rose and put out his hand to shake mine, and I accepted it. With that he wished me good night and disappeared to his room.

"I tried to make myself comfortable on the sofa with the blankets and pillow Auntie had left for me, but it took a long time before I finally nodded off. I was torn by what Uncle wanted, but already I sensed his victory over me."

As he had been on the subway in London, my father was clearly anguished over what had happened so many years before.

"I woke early the next morning. It was still dark. Then I noticed a thin line of light coming from the partly opened door to Uncle's study. I remained as I was, with my head on the pillow, but through the crack I could see that Uncle was already up and dressed. He was at his desk scrutinizing something.

"I got up and went over. He hadn't heard me stir, so I tapped lightly on the door. The instant he saw me he stood up and beckoned me in.

"Before I could even wish him good morning, he thrust a sheet of paper into my hand, saying, 'It needs to be signed and witnessed before I send it off.'

"I read what Uncle had prepared for me. It stated unequivocally that I had no knowledge of Slonim, or of any other incident, adding that I had spent some years in close company with the commander during the war. I viewed Mr. Lobe as a man of good character, it continued, and I remembered nothing of Mr. Lobe as a violent man. I had never seen him kill anyone."

My father was subdued.

"Do you have a copy of it?" I asked, hoping that there'd be one in his case.

My father shook his head. "Uncle didn't offer me one," he said, "and

I never thought to ask. I was uneasy and wanted the matter to be dealt with as quickly as possible. Uncle told me that he was going to personally deliver it to a lawyer in Melbourne, a Latvian man, who would then forward it as evidence in support of Commander Lobe's appeal."

"Who was this lawyer?"

My father leaned back in his seat, squinting as he tried to recall the man's name. "Eglajs," he said. "That's it. Mr. Eglajs."

"I wonder if he's still alive."

"If he is, then he must be in his nineties," my father said.

"I'll see if I can track him down," I said.

"Why?" My father was surprised.

"To see the statement, of course," I answered. "It is a piece of evidence."

My father seemed uneasy. "Evidence against who? Why do you want evidence?" he asked.

"I don't exactly want it as evidence against anybody in particular," I said, trying to calm my father's growing anxiety. "But it is part of the jigsaw of your story."

He appeared to accept my explanation and returned to the events surrounding the affidavit.

"'We could get it witnessed now,' Uncle said. 'There's a police station nearby.' So I agreed to do it there and then. What choice did I have? Was I complicit? I looked up to Uncle. I always obeyed him, and now he wanted me to repay a debt. The Latvians did save me, and I didn't want to bite the hand that had fed me. To this day, I feel guilty about what I did."

My father shot me a despairing, almost pleading, look.

"Uncle coerced you that day. He made you feel guilty for being alive," I said, trying to console him.

My father's hands rested on the kitchen table but were gripped together so tightly that his knuckles had turned white. He stared at me intently.

"They forced you to keep silent throughout the war," I said. "They erased your identity and turned you into their little mascot.

"Lobe did save you," I continued. "From what you are saying I'm starting to think he did so for his own reasons. After the war, the Latvians kept you as an alibi in case things went wrong in the future. If the Latvian soldiers were called to account for their collaboration, what better way to bargain against their own guilt than with an innocent child?"

My father seemed shocked both by my analysis and by my vitriol toward the Latvians. He was silent for a moment. Then he said, "You know, worst of all, Uncle couldn't get me out of the house quickly enough. He didn't even give me a chance to say good-bye to Auntie. 'We won't be long at the police station,' he said. 'You may as well continue on from there. Gather your things. I'll tell Auntie that you wanted to get an early start. She'll understand.'

"When we left the police station, Uncle was anxious to be rid of me. He looked at his watch pointedly and told me that he had other urgent business at home. He didn't even offer to shake my hand. Perhaps he felt as uncomfortable about the affidavit as I did.

"He walked away from me briskly. Without thinking, I called out to him so that he stopped and turned to look back at me.

"'Every day I put the past behind me. Over and over,' I said. 'I never talk about it with anybody, not even Patricia. I hope I never have to again. To you or to anybody. You should know that.'

"Uncle didn't say a word. He stared at me for several moments as if registering something about me. Then he raised his hand and gave me a brief wave. I watched him until he disappeared around the corner, and then I picked up my case and headed in the opposite direction, toward the train station."

I could see that the question of his presence at the Slonim massacre had cast a shadow over my father. He felt guilty for having signed a statement exonerating Lobe when he may have committed a crime. Had his faulty memory prevented justice from being done?

Though he could not be certain that Lobe had been at Slonim, or indeed whether the massacre he himself had witnessed was at Slonim, the affidavit raised for him the question of his own complicity. I knew that we must find the truth about Slonim, if only to help my father come to terms with his decision to sign the affidavit. But I feared that my father would not forgive himself easily.

CHAPTER EIGHTEEN
NO ESCAPE

I'd reached rock bottom. For the greatest part of my life I had followed every order the Latvians had given me. Now they wanted more. I couldn't betray them. Perhaps what Uncle had said was true. I owed them my life. I thought that I'd never be free of them. They'd find me wherever I went. The past would draw me down and suffocate me."

"Did the affidavit reach Sweden?" I asked.

"I assume it did. I did hear later that Commander Lobe was cleared."

"Did Uncle ever mention this incident to you in later years?" I asked.

My father shook his head. "Never." He was quiet.

"So you think it highly likely that the Eighteenth was involved in Slonim?" I continued.

"Why would the Soviets pursue this otherwise?" he replied. "And as I said earlier, my instinct tells me that on the night I visited him, Uncle knew more than he let on, that the Eighteenth and Commander Lobe were there . . ."

"Lobe could be fairly certain that his own soldiers would not betray him after the war. They were as guilty as he was. But who might, if he remembered enough in the future?" I said.

We both went quiet since we knew the answer: my father.

My father mulled this over. "But the question remains," he said finally, "did the extermination of my family occur before late 1941? And where the soldiers captured me—was it anywhere near Slonim?"

"There's an atlas in my room," I said, rising to fetch it. "Let's find Slonim."

We hunched over the atlas, our heads close together, scanning the maps of eastern Europe. We finally located Slonim in central southwestern Belarus.

"This would mean the Eighteenth would need to have been somewhere in the vicinity of Slonim at the end of 1941 if it took part in the massacre," I said. "And if you were taken shortly before that, your village must not have been too far away."

"That's right," my father said. "I couldn't have traveled very far in a matter of weeks. I do remember going in circles as well."

My father pulled the atlas closer. Suddenly he stopped and pointed his finger at a spot on the map. "Look at this town," he said excitedly. "Stolbtsi. To the northeast of Slonim."

I didn't understand what had roused his interest so pointedly.

"Don't you remember?" he said. "I mentioned that the Eighteenth was positioned at a place known as 'S' when they picked me up. That was where I first met the commander. 'S' was about a day's march from the schoolyard where Sergeant Kulis took me out of the firing line."

My father continued to hold his finger on the spot but was staring at me intently. Then his finger began to move across the page again, as his eyes scanned the area surrounding Stolbtsi.

"The commander and the soldiers were careful to only ever refer to 'S' and not its proper name. Why on earth did they do this unless they were deliberately obscuring their movements for some reason . . .

"What if 'S' was Stolbtsi, Marky?" he said, barely able to contain himself. "What if my village was somewhere nearby as well?"

"We've got to find out the significance of Koidanov," I said. "Give me the atlas. My eyes are better than yours." I drew the map closer and examined it. There was no Koidanov in the vicinity of Stolbtsi.

"Perhaps it's too small a place to be recorded in an atlas, no more than a hamlet or tiny shtetl," I said, trying to be optimistic. "We need to get hold of a more detailed map," I added, recalling that I had been about to do so in Oxford when I'd been abruptly summoned back to Australia.

I leaned back in my chair and noticed my father was doing the same. We laughed. My father raised his glasses and rubbed his eyes.

"You're tired, Dad," I said.

"No," he protested, "not in the slightest." He returned his glasses to the end of his nose and stared down at his hands.

"So the affidavit was the end of your association with the Latvians, apart from the Dzenis family," I said.

My father screwed up his face as if tasting something sour. "It wasn't quite as simple as that," he said. "Of course, I didn't want anything to do with Mr. Lobe after what had taken place. But word had obviously got around the Latvian community, and there was a sort of pressure put on me.

"The commander was a national hero to all Latvians. You couldn't have said a word against the man in the Latvian community in Australia. Most of the threats were low-key: veiled references to my duty to Commander Lobe and how good he and the other soldiers had been to me.

"That would happen when I came into contact with some of the old soldiers at social functions at the Latvian Community House. They'd reminisce about their time in the army and then they'd turn to me and say, 'Isn't that so, Uldis?'"

"They weren't just being nostalgic with you?"

"Don't be absurd!" my father snapped. "I understood the nuance. They were reminding me that I was one of them and had been there with them, through it all.

"Some threats were more direct—anonymous letters sent in the mail warning me to remain silent about Commander Lobe and the battalion's wartime past."

I was shocked. This was the stuff of spy novels and films, not my father's life. "Have you kept any of them?" I asked.

My father shook his head. "I burned them as soon as I received them. I didn't want your mother to come across them. Even my case didn't seem secure enough. They must have come from old soldiers who'd emigrated to Australia. Or other Latvians who knew of my exploits with the army. It didn't end there, either. It got worse after I married your mother and we settled together in Melbourne.

"There was one man in particular who was more blatant than the rest—Arnold Smits. I'd first encountered Smits in Riga during the war. Even though I was only a child, I could tell that he was a deeply nasty person. He was a sports journalist on a newspaper in Riga, but he collaborated with Commander Lobe on some special projects as well. He was heavily involved in Nazi propaganda to incite hatred against Jews, demanding that Jewish vermin—that's the term he used—be barred from Latvian sports and other rubbish like that.

"Smits emigrated to Melbourne after the war and wrote for a Latvian newspaper. One day—it must have been around 1958 or 1959, when Mum and I were living in Pascoe Vale on the other side of the city— Smits appeared on our doorstep. I was immediately suspicious. I didn't want him in my home—I didn't want your mother to be exposed to this man—so I stood out front with him, out of Mum's earshot.

"He told me that he wanted to write a series of articles about my life in Latvia for the Latvian newspapers in Australia. I made it clear to him from the outset that I wouldn't cooperate. At first he tried to cajole me into it, telling me what an honor it would be. 'Don't you want your story to be read by everybody who doesn't yet know it?' he said. Of course, it was the official version he wanted to write about and not the truth.

"I didn't want anything to do with his plan, but he was like a dog with a bone. In the end I was frank with him. I told him that the story was a pack of lies, and Lobe was not the hero Latvians believed him to be. He laughed directly in my face, telling me that he was going to write the articles no matter what my objections.

"He did exactly as he said he would. The articles were published in 1959. I have a copy here if you want to see it."

Once again he dug deeply into his case. The articles were written in Latvian. He offered to translate them for me there and then, but at that moment, in the middle of the night, I felt too weary to listen to more of these men's lies.

"Later, after I've gotten some sleep," I replied. I could see that my response had disappointed him, but he didn't push me. Instead, as he returned the article to his case, he removed another tatty and yellowed newspaper cutting. "See," he said. "Smits and I."

He passed the scrap of paper across to me. It was a grainy photograph with a caption, printed decades ago. In it, my father, barely distinguishable, and another man were hunched over a chessboard, absorbed in a game and surrounded by a crowd of onlookers. As I examined it more closely to see if I recognized any of the faces in the crowd, he told me that he and Smits had belonged to the same chess club in Melbourne.

"I don't know whether or not Smits joined just to keep an eye on me," he said, "but whenever I ran into him there, he would insist on challenging me. I beat him every time, just as I'd beaten every soldier in the Eighteenth once they'd taught me to play.

"He always demanded that we sit in the far corner of the clubrooms, as far as possible from the other players, saying that he needed silence in order to concentrate on his strategy.

"As we entered into the depth of our game, he would make it very clear to me, smiling his death's-head smile, that nobody would believe my word against that of real Latvians, and that I would make certain people very unhappy and risk dire consequences if I tried to discredit Latvia or any of its people in any way. I would sit there with my head down and try to focus on the game in front of me, though more than once I came very close to sweeping the pieces off the board and denouncing him. But I never did. Who'd have listened? Nobody would have been interested. In those days Australia was a sleepy backwater, full of immigrants who'd come to forget the past, not dig it up.

"After the war, Australia welcomed thousands of people from the Baltic States. 'Balts,' we were called. We were seen as refugees from Stalinism and thus on the Aussies' side. The authorities weren't suddenly going to have a change of heart and stir up a hornet's nest by hunting for war criminals."

It wasn't until the 1990s that the Australian government examined with any vigor how many Baltic war criminals had come to its shores.

"Once Smits's articles were published," I heard my father say, "I felt more locked into the official version of my story than ever. Having made it all the way to the freedom of Australia, I felt that the right to be left in peace had been taken from me. As I'd feared, these men kept in touch with each other, and each in his own way was set against me."

"The last threat I received was almost two decades ago. I guess they thought that if I hadn't said anything by then, I wasn't going to talk at all. And many of the old soldiers were starting to die off.

"God knows what will happen if my story gets out," he mused, trying to make light of the situation. "They'll all turn over in their graves and come back to haunt me."

For a moment I felt a surge of anger not only toward the Latvians but toward my father as well. I felt that his choice to remain silent about these threats had somehow added to his betrayal. He appeared to sense this, and he opened his case and began to fumble absently with its contents, obviously keen to avoid my ire. It was a cunning, theatrical move, but it also struck me as rather desperate, and my anger turned to pity. I imagined myself subtly tormented as he had been for most of his adult life. During those early years in Australia he had looked to the future and resolved to make a new life for himself. But the tentacles of this Latvian nationalist network, unable either to leave its past behind or to face it honestly, had stretched out and ensnared him.

As if he had followed my train of thought, I heard my father say, "I was to blame, too." He shifted uncomfortably in his seat. "Even though I looked to my new life here, I held back from breaking those bonds completely. These men were the only link to the past, for better or worse. I used to have fantasies that one of them somehow knew my real name—don't ask me how—and that one day he would take pity on me and tell me.

"I let them behave as if they owned me because I didn't want to alienate them. For years that tore me in two inside. That's the truth of it."

"Dad, you've never said a single word to any of us," I said. "Not even Mum."

My father ignored my words and instead gave a deep sigh. "Even though the old soldiers are all gone now, the idea that they might have been able to tell me who I was taunts me from their graves."

My father looked at me searchingly. "I've been naive, haven't I?" he said.

CHAPTER NINETEEN

STOCKHOLM

My father seemed oblivious to the passing hours. I cast a furtive glance at the clock on the kitchen wall and saw that it was almost four in the morning. I was exhausted but now that my father had finally broken his silence, I was reluctant to stop our conversation.

"Hearing all of this makes everything fall into place," I said. "Even though Lobe avoided a trial and extradition, he must have lived in constant fear of retribution. That would explain his behavior when I visited him in Stockholm."

My father gave me a questioning look.

"What did happen?" he asked. "You simply said that the visit was fine."

"I decided not to say anything, because you'd seemed so set against me going there at the time."

My father simply nodded. I began to tell him about my visit.

I first described to my father in detail what had gone on in the Lobes' apartment that day. He listened intently, without interrupting me. "After I left the Lobes," I told my father, "I hurried along the path that led away from the apartment complex. I was excited and wanted to get back to the city so I could call you in Melbourne. But as I waited for a tram, a number of things began to nag at me, and my euphoria gradually evaporated.

"Above all, I was alarmed by Lobe's first reaction to me when I'd knocked on his door the previous day. I realize now that after I'd slipped the note under the door, he must have been fairly sure that I knew nothing of the truth of who he was and who you'd been. No wonder he was so suspicious initially and so exaggerated in his welcome later. Added to that was his semideranged tirade about his association with Nazism. I began to wonder how closely he was personally associated with the Nazis, and, more to the point, how closely you had been.

"I was unsettled as well by something in Lobe's and your description of your discovery by the soldiers."

My father became alert and sat upright in his chair. "What was that, son?" he asked.

"It was eerie," I answered. "The words you used were almost identical. And there was another thing that occurred to me as I stood there in the freezing wind—the perspective of your description. It was as if you had been one of the soldiers who witnessed the boy step from behind the tree. From the outside looking in, rather than from the point of view of the frightened child stepping out to be confronted by a band of soldiers brandishing rifles and bayonets."

"As I told you," my father said, "Commander Lobe had drummed that version into me, and the only way I could believe it was to memorize his every word and repeat it exactly. Still, it's amazing that you picked up on that."

"Yes, but I was mystified at the time and could find no explanation for it. As I journeyed back into the center of Stockholm, I decided to put this unnerving observation to the back of my mind. In fact, I hadn't thought about that day until you spoke to me in London. I realized then that there might be something complex in your association with Lobe and Uncle.

"Of course, it's only now that I've got some inkling of why you seemed so apprehensive when I called to tell you that I intended to visit

Lobe," I ventured. "You must have been petrified that I'd learn the truth about your life with the Eighteenth Battalion, and what sort of men they were."

My father was silent. My last comment must have seemed accusatory, and I sensed his reluctance to engage with me. I returned to the affidavit.

"When Lobe decided to get me to make a statement on his behalf, he must have wondered more and more what I had witnessed all those years ago and how incriminating it might have been. And certainly after my visit to him in Melbourne, Uncle must have conveyed to the commander that I did have recollections that could incriminate him.

"So even though I signed the statement, that must have played on Commander Lobe's mind as well for all those years, along with the chance that more of my memory might return. Perhaps in his mind the question of my loyalty was never really settled with the signing of the affidavit."

I nodded. "So when I appeared on his doorstep, identifying myself as your son, he must have feared the worst. He must've thought that you'd told me, your son, the truth, and that I'd come seeking something. Revenge, perhaps? Why else would Uldis's son visit him?"

My father agreed. "It looks that way. How else to explain his response? One thing is clear, even though Commander Lobe had been able to fight off his extradition years earlier, he'd probably spent the remainder of his life in fear that somebody would eventually come after him."

"He promised to stay in touch, but I never heard from him," I said.

My father looked sheepish. "Shortly after your visit," he said, "a letter came from out of the blue. I was surprised when I saw the envelope and realized it was from Commander Lobe. He'd never written to me before."

He raised the lid of his case slightly and with his usual adroitness produced an envelope. He removed a sheet of paper and smoothed it out on the table. He lowered his eyes and began to read, translating as he did so.

" 'My dear Uldis Kurzemnieks.

" 'It is a long time since we last saw each other. I hope that you are in good health. From time to time, I hear news of your life in Australia from Mr. Dzenis. I am happy that you are successful and have your own family.' "

My father paused. "I'll skip the pleasantries," he said, "and go to the nitty-gritty."

I watched him as he scanned the page. "Here we are," he said and began to read again.

" 'Recently I was pleased to meet your son Mark. A fine boy! We spoke a lot about the war, and I told him of the special bond between us. I am sure that there is no need to remind you of it, my little Corporal . . .' "

My father raised his head and looked at me. "Can you believe that?" he said, slightly astonished. "He called me corporal, as if to remind me that I still belonged to the battalion and that he was my commanding officer."

My father didn't seem to need any reminder. I had noticed that even though Lobe had been a civilian for many decades, my father still called him "Commander."

He took up where he had left off.

" 'We were all very fond of you. Mr. Dzenis loved you—you were the son he'd always wanted. His wife, Emily, adored you. Mrs. Lobe and I did, too.

" 'When I said farewell to you in Riga, we agreed to bury the past. But I am worried that one day before too long, you, Corporal, will forget your promise to me. It would break my lifelong trust in you if you spoke of your memories now. Besides, memory is a strange thing. It can play tricks on all of us, so that we are unsure of what we remember and what we do not.

" 'Do you really want to destroy our reputations? You cannot betray all that many of us have done for you. Your debt can only be repaid by loyalty—nothing else!' "

My father ceased reading. "That's it, more or less." He folded the letter slowly and returned it to its envelope.

In the ensuing silence, my mother's faint snoring could be heard from their room on the far side of the house. Suddenly the kitchen clock on the wall caught my father's attention.

"Crikey, Mark," he exclaimed. "It's six a.m. The world is going topsy-turvy. We should both get some sleep." He rose from the table.

"One thing, Dad . . ." I stopped him.

My father looked at me expectantly.

"Was I right?" I said.

He looked confused. "Right about what?"

"Would you have wanted revenge?"

My father did not hesitate. He shook his head in dismay. "Revenge?" he said. "What's that worth? Nothing! It only makes you bitter and sick inside—and as bad as them! I never started out by wanting to point the finger at anybody."

"What about justice, Dad?" I asked.

"Justice? I don't even know what justice would mean for these sick, elderly men. Better to let them face their own conscience, if they have any."

I rose to join my father.

Just then the kitchen door opened and my mother peered in. She must have heard our voices in the kitchen.

"You're both up early," she said.

CHAPTER TWENTY
FEAR

At times during my stay in Melbourne my father appeared willing to reveal more about his past to me. Then abruptly he would turn in on himself. Sometimes he seemed so worn down by the burden of his secrets that, irresistibly, the floatsam of his memory would float to the surface of his consciousness like debris from a submarine disaster.

He still hadn't told my mother anything. Nonetheless, she seemed to tire very easily and frequently went to her room in the early evening. My father and I often found the night stretching out awkwardly before just the two of us.

After saying good night to my mother, my father would turn the television off and quietly retrieve his case from where he had placed it outside their bedroom door so that he wouldn't disturb my mother's sleep. Case in hand, he would pass me in the living room and head for the kitchen.

I would listen as he seated himself at the kitchen table and switched on the reading lamp as if to announce that he was ready to speak and that I should jump to attention and join him. Perversely I would remain seated, vainly attempting to assert my independence. The moment I heard the familiar clicking sound of his case unlocking, however, I would waver, then rise to join him.

Later that week, as I entered the kitchen, I noticed that he had opened a thick volume on the table before him. He furrowed his brow and squinted at the book.

He concentrated so intently on one page that he didn't even bother to acknowledge my presence with his usual grunt.

I sat down beside him at the table. "Dad?" I whispered.

He gave a slight start.

"What's the book?" I nodded toward it.

He looked at the cover as if he, too, were noticing it for the first time. "An atlas," he mumbled.

"Koidanov and Panok?"

He regarded me silently for several moments.

"The most important thing is I've got to find out what these words mean," he said. He sat, isolated and discouraged, in the small circle of light thrown by his reading lamp.

"Dad," I said. "I promised you in London that I would help you."

He nodded but continued to scan the book in front of him.

I hadn't yet told my father that I had begun my own investigations in Oxford. I kept silent principally because I felt I'd dug around without his permission.

"Any luck?" I asked.

"Nah," he said, rubbing his fists over his eyes liked an overtired child. "Like looking for a needle in a haystack."

He sighed heavily. Then, without looking up at me, he pushed the atlas across the table in my direction. "Pages twenty-three and twenty-four," he said in a matter-of-fact tone. "Eastern Europe. See if you can spot Koidanov or Panok."

I turned to the pages in question. They were densely inscribed with a vast array of foreign words tumbling over each other higgledy-piggledy. "The first thing we'll need is a magnifying glass!" I exclaimed, trying to make light of the situation.

My father didn't laugh.

Sobered by his response, I buried my head in the book once again before concluding aloud, "We're going to need far more detailed maps than this, for starters."

I decided that it was time to tell my father what Frank had discovered in Oxford. "In any case," I said, "we won't find Panok anywhere on these pages."

My father gave me a questioning look.

I hesitated for a moment. I felt cautious about Frank's revelation—I had heard nothing further from Frank since my arrival in Melbourne, and there was nothing to confirm that my father was a Panok. I feared that my father would jump at even the simple likelihood that he was a Panok and that he would be bitterly disappointed if we couldn't prove it.

"Come on," he urged, becoming impatient.

Cautiously I told my father about what Frank had unearthed, that there was a family of Jews known as Panok who had lived in the vicinity of Minsk in the prewar period. And just as I had feared, my father's face reddened with excitement.

"I told you, son," he said, rising from his chair and moving around the room. "I remembered these words for a reason. I bet it's my name. I must be a Panok."

My father repeated the word several times, savoring it, while he paced back and forth. Then he sat down again, and I saw that he was so moved by the news that his entire body was trembling slightly. Without thinking about the usual physical reserve between us, I reached across and gripped his forearm to steady him and to get him to look at me directly.

At that exact moment my father jerked backward and removed a handkerchief from his pocket. He threw back his head and held the cloth against his nose, which had suddenly, as if under pressure from the news, begun to bleed profusely.

"Some tissues," came his muffled order.

I fetched some and then waited in silence, watching him. The bleeding was so strong and voluminous that it took several minutes to subside.

When it did, my father immediately picked up where he'd left off, still gripping his bloodied handkerchief.

"I must be a Panok," he said emphatically. "Why else would I remember this word?"

I smiled at him, but my father must have sensed my inner reserve. He stared at me shrewdly. "What's bothering you?" he asked.

"I don't want us to jump the gun," I said. "That's all. We should take it one step at a time. Find a way to confirm whether you are a Panok or not."

He looked at me, as if to dismiss my caution, and then reached for the atlas. "Minsk, you said?" he asked. "Where the hell is that?" He stared at the open page in front of him.

"Belarus," I answered, deciding to feign enthusiasm rather than dampen his spirits. I pointed to a spot on the map. "Here it is."

After Frank's discovery, and prior to my sudden departure for Australia, I had crammed in a small amount of reading about the country. I now recounted it to my father, who sat attentively opposite me.

"The country is falling apart," I began. A former satellite state of the Soviet Union, Belarus is now ruled by a despotic Communist dictator, Alexander Lukashenko. Lukashenko has chosen to align the country economically and culturally with its Russian master. It seems to be the only country in eastern Europe not to have benefited from the collapse of the Soviet empire. It is still impoverished and largely underdeveloped.

My father's attention began to waver, and he interrupted me. "Let's get back to this Koidanov. It could be where I'm from and, if so, it must be somewhere here if I am a Panok . . ." My father hunched over the atlas like a diamond merchant over a jewel. After several minutes, he leaned back. "No luck," he said. He looked tired and drawn, and his optimism seemed suddenly to have faded.

"We'll crack this, Dad," I said feebly, trying to reassure him despite my own feeling of discouragement.

"I've already waited a lifetime," my father said ironically, then fell silent.

I took advantage of the hiatus to change the topic to one I'd been

dying to raise. "Now that there's even the slightest chance of a name," I said, "you must tell Mum and the boys. Now." I was shocked by my challenge.

My father shrugged and stared straight ahead, avoiding my gaze. In the odd, flat silence between us I waited for him to say something. In the end all he said was, "I'll tell them sometime soon."

"What's wrong with now?" I demanded.

My father pretended not to have heard me and instead turned the pages of the atlas as if searching for something.

"This can't go on," I insisted. "They deserve to know."

His eyes began to move slowly from one object to another in the room, as if he were keenly interested in each.

"You're avoiding even listening to me?"

"I didn't hear you," my father blustered. But I knew that he had.

Annoyed, I said, "I can't keep covering for you." Then I changed tack. "What's bothering you, Dad?" I asked, trying to sound conciliatory.

My father shifted in his seat. He closed the atlas and reached for his case, snapping it shut and placing it between us on the table. His head dropped forward as if he were being forced to own up to a felony.

"It's that I am . . ." he said, "you know . . ."

I waited for him to finish the sentence. But he didn't.

"You're what?"

"Jewish."

He winced at being forced to say the word.

I didn't understand.

"Will they accept it?" he asked, as if ashamed. "Your mother didn't know she was marrying a Jew."

"I don't think that it will make a scrap of difference to Mum," I said. "What will disturb her is that you kept your past from her for so long."

My father gave me a sharp look but then nodded, grim-faced. "I'm worried that it'll be too much for her," he said. "She's not strong at the moment."

I'd noticed this myself. I had never seen my mother so low-spirited. "Still no idea what's wrong?" I asked.

My father shook his head. "She feels weak and unable to breathe," he replied. "She's been to the doctor, but he can't find anything wrong with her."

I wondered whether it was her intuition that something was wrong with my father that was causing her symptoms. My mother had a keen loyalty to my father and rather than confront him and bring a matter to light—she was awkward with emotional language and mistrusted it—she chose to internalize her doubts.

"Martin and Andrew will be fine about it," I said. "When will you tell them?"

My father held his hands together as if praying and then rested them on his case.

"This week then," he said with finality. "The same time as I tell Mum. God knows how Martin will react . . ."

My father noticed my puzzled look.

"Think about it," he said. "Martin's married to a German girl." I could see that he was uneasy about the possibility of her discomfort. My father screwed up his face.

"It's not your problem," I said tersely.

"I don't want to make him feel awkward. Or anybody, for that matter. Think of Uncle's family. Mirdza, Edgars, and their children. All the other Latvians who've helped me. They'll say that I've betrayed all their kindness. And what about other Latvian nationalists—you know, some of the old soldiers have threatened me before."

I did understand my father's reluctance. I feared, too, that their oft-expressed patriotism for the mother country would blind some of the Latvians to the truth and provoke their condemnation. My father would risk losing the last remnants of the only family he had known as a boy. But my intensifying desire that the truth come out fueled in me a new bravado. "You've done nothing wrong," I snapped. "If they can't accept you, then screw them!"

My father rubbed the back of his neck.

"There's more to this, isn't there?" I said.

"What?"

"About being Jewish . . ."

He nodded. "I can't explain it," he said in a low voice. My father gripped his head in his hands, with his elbows resting on the table.

"Are you afraid of being Jewish?"

My father raised his head and looked at me sharply. I had hit a raw nerve.

"I don't know, son," he said. "All the time I was with the soldiers they spoke of Jews as vermin. Jews were evil, they said. I had to listen to this day in and day out—and remain silent—until it was drummed into my soul, until I felt ashamed of being Jewish."

With their insults against Jews and, more frighteningly, in *"Aktionen,"* or "actions," against them, the soldiers and other Latvians had terrified the little boy in their midst. Worse, perhaps, they had shamed this child to his very essence. Not only did my father have to hide his identity from others, he'd had to hide away from himself for all these years. It was a terrible self-obliteration.

My father hesitated, struggling to describe something else.

"When I summoned the courage, or stupidity—I don't know what you'd call it—and went to the Holocaust center, I'd imagined that the shame would lift. But it didn't. Somehow within myself I didn't feel comfortable there, as if I'd betrayed my Jewishness. I was somehow unworthy of being Jewish, even though I'd been born Jewish, and had no right to speak about who I was. By the time I'd left the center, I realized that I was completely and utterly trapped by who I was. I felt doubly cursed by my fate."

I felt almost uncontrollable anger rising at what a child living with a hidden identity must have gone through. Over fifty years later, it seemed that he was still struggling with himself to reclaim it.

"What about the interviewers?" I asked. "Did they understand what you'd been through?"

"They had their questions to ask," my father said.

I realized that he was staring at me intently.

"Perhaps, after all," he said, "it's been wise to have stayed silent all these years . . ."

"I understand, Dad. At quite a few moments my instinct was to tell you to get up and leave the interview."

"You felt that, son?" My father's face became more animated. He seemed relieved that I'd wanted to support him. He looked down at his hands.

"I couldn't bear it," he said. "I felt like I couldn't breathe. I just fled. I can't remember clearly what happened after that. I didn't black out, but it is a blur.

"The next thing I *do* remember clearly was being on the street. I had enough sense to make it to my car parked on the other side. I got in and locked the doors, but I wasn't capable of driving anywhere. And that's when somebody knocked on the car window. A woman. She introduced herself as Alice Prosser.

"Will you meet her?" my father asked. "She's a Ukrainian Jew from Odessa. She came to Australia in the early 1970s as a political refugee. She won't go into much about what happened to her. All that she was willing to tell me was that she'd been arrested there, declared an undesirable, and quickly deported. After being shunted from country to country, she finally found asylum here."

My father paused. "I'm sure they tortured her," he said quietly. "Anyway, Alice is a volunteer at the Holocaust center, and that's where I met her. You know what she told me?" he asked and didn't wait for my response. "That I have the 'true spirit of a survivor.'"

"Those were her exact words. I've never thought of myself in that way. Imagine her saying that to me after all that she'd been through herself!"

"Too bad those interviewers didn't seem more sympathetic," I couldn't restrain myself from commenting.

"They had their questions to ask," my father repeated.

I remained unconvinced.

"They've been made bitter by their suffering," my father said gently. "You can't blame them."

I found his generosity of spirit hard to accept—even though I was not surprised by it. I only wished that he was more forgiving toward himself.

"I told her about you," my father said. "She wants to meet you."

I sensed that he had already set the wheels in motion for a meeting with Alice, and I was annoyed.

"Go on," he cajoled me. "You won't regret it."

I felt cautious about meeting Alice. Since his brief visit to Oxford months earlier, I'd been slowly drawn into a world dominated solely by my father's quest. I had a brief vision of this Alice as an usher checking my ticket before escorting me to the seat where I would watch the rest of my father's story play out.

"Make the arrangements," I sighed.

"I'll call her in the morning," he said, pleased.

My father glanced at the clock on the kitchen wall.

"Look! It's almost two in the morning. Get to bed, you rascal," he whispered with affection. "Keeping me up this late!"

CHAPTER TWENTY-ONE
ALICE

When I got up late the next morning, my father was in the kitchen drinking coffee. He looked up when he heard me come in. "Get dressed, Mark," he said. "Alice wants to meet you this afternoon." He told me that she'd wait for me on Acland Street in St. Kilda, a beachside inner suburb of Melbourne that was his old stomping ground.

"Two o'clock at Café Scheherazade," my father said. "I usually meet her there. She loves it. 'It's very kosher,' she says."

The Scheherazade was renowned for both its Jewish food and its atmosphere, which was redolent of prewar eastern Europe—members of the Jewish community would congregate there for coffee and cake. When I was small, Scheherazade's front window attracted me more than any other on Acland Street. We would pass it on the way to the Monarch cake shop to buy what my father maintained was the best cheesecake he had ever eaten. I would dawdle in front of Scheherazade's window and stare in, instantly hypnotized by the vivacious ladies inside.

It was just before two when I stepped into the Scheherazade. The interior had been modernized since I was a child, but it somehow seemed shabbier than I had remembered. As the last of the lunchtime crowd cleared, I found a table at the rear of the main room and ordered coffee with the inevitable piece of cheesecake.

A few moments later, a stocky woman in her late sixties entered. She was tiny, almost dwarfish, and used a walking stick to steady her lopsided gait. On one arm, she nursed a shopping bag that appeared to be stuffed with clothing, books, newspapers, and tins of soup, as if she carried all her belongings with her.

"God, no!" was my initial, uncharitable reaction. "Another one of my father's crackpot friends."

She headed directly across the room toward me, smiling broadly, her hand outstretched.

"I'm Alice Prosser," she said. "You're Mark. I recognize you from your photo."

I must have looked surprised.

"Oh yes," she said. "Your father carries a photo of you with him. He's so proud. His son who studied at Oxford."

I laughed, embarrassed. Oxford seemed far removed from my life at this moment.

I exchanged a few pleasantries with Alice about the weather and the like, in an effort to break the ice, but she didn't seem to have much time for idle chitchat, so I jumped right in. "So you know my father from the Holocaust center?"

Alice nodded. "But sadly not under the best of circumstances," she said heavily.

I stared at her, waiting for her to continue.

"Your father's told you about what went on there?"

I shrugged.

"What did happen, Alice?"

Our coffees arrived at that moment. Alice took a long sip and rummaged in her bag for something. She pulled out a small leather pouch, plucked out some tobacco and papers, rolled a cigarette, and lit it.

The waitress who had just served us approached tentatively. She looked down at Alice, giving an apologetic smile. Alice looked up at her. "Is something the matter?" she asked.

"The cigarette, madam. I'm sorry," the young woman said. "This is a no-smoking café."

Alice nodded, contorting her lips into a tight grimace. She stubbed out the cigarette on my empty cheesecake plate.

The waitress removed the plate, holding it at a distance as if it still gave off noxious fumes, and disappeared.

Alice remained slightly hunched over her part of the table.

"You know," she said, shaking her head in disgust, "every time I come here they say the same thing to me—no smoking. It's worse than the old Soviet Union. At least there you could smoke wherever you wanted."

I watched her as she returned her tobacco pouch to her bag and wondered at her stubbornness.

"It just wasn't a place that suited your father's character," she said cryptically, finally responding to my question.

She fell silent for a few moments and then continued much more quietly. "I was working in the back near the interview room when I saw your father come in with one of the interviewers," she said. "I couldn't help but notice him because of his face. You must know what I mean . . . he looks like a sad clown, and those expressive blue eyes."

I knew exactly what Alice meant. It was not the first time I had heard my father described in this way. I recalled when he had taken my brother and me to visit his old friends at the traveling circus he'd worked with, how fond he was of the clown act—the Zakkini Brothers. To me they were the saddest people I'd ever laid eyes on—four Italian Jewish émigrés from the war. My brothers and I would always tease my father, telling him that he should quit his job and become Zakkini Number Five. He would always laugh and nod in agreement. "That's me, boys," he'd say, "a sad clown, too."

"I guessed that he'd come to give his testimony," Alice said. "That's where they usually did them. Anyway, because I am a volunteer at the center, I do all sorts of jobs around the place. That day, I couldn't help but overhear parts of your father's testimony. And the parts I heard astonished me. An amazing story, one of the most remarkable I have ever heard. Imagine! A child could survive like that. As I listened I could hear him struggling to explain things clearly to the interviewer. I felt terribly sorry for your father."

At that moment Alice set down her coffee cup with such a clatter that some of the other customers in the Scheherazade stopped what they were doing and glanced in our direction. She was oblivious to their stares.

"But it was your father's destiny to live to tell the story," she declared, opening her eyes wide to reveal her yellowish eyeballs. Despite the seriousness of what Alice was describing, I didn't know how long I could suppress a smile at her theatrics.

"Tell me," I said, "why wasn't the visit to the center"—I searched for the right word—"successful?"

"Put it this way," Alice replied, "in my opinion I think your father felt uncomfortable at the center, that he believed that somehow he didn't fit in. Perhaps he felt that because he was not after all raised a Jew that he didn't belong there. Who knows? Even though I am a volunteer there I don't think it was the most appropriate place for him. I'm not saying more than that."

I reflected on how Alice's words resonated with my father's. Then she spoke again.

"In the short time I've known your father," she said, "I can see that he is an exceptional man. He embraces life, I could tell that immediately. But it doesn't mean that he hasn't suffered—he's been exposed to things that a child should never be—or still suffering. But your father isn't the type of man who wants or needs to dwell on it. He simply wants to tell his story, and even then not just for his own benefit. He told me later that his story was a lesson for everybody, Jewish or not, about cruelty."

Alice lit another cigarette, taking a long drag on it, and then quickly put it out.

"At one point I noticed that the interview room was empty. The testimony had come to an end, only a few minutes earlier according to the interviewer whom I'd come across in the corridor. I felt very sorry for your father after hearing his story. I decided to look for him. With a bit of luck, I thought, he might not have left the premises.

"I was right. I found him in the museum. He was wandering among the exhibits, taking in their horror. They must have reminded him of things he'd seen as a boy. Even the images of life in the prewar shtetl must have upset him—what a terrible sense of loss he must have felt looking at the world fate denied him—because as I approached him I could see that he was shaking slightly.

"I touched him gently on the shoulder. I didn't want to alarm him. 'Do you remember me?' I asked. 'I was the one working back there.'

"Your father nodded. I extended my hand to him.

"There was an awkward silence. Your father was lost for words but it didn't matter. I knew what he was going through. Then, before I knew it, he gave a weak smile and turned away from me, blank-eyed, in a daze."

Alice became agitated and breathless as she related this to me.

"Alice, are you okay?" I asked.

"Of course I'm not," she answered heavily.

Alice was then silent for several moments as she gathered her breath. Then she continued. "I watched your father slip out the exit, and I decided to follow him to make sure he was okay. He was on the doorstep outside the museum entrance. Then he walked back to his car, which was parked on the opposite side of the road. He climbed in and started the car, but after several minutes the car hadn't moved, so I decided to check on him."

I pictured Alice hobbling across the street, her walking stick in one hand and shopping bag in the other.

"I reached the driver's side. Your father seemed to be in a state of shock.

"He stared straight ahead, oblivious to the world around him. He didn't even seem aware of me. I tapped lightly on the window. He snapped out of his state and wound it down, giving me a questioning look as if he didn't recognize me.

"'I'm Alice Prosser,' I said, introducing myself properly. 'Can I join you?'

"After a moment's hesitation, he simply nodded.

"I climbed into the car, and we sat there together in silence, your father still unable to drive off.

"In the end I had to tap on his arm a number of times before he turned toward me. I sensed that your father wanted to talk and suggested we move on to somewhere else. Within minutes we pulled into a parking lot that looked out at the sea. It was a bleak afternoon, and the place was deserted. We sat in silence, watching the waves. I had to say something to break their spell, so I told your father that I'd overheard some of his story. It was unavoidable: the walls at the center are paper-thin.

"I believe your father's story and I told him so. He was so taken aback that he asked me two or three times, 'You believe me?' and then added, 'Even though my memories are patchy?'

"'Memory is a strange thing, Alex,' I said.

"'I know,' he said. 'Do you know, I can still taste the *kes* my mother would make for the family, as if it were yesterday, but something important, like my mother's face, I cannot remember at all.'

"Your father had used a Yiddish word, and when I told him so, he was baffled.

"'I don't know where the word came from,' he said. 'Maybe I heard it as a child.' Your father repeated the word over and over—'*kes kes kes*,' he said, as if he were relishing the cheese itself.

"'Do you remember the taste, too?' he asked me excitedly. His eyes were moist with nostalgia for its taste.

"I nodded. Your father was overwhelmed that I shared an experience from his past. Perhaps he realized that he was no longer alone, as he had been in his silence."

Alice shifted slightly in her seat, taking the weight off her bad hip.

"At that moment," she said, "I lost any doubt that your father was telling the truth about his past. The task was only to uncover it.

"I've met your father here a couple of times since then. I tell him little things about being Jewish, life in the shtetl and Jewish ceremonies, and he is always fascinated. Who knows, we might make a good Jew out of him yet, and turn you into a good Jewish boy as well!"

I laughed.

She seemed disconcerted, as if she'd misunderstood my response.

I leaned forward. "My father and I," I joked, "we're a couple of old dogs. Too old for any new tricks!"

For a moment I feared that she was going to pinch my cheek.

"We'll see about that." She smiled, as if she knew me better than I knew myself.

Alice took a sip of her cold coffee and made a sour face.

We sat in silence for several minutes.

Finally she rose and gathered her bag, suggesting that we meet again soon.

"I'd like to come to the house," she said, "and meet your mother."

I said nothing.

"Your father's still not told her then?"

I shook my head.

Alice made a tutting sound.

"I must go," she said.

I watched as she hobbled across the café, and out the door.

I remained in Scheherazade for some time, drinking another coffee and reflecting on my meeting with Alice. I felt that I'd been in the presence of a magical dwarf who'd appeared from somewhere deep in the forests of eastern Europe. I tried to make sense of what she had told me.

Through the window I could see that Acland Street was busy with early-evening crowds. I could understand my father's lifelong attraction to Acland Street with its vibrant street life—it must have reminded him of the mood and communality of the shtetl of his early years. It was utterly unlike the atmosphere of the suburb where he lived now.

It struck me then that my position in Acland Street had diametrically shifted. I was no longer a little boy peering into the Scheherazade. Now I was a man, still my father's son, but I was inside looking out.

CHAPTER TWENTY-TWO
THE LETTER

When I turned into the driveway, I saw that our house was dark. I wondered where my parents were, as it was unusual for them to be out on a weekday evening.

I parked the car and went inside. I made my way to the living room, not bothering to turn on any lights, and called out their names, but there was no reply.

I sat down in one of the armchairs. Outside I could see the headlights of cars as they passed by and expected that, at any moment, I would see the lights of my parents' car coming up the drive.

Sitting alone in the dark, I had an image of Martin, Andrew, and me waiting expectantly for my father to return from work, when suddenly I saw the headlights of my parents' car. They were home from wherever they'd been.

My mother seemed subdued when she came in. "I'll get some dinner for us," she said quietly, going straight through to the kitchen.

My father turned on the television—it was time for the evening news—and sat down in the chair opposite me.

"Where have you been?" I asked.

"Just dropped by Mirdza's," he replied.

"How are they?"

"They're getting along fine . . . nothing new."

After dinner the three of us watched television, but none of us seemed very interested. Nor was there any of the usual banter that accompanied our evenings at home. My mother remained as dejected as she had been earlier in the evening, and my father seemed unable to settle. He rose constantly to fetch small electronic gadgets that he repaired on the floor in the center of the room. Eventually my mother rose, pleading tiredness, said good night, and went to her room.

My father continued to tinker with an old camera on the floor while I stared at the television, halfheartedly trying to follow the plot of a police drama. I gave up and looked away from the screen.

"So what did you talk about with Mirdza and Edgars?" I asked.

My father was evasive. "This and that," was all he said. He continued to tinker with the camera.

"What did you think of Alice?" he asked without looking up. "She's a nice lady, isn't she?"

"She is."

"What did you talk about?"

"This and that," I answered, imitating my father's response.

I could tell that I'd irritated him but I couldn't help myself. If he was going to keep things to himself then I would do the same, I thought stubbornly.

We both lapsed into silence once again, and before long we said good night and went to our respective rooms.

It was the middle of the same night. I'd always been a light sleeper, and the sound of somebody moving in the hall had awakened me. I thought that it must be my father, troubled by another nightmare about his past.

These nightmares were becoming more frequent: I would hear him stir and then make his way to the kitchen for a cup of tea. I would get up and follow him, pretending that I needed a glass of water, then feign surprise at finding him there. In this way, he slowly began to confide in me more of the memories that seemed to be triggered by his nightmares.

This night, too, I rose and headed toward the kitchen, expecting to find him. I was surprised to find the kitchen dark. "Dad?" I whispered. There was no response. Then I heard an indistinct noise coming from the adjacent utility room. I approached the closed door; there was no light coming from under it, but the muffled sound became stronger.

I put my ear against the door.

It was my mother, weeping quietly.

I was suddenly certain that my father had told her his story. I reached for the door handle. But then I stopped, unable to open the door.

I was petrified by my mother's grief: I had had the same feeling when I had first seen my father's tape. As I stood there, frozen to the spot, I knew that I should have done something, made even a single gesture to console my own mother. But much to my enduring shame, I did not. I didn't know how, and I feared that she was beyond comforting. Instead I left her alone: bewildered and frightened.

I lay awake for some time until I heard the sounds of my mother's footsteps returning to her room.

The next morning dawned sunny and unusually mild for early spring in Melbourne.

Over breakfast my mother was perky, but her features were drawn. My father seemed to be avoiding both her company and mine. No sooner had he gulped down the last of his cereal than he rose and headed off to his workshop.

My mother and I were left alone to face each other.

"It's a lovely day, Mum," I said enthusiastically. "Let's go down to Williamstown Beach."

We lived a couple of miles from the bay at Williamstown, one of the oldest parts of Melbourne. I parked on the foreshore close to where my mother had spotted a vacant bench. We made our way to it and sat down. We were silent, listening to the sounds of the waves lapping gently against the small boats moored just offshore.

Suddenly, out of the blue, my mother spoke.

"I've seen the tape," she said. "I know now what was bothering your father. All those years, he never said a word."

My mother told me that after I had left the house to meet Alice my father had simply left the tape on the kitchen table, telling her that he was off on an errand and that she should watch the tape while he was out.

"Your father didn't return until nearly four o'clock," she said. "He went straight to his workshop. I tried to speak with him, but he refused to say a single word about it. There was no choice, I left him to it. You know how obstinate he is—he'll only talk when he's ready to.

"Moments later the phone rang. It was Martin, and I'd no sooner hung up with him than Andrew called," my mother said.

Both my brothers had been at home when my father appeared on their doorsteps. Without even exchanging pleasantries, he had passed over copies of the tape. As with me, he had given neither of them a clue about the tape's contents.

Certainly my father was a shy man, and he must have known that its contents would be traumatic for us, but nonetheless it struck me as perversely reticent the way he had gone about revealing his past to us by videotape.

"How did Martin and Andrew react?" I asked my mother.

She turned away from the view of the bay so that I could see her full expression. It was clear that she was disturbed.

"Andrew was too upset to talk about it very much," she said quietly. "It really shocked him."

"And Martin?" I asked.

"Martin hardly said a word about it," my mother said. "He told me about the tape and then changed the topic. But that's Martin's way. He keeps things to himself.

"Your father was like a man possessed yesterday," my mother continued. "Not long after he returned home, he announced that he was going to visit Mirdza and Edgars.

"'Now?' I asked. 'Are you going to tell them?' He was desperate to have it all out in the open.

"'Will you come with me?' he asked.

"Of course, I couldn't let him go by himself: Edgars is a reasonable

man, but I worried about how Mirdza would react. This would be difficult for her to accept. He was so impatient to get over there that he
jumped in the car and waited for me there—beeping the horn several
times to hurry me up.

"Mirdza answered our knock. She was startled to see us standing on
her doorstep, but welcomed us inside. Edgars was home as well, reading
the newspaper in the kitchen.

"Your father didn't even wait for Mirdza to prepare coffee. We'd
barely sat down when he started telling them his story.

"Mirdza and Edgars sat in silence staring at him the entire time. I'm
not even sure how much they absorbed of what he was saying; he was
speaking so quickly and jumping from event to event. When he'd finally
finished, they looked shell-shocked. They didn't say a word.

"Then after several moments your father looked at his watch.
'We'd better be going,' he said. 'It's almost seven. Mark might be home
by now.'

"Your father rose, and as he did so, he produced a copy of the videotape from his case. 'Let me leave this with you,' he said, putting it on the
table.

"With that, we were out the front door and on our way home. I felt
sorry for Mirdza and Edgars as they waved us off from their front gate.
Your father had swept in like a whirlwind and then disappeared as
quickly.

"What I don't understand," my mother said, turning to look at me, "is
that I saw on the tape that it'd been recorded over two months ago. Why
didn't he tell me sooner? He's kept it from me all the years we've known
each other, and even after he'd told those characters on the tape?"

I had no answer to her question.

"How long have you known, Mark?" she asked.

I'd been put in an awkward position once again. I did not want to tell
my mother about my father's visit to Oxford. Somehow his muteness
about the past was one thing, but its offense would be worsened by the
revelation of a secret journey to the other side of the world.

"Just this week, too," I answered instead.

"Still, for better or worse, we all know now," she said. "But he owes people more of an explanation than simply thrusting a tape at them, don't you think?"

I nodded.

"It's funny," my mother said pensively on the way home from Williamstown. "You know how your father's been about chocolate all his life? He wouldn't share it with anybody, or if he did, he had to be in charge, handing out a piece at a time."

My father had always been a "chocoholic." He would hoard supplies of chocolate, hiding little stashes all over the house. His addiction to it had become a family joke.

"A few weeks ago," my mother said, "he gave it up completely. In one go. I came home one day and found him clearing out his various stashes. Bars and slabs and boxes of the stuff were piled up high like a treasure. I thought he'd lost his mind.

"'In God's name, what are you doing?' I asked.

"'Disposing of it,' he said. 'You can have it. Or give it to the grand-kids, if you want.'

"'But why on earth?' I asked, but your father only shrugged. 'Lost my taste for it,' he said."

We turned into the driveway. "You okay, Mum?" I asked. I didn't know what else to say.

"I'll be okay," she said. "I'll be as right as rain. Just need time to take it all in."

I admired her attitude, but I wondered if she would be "as right as rain." Her mood was somber and she shook her head resignedly. "This world . . ." she said.

I don't believe that she ever really recovered, despite her best efforts to put on a brave face. I still wonder if it would have been easier for her to deal with my father's revelations if I'd not been so fearful of her emotions during those days.

Now that my mother and the rest of the family knew about my father's past, it was as if a brief Indian summer had descended on our house: the curtains had been tied back and the windows thrown open to let in the fresh, mild air.

My father's decision to speak gave me the tacit go-ahead to begin a more concerted search. Two mornings after he had made his disclosures, I was reading the newspaper in the living room when I heard what sounded like a minor explosion in front of our house.

"What on earth?" I heard my mother exclaim as she came into the room, hurried to the front window, and peered through the curtains.

When I joined her there, I saw a dilapidated car shudder to a stop.

The driver's door opened and Alice Prosser got out, collected her bag from the passenger's side, and struggled up the driveway. She was carrying a rolled-up map and a number of books under her arm.

"Poor thing," my mother said sympathetically. "She looks like she's in constant pain with that leg of hers. I wonder who she is . . . she must want your father to repair something for her."

Evidently, my mother had no idea who Alice was.

"Come away from the window or she'll see us staring at her," my mother said, giving me a nudge. "I'll get your father. You look after the lady."

"Alice!" I exclaimed as I opened the door. "This is a surprise. Come in." At that moment I heard my father enter the kitchen.

It was an awkward moment. I could see my mother wondering about this goblinlike woman whom we'd befriended.

"This is my wife, Patricia," my father said. Alice reached out for my mother's hand. My mother seemed momentarily nonplussed.

"Alice has been helping me with my story," my father added, noticing the question in my mother's eyes.

"Oh," she said, before collecting herself and offering Alice a chair.

"Fine to smoke?" Alice asked. When my mother nodded, she got out her tobacco pouch and rolled a cigarette.

"Coffee, Alice?" my mother asked.

"Please, Patricia. May I call you Pat?"

"Yes, you go ahead, dear." My mother seemed to have shed her suspicious attitude.

Alice placed her hand on top of the pile of books.

"I haven't had a chance to look at these yet," she said. "The target is Koidanov. We've all got to put our minds to it."

"I'm not clever enough for that," my mother said from where she was preparing coffee. "I'll make the drinks and sandwiches instead." After she brought our coffees to the table, she retreated to her territory on the other side of the kitchen counter, near the stove and the sink.

In the end, the discovery of Koidanov was surprisingly easy, if not quite straightforward. Once we had finished our coffee, Alice reached for one of her many books, all of which were written in either Yiddish or Russian. She popped her reading glasses on the end of her nose, put a pen behind her ear, and got down to business. Hunched over the table and squinting at the pages of the book in front of her, she reminded me of a Damon Runyon character, perhaps a bookie taking bets on my father's past and future.

"Let me see . . ." she said, going through various possible spellings, "Koidanov . . . Kuidnov . . . Koydanev." Within about ten minutes she had found mention of Koidanov in a list of the various *samulbuch* that had been published. "A *samulbuch*," she explained, "is a collection of historical information—photos, anecdotes, essays, and memoirs—that were kept by the Jewish communities of many towns and villages in eastern Europe.

"Here," she said, pointing at a word on the list. "There's one for a village called Koidanov in the Minsk region in Belarus. Aah . . . I know why you couldn't find it on any map. It states that just before the Second World War the name of the village was changed to Dzerzhinsk. Named after the ignominious founder of the Cheka. Stalin must have been keen to give the place a more Soviet flavor."

In the atlas I'd scoured with my father nights earlier I had in fact come across the name Dzerzhinsk.

Alice shifted her attention to another book among the stack on the table. This one contained maps of prewar Europe, and she consulted one in particular. She had no difficulty in pinpointing Koidanov, and we gathered around her, staring at the spot where she had placed her finger. I was unsure. Koidanov lay some distance to the northeast of Stolbtsi—the town that my father thought might have been referred to as "S" by the soldiers and the site of their base camp, not far from where they claimed to have "discovered" him.

But it was possible, especially if my father had wandered for months on end in a wide circle before being picked up by the Latvian police brigade in the vicinity of Stolbtsi. Taken there by Kulis, who received permission there from Lobe to adopt the boy as the troop's mascot, he was tidied up, given a uniform, and could easily have been dispatched to Slonim, where the massacre had occurred. Of course, it was feasible only if my father had been picked up by the soldiers earlier than they claimed. Professor M. at Oxford had conjectured that any extermination in my father's village would have to have occurred before December 1941 if my father was also to have witnessed the Slonim massacre, which has been variously dated from late 1941 onward. That is, of course, assuming that the Soviet accusation against Commander Lobe and the Latvian police battalion was justified. Or perhaps my father had been picked up in June 1942, as Lobe and others claimed, and was not a witness to the massacre at Slonim but to another unnamed incident.

I scanned the map further to reconfirm what my father and I had already discovered: that to the west of Stolbtsi lay Slonim. Was this distance also too far for the Eighteenth to have ventured on duty?

I cast a quick glance at my father, who was already staring at me. He must have had a similar train of thought. I was on the verge of commenting on this when my father indicated with his eyes and an almost imperceptible shake of his head that I should say nothing.

Fortunately, Alice hadn't noticed our exchange. She continued to stare at the name on the map as if it would somehow magically transform into a window through which we could see Koidanov, past and present. We were all buoyed by the discovery that Koidanov was an actual place. Alice rifled enthusiastically through her books, trying to learn more about Koidanov, while we hovered expectantly around her.

My mother placed another cup of strong black coffee on the table for Alice, who sipped it gratefully. Then she reached across for another of her tomes, this one written in Russian. In it she found a brief reference to Dzerzhinsk and a massacre that had occurred there on October 21, 1941. It spoke of the killing of sixteen hundred patriots by Fascists during the Great Patriotic War.

Alice grunted in annoyance. "In other words," she said, "translating from Sovietspeak, sixteen hundred Jews were murdered in the Holocaust."

"What do you mean?" my father asked.

"The Soviets didn't acknowledge the Holocaust," Alice explained. "Exterminations of this sort were just called crimes against patriotic citizens. And the Second World War was referred to as the Great Patriotic War."

She leaned back in her chair and took another sip of coffee. "The next thing we need to do is to establish contact with Koidanov. I have one contact in Minsk: Mrs. Reizman, a historian who works at a Holocaust research center there. We've exchanged letters a couple of times." She plucked her address book out of her bag.

"Here it is," she said. "If anyone has access to information about Koidanov, then Frida Reizman will be the one."

Alice rolled another cigarette and took a long drag.

"Why don't we write to her now?" she suggested.

"This minute?" My father seemed shaken by the immediacy of it.

"What do they say in English?" Alice asked, looking at me cheekily. "Strike something while it's hot . . ."

"Strike while the iron is hot," I corrected her.

"Okay . . . Okay," she said. "We need to get all the details of your story written down and then send it off to her."

My father's face started to brighten at the possibility opening before him. He nodded in agreement.

I felt my mother looking at me from across the kitchen. She gave a smile when our eyes met, excited in her own cautious way. She reached into one of the drawers under the kitchen counter and pulled out a pad of paper and envelopes.

———

I sat alone in the living room, listening to the soft murmur of my father's and Alice's voices as they composed the letter. I began to plan the logistics of the journey to Minsk. My thoughts were interrupted when I heard Alice call my name. I went to the kitchen, where my father sat anxiously by her side.

"It's finished," she said, looking up at me. "Tell me what you think. You're the young man with the good education."

I laughed, and returned to the living room to proofread the letter. It was fine, describing as much as it could of the details we had to go on— the words "Koidanov" and "Panok" and a description of the massacre my father had witnessed in his village.

I heard the sound of Alice's walking stick on the polished kitchen floor as she hobbled around, stretching her legs. Her face appeared around the doorway, followed by my father's.

"You approve?" she asked.

"Of course," I replied.

"It's great, Alice," my father added.

Alice smiled shyly, pleased with our praise.

"You must post it yourself," she said to my father. "It will be symbolic."

"Do you think something will come of it?" my father asked. His words had a hopeful tone, but Alice only shrugged.

"Time will tell," she said.

"I'll take it to the post office straight away," my father said, already heading for the front door. "Be back soon."

"I'll come with you," I called after him, grabbing my jacket.

I tried to keep up with my father's stride; shamefully, he was in better shape.

"Why didn't you want me to mention Slonim to Alice?" I asked, already slightly breathless.

"I don't want Alice to think that I was associated with something like that," my father answered, maintaining his speedy pace.

"You mean suspect that you might've killed people yourself?"

My father nodded.

"You didn't, did you, Dad?"

It was a question I had always dreaded asking him. I was relieved that we were both facing ahead, and I didn't have to look him in the face.

"Never," he said. I saw him shake his head.

"Never," he repeated. "Not once did I lay a hand on another person, even though the soldiers tried to get me to do so. Much to their amusement I would always run away, petrified."

We continued to walk side by side.

"There was one incident, the worst of all," my father said quietly, as if he feared the neighborhood would hear him. "We were on patrol in a forest. I'm not sure where. The soldiers had captured a Jewish lad—he must have been with the partisans. He was no more than sixteen or seventeen, a teenager, really. They bound his hands together and led him back to our camp.

"When we got there, they tied him to a tree with a long piece of rope. Then they started firing their pistols on the ground around his feet to make him jump and dance around the tree. They were laughing, as if it were a game.

"I couldn't bear to look. I'd caught a glimpse of the terror in the boy's face. Just as I was trying to slip away, one of the soldiers thrust a pistol into my hand. 'Shoot!' he shouted at me. 'Shoot!'

"They all began clapping their hands together, chanting 'Shoot' over and over.

"I was almost as terrified as the boy. I was trapped. There was no way out.

The only thing that came into my head was to aim badly at the boy's feet, so that's what I did. The bullet struck halfway up the tree instead.

The soldiers let out a groan of disappointment, and one of them demonstrated how I should aim the pistol. I nodded my head confidently, as if I'd now grasped what I should do.

"I took aim again—mind you, I was already an excellent shot from target practice with the soldiers—and this time I deliberately fired just over the head of one of the soldiers standing on the opposite side of the tree.

"He ducked, but I knew I wouldn't have hit him anyway. A few of the soldiers began to hurl abuse at me, but I believe that Sergeant Kulis realized that I'd misaimed deliberately. He gave me a furtive warning glance and then strode quickly over to me and gave me a clip around the ear. 'He's a fool,' he called to the other soldiers. 'He needs more pistol training.' With that, he began to push me toward the barracks and out of harm's way.

"He'd defused the episode, but I knew that he viewed what had gone on as a test of my willingness and loyalty to the squad. And I'd failed. I wasn't capable of killing anybody, Jewish or not. I must have had something in me that resisted that."

We reached the post office and stood outside the entrance.

"The soldiers killed everything they could lay their hands on. Incidents like that made me feel that I was a killer just because of what I witnessed. Just because I was with them. Perhaps those interviewers are right. I am a killer of Jews, not literally, but because I stood by and did nothing."

"Dad, you were only five or six then," I tried to reassure my father. "What could you have done to stop them? You would have been powerless against grown men. They would have turned their guns on you and killed you."

My father nodded. "Perhaps that would have been a better solution to my fate," he said. "To have died as a child, a forgotten, unknown martyr, rather than face their hate and accusations now."

My father was quiet.

"What happened to the boy?" I asked.

My father shook his head. "When I returned later in the day, the rope was still tied around the tree, but there was no sign of the boy."

CHAPTER TWENTY-THREE
NIGHTMARES

After his initial enthusiasm at sending the letter, my father's spirits began to flag. One morning I found him alone in the kitchen, staring bleakly into space.

"Even if Koidanov turns out to be my village," he said, "what will be there for me but a handful of memories? And they are here with me." He tapped his chest.

"So what do you hope for from the letter?" I asked.

"To be honest, son," my father replied, "I don't know. Are we clutching at straws? Who would remain there to miss me, or remember me? My entire family perished . . . though I still cannot place my father at the extermination."

I had no answer for that. I also suspected that working from the scant, nonspecific clues that we had provided would stymie Frida's efforts, no matter how enterprising.

The question of Panok remained especially oblique and intriguing for us all. Frank had finally contacted me with the news that his search had failed to establish any definite connect between Panok and the village of Koidanov. Yet why were the two words so strongly associated in my father's memory? Frank also told me that the Panoks who had lived near Minsk in prewar times had all perished in the Holocaust. It seemed that there would be no Panoks to find.

Yet my father would not let go of the mystery of the Panoks. On several occasions he insisted that Panok must be his name, only to retreat moments later into a state of stoic resignation, claiming to have no interest whatsoever in who he might have been.

I began to worry about his mental and emotional fragility.

Despite the somber mood that had descended over the household as we waited for a reply, by day, at least, we maintained a semblance of normality. My parents tried to return to the routine of their daily lives. My father spent his days in his workshop tinkering. On Sundays he and my mother went out for lunch or visited friends. Often they were drawn to the secular synagogue of Café Scheherazade. My mother would browse through her women's magazine over coffee and cheesecake, while my father sat on the edge of his chair, restlessly observing the comings and goings of other customers. He seemed eager, almost desperate, my mother said, to talk to the ones with sympathetic faces and tell them his story.

I was somewhat buoyed by the hours I spent in research at the library trying to get a picture of the historical context of my father's fate. At times, rather frustratingly, the research itself threw up different versions of the same event. In the end, I could construct only the very broadest of canvases based on indisputable historical evidence.

For example, records revealed that in July 1941 Heinrich Himmler had visited Minsk. The purpose of the visit was ostensibly to facilitate "living space" for western European Jews deported to the east. Himmler was keen to see the eradication of Jews in Belarus for that reason, and during that period he ordered *Aktionen* to begin in the region. (This was prior to the Wannsee Conference of January 1942, and the Final Solution, the systemized efficiency of the gas chambers and death camps, had yet to be implemented. In the pre-Wannsee period shooting the Jews one by one and leaving them in mass graves had been the predominant means of clearing the Jewish population out of the villages and towns of eastern Europe.) The killings were carried out by Einsatzgruppen, composed variously of Baltic police battalions and other military units. These groups were ultimately under the command of the German SS but had an internal hierarchy of local commanders. I learned that Einsatzgruppen had entered parts of White Russia, especially the area surrounding Minsk, and begun their *Aktionen* in the late summer and early autumn of 1941.

During subsequent days I learned also about the Latvians in the region. A police battalion, commanded jointly by Commander Lobe and Captain Rubenis, had been dispatched to the region in November/December 1941 to assist in "mopping up duties" and hunting "partisans," an umbrella term used along with "Bolsheviks" as a euphemism for the Jewish population. These facts coincided exactly with my father's confused memory of the presence of both Lobe and Rubenis when he was with the soldiers. It also accounted for the fact that my father had initially insisted to me that his battalion had hunted for only "partisans" and not Jews. As a boy of five, he would have accepted at face value what the soldiers had told him. What was most significant was that different versions contradicted each other as to whether the Latvian police brigade could have been present in time for the Slonim massacre.

In mid-1942 the brigade was incorporated into the Wehrmacht as the Eighteenth Battalion. It was eventually recalled to Riga in the late spring of 1943, where after a brief period it was again transformed, this time into an SS unit, the Kurzeme Battalion, under the command of Kārlis Lobe. In July 1943, the Kurzeme Battalion was sent to the Russian front south of Leningrad to a place called the Volhov swamps, north of Velikiye Luki, exactly as my father had remembered. Crucially, the transformations of the Kurzeme Battalion had involved at least two changes of uniform, which again resonated with my father's memories.

I verified in a number of sources that there had been an extermination in the town of Koidanov, and that it had indeed occurred on October 21, 1941. This date seemed familiar; but later, going through my father's documents, I noted that it was two years later almost to the day that my father became Dzenis's ward.

Each night after dinner, my mother would wash the dishes or do the ironing while my father sat at the kitchen table in silence as I, much like

The certificate from the Orphan's Court of Riga that gave Jekabs Dzenis guardianship of Alex.

a private detective reporting to a client, related the grisly details that had come to light that day.

On one such occasion, after learning of the Koidanov massacre and recounting it to my father, something very sinister occurred to me.

"Perhaps . . ." I began, and then stopped myself.

"Perhaps what?" My father was suddenly alert.

I didn't want to let my father into my train of thought: what if the Latvian police brigade had committed the Koidanov massacre? In other words, what if my father had been adopted and cared for by the very men who had murdered his mother, brother, sister, and extended family?

The thought sent a shiver through me. I didn't want my father to have to even contemplate the terrible possibility that Lobe and Kulis may have murdered his family.

In the end, I was glad that I'd held this suspicion back from him. I learned later that the Koidanov extermination had been perpetrated by the Lithuania Second Brigade, which was also operating in a number of villages southwest of Minsk during 1941.*

During my research, I came across a controversy about the actions of the Latvian police brigade that directly touched upon my father's memories. It pertained to the massacre in Slónim, which may have been within striking distance from "S," where the brigade had set up temporary camp.

According to what Uncle told my father and to the records, in the postwar period the Kurzeme Battalion had been held responsible by the Soviet authorities for a massacre that had taken place there in late 1941 (though again I found a number of conflicting dates for the incident). A war crimes trial had resulted in the execution of several members of the battalion who had not managed to escape from Latvia. Others, including Lobe, claimed that the battalion hadn't been involved and had never been in the vicinity of Slonim. Judging by what I read, their involvement was still a matter of controversy among historians and Latvian patriots alike. What attracted my attention above all, and most troubled me, were several eyewitness accounts of the massacre. Witnesses stated that they saw Jews—the elderly, women, and children—herded into a synagogue and burned alive. This account perfectly reflected the memory my father had recounted to me. It had taken place on the day he'd been tied to the

---

* I also learned much later that the Lithuanian troop had been led by Antonas Gecevicius. Now known as Anthony Gecas, he had been found in 2001 alive and well in Edinburgh, under the auspices of the British government. Our subsequent involvement in the intricacies of the Gecevicius affair would bring us into contact with the Lithuanian government. Although this incident and others related to the whitewashing of Latvia's past were merely peripheral to the story of my father's quest for his identity, they were central to our efforts to validate my father's search, because accusations against my father were made public and never retracted; the resulting damage to his reputation distracted us from our pursuit of the truth. However, these incidents speak of the impact of a small boy's story on contemporary political and national self-interest and the ends to which my father and I had to fight for the truth of his memory.

soldier on the roof of a train and transported with the brigade to an un-identified location. It was also the day when soldiers had jostled for a chance to be photographed with the unusual boy soldier in his uniform.

Had my father in fact been taken to Slonim, where he witnessed the massacre?

When I put the question to him, my father had prevaricated.

"It could've been another time and place."

And that may have been the case. Certainly many synagogues would have been set alight as the troops went about their dirty business.

But then my father had a change of heart.

"The soldiers claim to have picked me up in late May 1942, but what if it had been sooner, much sooner, even before Slonim? The key question is how long I was in the freezing Russian forest, and you know I still find it hard to believe that I was alone there throughout the entire winter. How could a child survive such deprivation?

"It was Commander Lobe who told me about how they rescued me, even that it was the summer season. Perhaps with time I've grown confused. I remember clearly that Kulis rescued me from the firing squad, but in my mind I've pictured that it was summer because that was what Lobe insisted. But, you know, I am sometimes troubled by a sense that there was snow on the ground when I was dumped in the firing line. That's my problem: my memories blend together between what I actually remember and what I was instructed to remember."

My father paused. "Why would they have lied about such a thing?" he asked.

"To cover their tracks," I reminded him. "You could have been a witness against any of the men who were there. I wonder what happened to the photographs that were taken that day. I wonder if any of the soldiers kept them."

My father shrugged. "Who would be crazy enough to keep something that implicated them as a war criminal?"

The fragile silence of our household was disturbed almost nightly by the wails and shouts that emanated from the spare room where my father had taken to sleeping to avoid disturbing my mother. I would lie half-awake in fear and anticipation of what that night's dreams would bring to my father. My mother and I often found ourselves together outside his room, our ears pressed against the closed door, eavesdropping on the tormented man.

Sometimes we would hear my father stir and begin to move about the room. At that point my mother would tap lightly on the door.

"Alex?" she would whisper, as if unsure it was her husband on the other side. "Alex? Are you okay?"

We would hear his muffled and drowsy-sounding answer: "I'm fine. Just a bad dream. Go back to bed."

"I'll talk to him," I would say to my mother. "You get some sleep."

"Tea?" I would say to my father through the closed door.

His usual response would be, "Okay, son, I'll join you shortly," though on a few occasions he ordered me to go back to bed. He needed his privacy, and I wondered what he had seen in his dreams that he couldn't share.

On most occasions, however, I would prepare tea in the kitchen. My father would enter some minutes later, after what I imagined to be a process of recovering himself, literally, from his dreams.

Sometimes he sat silently, as if in shock, sipping from his cup. I would sit opposite him, waiting for him to speak. These moments were both ghoulish and titillating because I didn't know if my father would be able to recall what he had just dreamed and if it might somehow be another clue to unlocking his past.

But that past was beginning to overwhelm him.

One night I woke with a start. For a moment, as I lay in my bed, the house was quiet. I rose and tiptoed down the hallway. The door to my father's bedroom was open. The room was dark. I softly called his name, but there was no reply. I continued toward the kitchen, where I could see light coming from under the closed door. I gently opened it, just a fraction. My father was sitting at the table with his head in his hands. He was utterly still and was so absorbed in his thoughts that he had not heard me. I opened the door farther.

"Dad?" I whispered.

He gave a slight jump and turned toward me.

"Another nightmare?" I asked.

He nodded.

"Recall any of it?"

He shook his head. "But a memory came to me the instant that I woke up. In fact, I wasn't sure if I was awake or not." He laughed darkly.

My mother suddenly appeared in the doorway and stayed, listening.

"For a moment I was back in the town where the synagogue had been set on fire with all those poor people inside. But this time everything was more vivid."

My father stopped speaking and screwed up his eyes as if to avoid seeing what was in his memory.

"I could see the expressions on people's faces, the little children. And the cries as people burned. I can hear the screams even now as they clawed at the burning doors trying to get out. And then the silence that followed, apart from the sound of the wood crackling, I can still hear that, if that makes sense."

For an instant my father seemed to struggle for breath, as if he, too, were being immolated inside the synagogue, deprived of oxygen.

"And there were other flashes of images. Men and women stripped naked and shot in the back of the head. I think that happened on that same day. I thought that it had gone from me, as you said, that I'd blocked it out, but there's no escape from it this time. It's like a film that plays itself over and over, and I cannot control it. Now that I remember I will never forget it . . ."

My father was silent for several minutes and then he seemed visibly to gather his spirit together.

"You still don't know where and when this was?" I ventured.

My father shook his head despondently. "I want to remember," he said reflectively, "but not this. This is madness."

I turned to my mother, who was still standing in the doorway. She was weeping quietly.

The strain of nights such as these eventually made it difficult to maintain even false cheer.

But the dreams were not always alarming. Ever since we found Koidanov, my father had gone through phases of excitability that opened up more pleasant and nostalgic memories and dreams of life in his village. Yet even then he sometimes found himself traumatized by a growing sense of what he had lost, and a growing bewilderment over why he alone had survived.

One night I made my way to the kitchen, where I found my father standing by the sink, waiting for the kettle to boil. He was staring at his own reflection in the kitchen window, and he must have heard me enter because he didn't startle as I came up behind him.

As I came closer, I realized that he was not staring at himself but outside. "Dad?" I whispered.

He raised his hand in the air, indicating that I should be quiet.

I waited expectantly and suddenly he spoke, or rather exclaimed, "An apple tree! I've just had a dream about one. It's jolted my memory. There was an apple tree in our back garden. I'd always be climbing it, playing in it, picking apples for my mother."

My father was elated. "I can see my hands in front of me," he continued, "trying to get a grip on the trunk as I climb it. Then suddenly I am in a fork of the tree and looking down through the branches and leaves to the earth, which seems miles below me.

"My mother is down there, looking up at me. I'm reaching out and plucking apples and then tossing them down to her. She catches some in her apron, but she misses others, which roll on the ground."

I noticed that my father was recounting his dream to me in the present tense, as if it were happening at this moment, as if he had returned to a past more vivid and real to him than the moment I shared with him.

"I can see her lips breaking into a smile and then she laughs as her apron begins to overflow with apples. She is calling out to me 'Enough! Enough!' But the eerie thing is that I can't hear her voice. I've no idea of how it sounds. Then she calls out my name, but again I cannot hear her.

And, worst of all, I am looking at her face, but I can't see her features. They will not crystallize for me.

"I look away for a moment. Something has distracted me."

My father gripped my forearm tightly. "It's below me and slightly to the left," he said. "It's a shed and a man is moving about inside. I can't get a clear view of what he's doing."

My father moved his head to one side as if trying to get a clearer view into the shed.

"Wait!" he exclaimed, raising his hand to silence me before I had even uttered a word. "The man has heard my mother's and my laughter and he's come to the doorway. He's looking up at me. It's my father, Mark," my father said excitedly. "My father!"

"Can you see his face?"

"No. He's gone. He's turned away. But I can see inside the shed now. Skins! Skins of animals. They are hanging behind him. These are what he works with. He makes things out of them. People come to the shed to buy things from him. He must be a shoemaker or tanner of some sort.

"The dream didn't end there. Suddenly I was flying. I soared high into the sky so that I could see all the houses in my street. I caught sight of the house with the apple tree and the shed. It was wooden and there was a drive running alongside it, wide enough for a cart. I know that this house is where I lived.

"I descended like an angel so that I hovered just above the height of the roofs. I could see people—ordinary-looking village people, not dressed fancily or anything—walking, chatting with each other, and going about their business. But again it is deadly quiet.

"I wanted to look at their faces but I couldn't. I could only see the tops of their heads. But I'm certain I knew them.

"I had no control over my flight and suddenly I was back in the tree . . ."

My father rubbed his eyes as if he had only just now roused himself from his dream. His sadness was palpable.

I began to question him, hoping that he would remember more, even if only a single signpost that might help us both. My concern frustrated him.

"No," he sighed wearily, "I didn't see the name of the street I was on."

He gripped his head in his hands.

"Or the town or what country it was," he added.

"It was a town?"

"I don't know," he said tetchily. "I don't even know if the place was large or small. It seemed small but that was because I was high in the sky."

He paused for an instant.

"But I'm absolutely certain that I would recognize the house and the area if I ever came across it."

I was concerned. Was this simply a dream in which he had imagined how his life might have been? Or had sleep itself triggered a real memory of his past?

"I wonder if we'll find it in Koidanov . . ." I ventured.

My father didn't respond at first. He was lost in thought.

"I associate the tree with happiness. I climbed it all the time. That's where I played with my friends as well." My father smiled.

I was grateful for his expression. I wanted him to recapture some sense of happiness, however tenuous.

"We'll have to wait and see what comes of the letter to Minsk," my father said soberly, "before we can solve the mystery of this dream."

He was right. Hard footwork alone would help us uncover the enigma of Koidanov.

Whenever Alice visited us during these weeks she, too, would quickly succumb to the solemnity that had pervaded the house. She would sit slightly hunched and frowning at the kitchen table, rolling herself cigarette after cigarette as my father recounted each and every memory that had come to him the night before.

She was galvanized by even the slightest of his recollections: she would fix him with her shrewdly observant gaze and pat his hand gently as he spoke.

My father told her about the dream of his home.

"We must send these details off to Frida Reizman immediately," she said. "Who knows? With some luck . . ."

I voiced my concern. "Those little bits won't give an investigator much to go on. It could be any apple tree in any village anywhere. How many houses in Russia have apple trees in their back gardens?"

"You stay the pessimist," she replied. "I'm sending a telegram to Frida Reizman with news of the apple tree and the man who might have been a tanner."

Alice stubbed out the cigarette she'd been enjoying and placed its remains back in her tobacco pouch.

CHAPTER TWENTY-FOUR
A TELEGRAM

I t had been more than six weeks since the letter and the follow-up telegram had been sent to Frida Reizman in Minsk.

One Saturday afternoon my parents and I were in Scheherazade when my father's cell phone rang. He pushed the answer button with his stubby, arthritic fingers.

"Yes?" he said. His face reddened suddenly.

"Truly?" he said excitedly. "We're in your neighborhood now. The usual spot. Okay, see you soon." My father signed off.

"Alice," he said. "She sounded breathless. She wants us to stay put. News from Minsk."

Suddenly he seemed more apprehensive than excited. We sat in silence waiting for Alice. My father fidgeted with his phone while opposite me my mother tapped her fingers lightly on the table, staring into space.

Finally, Alice appeared at the glass door, grinning. She hobbled across to us and, before she'd even sat down, slapped a piece of paper down on the table.

"A telegram," she announced with finality. "From Minsk."

We each read it slowly, absorbing its few words.

"Regarding the man from Koidanov with the unusual fate. A possible family member living in Minsk. A letter to Alex Kurzem will follow."

"Who have they found?" I exclaimed. "Who exactly? A cousin? An aunt? Who?"

My mother was slightly vexed too. "She should've included more information rather than leave us on tenterhooks like this."

Alice nodded in agreement.

Typically, my father was the most pragmatic among us. "We'll just have to be patient," he said stoically. "One step at a time."

"Good God, Alex!" my mother said. "Don't you want to know as soon as possible?"

"It says 'possible family member,'" he replied, reaching for the telegram. "As I said, all in good time."

My mother and I rolled our eyes in frustration, but we both knew that my father was grateful for any delay allowing him to brace himself for whatever came to light.

A week later, just after my father had left the house on a repair job, the postman delivered a letter from Minsk.

"Should we open it?" I asked.

"Keep your shirt on," my mother said, gripping the letter tightly. "Your father will be back shortly."

But I could tell that she was as anxious and excited as I was.

We were in the kitchen when we heard my father come in.

"The mail is on the coffee table, luv," my mother called out.

There was silence in the next room for several moments before my father joined us. He held the envelope aloft.

"From Minsk," he said. "I guess you know that already."

My mother and I waited with bated breath, like excited schoolchildren, as my father fumbled with the envelope for several seconds before giving up.

"Here," he said, thrusting it at me. "Read it to Mum and me."

I objected. I thought he should be the very first to lay eyes on its content.

"But I can't find my reading glasses," he protested, pretending to look for them. "Where did I put them?"

I was sure that he was stalling.

"I need a cup of tea," he said, turning to my mother.

My mother hastily prepared tea and brought it over to him.

"Are you ready now?" I asked, reaching into the envelope.

"No," he said. "One more thing. I must let Alice know at once." He reached for the phone.

"Just a message for you, Alice," he said. "Come over as soon as you can. A letter has come from Belarus."

"We may as well get on with it," I said, growing impatient.

When I tore open the envelope, something fluttered to the floor. It appeared to be a photograph. Before I could react, my father bent down and snapped it up, looked at it, and went deadly pale. He stuffed it into his shirt pocket without a word.

"What have you got there, luv?" my mother asked.

"Nothing important. I'll show you later."

My father sat down and sipped his tea while my mother stood behind him, gripping the top of his chair, eager to hear the news.

I pulled out the letter and saw that it was written in Russian. We would have to wait for Alice to arrive. This time I called Alice's cell, and she picked up immediately.

"Yes," she said. "I've heard your father's message. I'm already crossing the Westgate bridge. I'll be with you soon."

I hung up and relayed the news of Alice's imminent arrival to my parents.

My father looked drained and decided to go to his room to rest.

"But Alice'll be here any moment," I protested.

"Don't worry," he replied. "I'll listen for her old bomb."

My mother and I waited for Alice in the kitchen. Soon we heard the telltale rattle and bang of her car as it turned into our driveway. Moments later I heard my father greet Alice as he let her in.

"What's up?" I heard her reply as she hobbled into the kitchen. For an instant I was startled by her appearance: she could have easily passed for an eccentric private detective. She looked slightly disheveled in her raincoat and carried an oversized tote bag; a lit cigarette drooped from the corner of her mouth. For an added touch of eccentricity—deliberate or not, I am uncertain—she wore a large black fedora with a yellow feather tucked into its silk band.

Taking a long drag on her cigarette, Alice began to translate in a quiet voice.

" 'Dear Alex Kurzem. It is an act of G-D that has brought you to us in Minsk.

" 'My name is Frida Reizman. I am a historian at the Holocaust research center here.

" 'One morning, three weeks ago, I was at my desk at the center, reading through the manuscript of my book, when there was a knock at the door. It was a letter for me.' "

"Only three weeks ago?" my father interrupted. "That took some time to reach her." Alice shushed him and continued.

" 'I opened the letter and soon I couldn't believe what I was reading with my own eyes. When I had finished learning your remarkable story, I had to sit and think about it for some time.

" 'Suddenly there was another knock at the door. It was my printer-publisher, Mr. Erick Galperin, with a printout of my book. Erick and I got down to business. After a while, we took a break. I had only recently become acquainted with Erick but had to tell somebody about your extraordinary letter.

" 'I told him that a man from Australia was searching for his identity. He remembered two words that might be clues, Koidanov and . . . before I could say another word, Erick interrupted me. "Koidanov?" he said, surprised. "I was born there! My family were from there." We were both truly amazed by this coincidence.

" 'Erick's father's family all perished in the liquidation in Koidanov, and he was moved by your terrible fate and the fact that your family may have died alongside his own father's original family, and, worst of all, may share the same grave.

" 'Before the war Koidanov was not much bigger than a village. So if you were from Koidanov, Erick believes that your family may have known his father's first family. They might have been neighbors or visitors to each other's homes.

"'According to Erick, if you were about five when the massacre happened, then you may have even known Erick's father's three children who died that day. His father's eldest was a boy about the same age. Ilya Solomonovich was his name. Who knows, perhaps you and Ilya played together when you were young. You may have been best friends.

"'I told Erick not to be too hopeful. But still, you never know, do you?

"'Then I told Erick about the second word, Panok. Erick thought he had heard this word, but he could not remember where.

"'Erick wanted to know more about your family, and the only other thing I could tell him was that your father might have been a tanner. It was good fortune that Alice sent the telegram with the extra details . . .'"

Alice gave me a look of vindication.

"See," she said. "I told you every little bit helps."

I raised my hands in surrender.

Alice adjusted the reading glasses on the end of her long nose.

"Now, where was I?" she said. She began to read again.

"'Again Erick interrupted me. He was surprised because his father, Solomon, was a tanner, too, who repaired shoes. Koidanov was a small place. It barely needed two tanners. Your fathers must have known each other, even if they were in competition.'"

"True," my father interrupted. "Surely they knew each other."

"Listen to this!" Alice said. "According to Erick, Solomon had a workshop next to his home, where he worked on the skins."

Alice peered over the rim of her glasses. "Just like the little shed next to your house . . ."

"That's right!"

Alice put the letter down. My father's expression was a mixture of shock and pleasure.

"Shall I go on?" Alice asked.

"Please."

Alice brought the letter closer to her eyes. "'Erick had the idea of sending a photo of his father to you,'" Alice read. "'He hopes you might recognize his father from when you were a child.'"

Alice examined the envelope. "It's not here," she said, shaking it vigorously.

"I have it," my father said, removing it from his pocket. After glancing at it briefly, he passed it to my mother. She was startled by what she saw and, with shaking hands, passed it to me.

I looked down at the picture of a man sitting with a small boy. I was stunned and passed it quickly on to Alice, who held it at arm's length and then drew it closer to her. She, too, was transfixed by the image in the photograph. She pulled out a tiny magnifying glass, held it up to the photograph, scanned it thoroughly, and finally looked up.

"I have never seen such a likeness before," she declared.

The room was quiet for several moments.

"Does Frida give any more details about the photo?" I asked, breaking the silence.

Alice perused the letter.

"The man is Solomon Galperin, Erick's father. We know that," she said. "The photo was taken in 1961. Apparently he lived all his life in Koidanov, apart from the war.

"'Although you were only a small boy,'" Alice read from the letter, "'do you remember his face?'"

My father examined the photo closely for several moments but then shook his head.

"What about the name Galperin?" Alice asked. "Does it ring a bell?"

My father shook his head.

I blurted out what was surely on all our minds: "I think the man in the photograph is your father."

"Look at the resemblance," my mother said. "You're almost identical."

My father nodded without hesitation. "But I can't remember my father's face at all," he said. "Nor my mother's. It bothers me that I can't

The photo of Solomon Galperin, possibly Alex's
father, that arrived unexpectedly in the mail in 1997.

when I do remember the faces of so many of the soldiers and scenes from
the war. Why can't I remember my own family?"

Unexpectedly, my father had a change of heart. "How on earth could
this be my father?" he snapped. "If the picture was taken in 1961, my
father would have been long dead by then. My mother told me that he'd
died long before she and the rest of my family had perished."

Suddenly Alice raised her hand to quiet us. "Listen to this," she said.
"Erick states that his father, Solomon, survived the war. Solomon fled
Koidanov to join the partisans but was caught and taken to Auschwitz
and later Dachau. He survived because he was a good shoemaker. After
the war, when he made it home, he learned that his entire family had
perished. He remarried and he and his new wife had a son, Erick."

"So Erick could be your half brother," my mother concluded. "You
might have the same father—Solomon."

"Could your father have survived the war?" I asked my father.

He buried his face in his hands. He was completely bewildered. "But why would my mother tell me my father was dead?"

Alice's attention shifted back to the letter, which she still held in her hand. Her eyes scanned quickly down the two pages.

"Amazing," she said.

Her eyes shifted from my father to my mother and then to me.

"Who'd have expected Erick to be in Frida's office the same day the letter sat on her desk? You'd have a greater chance of winning the lottery."

"I think we all need a brandy," my mother suggested and rushed to put out glasses.

While my mother poured the drinks, Alice put down the letter and slowly rolled herself a cigarette, gazing at the letter.

"Frida has included Erick's number," she said. "Shall we try to call him?"

"Now?" my father asked.

Alice nodded.

My father appeared thrown by the suggestion.

"Strike while the iron is . . . what do they say?"

"Hot," I offered.

Alice smirked at me.

"It's probably too late there," my father said hopefully.

"Not at all," Alice said firmly, looking at her watch.

The call did not go smoothly. Alice had to shout down the line in an effort to make herself heard and in less than ten minutes the call had ended.

"There were such crackling noises on the line," she complained.

"What was Erick like?" my father asked enthusiastically.

"Hard to say," Alice replied. "He seemed sane. I told him about your resemblance to Solomon and he was baffled. Then it was strange—he had the same idea that we have. What if you are Solomon's son? That you are Ilya Solomonovich, the eldest of the Galperin children, who everyone believed had died. Ilya would have been about five years old at the time of the extermination—the same as you. Solomon had often spoken of Ilya and had laid flowers on the mass grave in memory of the boy, his wife, and other children. He got carried away with the idea and pleaded for you to come to Belarus immediately.

"He said that there are many things that he can do for you, Alex. He can take you to Koidanov and introduce you to people who knew your father and who probably knew you as a little boy. People who know even more than he does about the past.

"After that the line was bad. The last thing I heard him say was, 'Tell him to come. All will be revealed.'"

We sat in silence, taking in the significance of the letter and now the call. Had we made direct contact with my father's past for the first time?

I glanced furtively at my father. He looked excited but grim. "I'm not convinced I'm a Galperin."

There was a note of hysteria in his voice as he continued, "I don't know who I am. Will I ever know?"

Then he wavered again. "Imagine if it were true," he said, looking hopefully at each of us. "I would have a brother. Erick would be my brother."

We listened as he repeated the word "brother," relishing it.

Then his caution overcame him again. "No, it can't be," he said. "Perhaps Panok is my name . . ."

Finally, Alice spoke. "There's only one thing to do," she said. "We have to get Alex to Koidanov."

She turned to look at me. "Any ideas, Mr. Oxford?"

My mother and father both looked at me expectantly.

"Let me think about it . . ." I faltered, secretly feeling daunted by the task.

"Well, don't take too long," Alice said with determination. "We need action on this. Now."

The letter and the phone call seemed to have ignited my father's psyche. No longer confined to his dreams, incidents and impressions from his past now flashed before my father at all hours.

One night in particular, my parents and I were at home watching television, and my father was lying on the floor in front of the fire.

Suddenly he sat upright. His face was almost apoplectic: his eyes bulged wide.

"Alex!" my mother exclaimed. "What's wrong?"

The sound of my mother's voice calmed him. He rose to sit on an armchair, shaking his head to rouse himself.

"I'd been asleep in a bed. Something has woken me. There's another child next to me. He must be my little brother. Then I hear a sound, this time coming from the ceiling."

My father's eyes were feverish and, again, he spoke in the present tense.

"'Mama,' I call out, and my mother comes into the room. It's not really a room, it's—how do you say?—it's partitioned off from the next room by a curtain. 'I can hear something,' I tell her. 'No,' she whispers, 'you must have been dreaming. Go back to sleep.' She kisses me. I watch as she leaves the room.

"I hear the sound above me again. Something is moving up there. I can just make out a shadow through a gap in the curtain."

Involuntarily my father moved his head to one side, as if trying to peer through the gap from a different angle.

"Legs!" he exclaimed. "Somebody's legs . . . a man's. They're coming out of the ceiling. They're wearing trousers and boots. I recognize them—they are my father's boots. Why are they hanging from the ceiling?

"I can hear something else now—the whispers of men's voices and my mother's, but I can't see from where I am. I get up and tiptoe to the curtain. My mother's there. And a man with a beard. And my father. I am confused. I haven't seen my father for ages. My mother has told me that he is dead. But he's not. He's not! He is here in front of me. Or is he a ghost? Am I dreaming? I am frightened and return to my bed. I feel safer there.

"Now I hear the sound of footsteps coming toward me. I open my eyes. Even in the darkness I know that it's my father. He's hovering above me, but he's not a ghost.

"He strokes my hair.

"'Papa?' I cannot resist saying his name.

"He doesn't answer me.

"He touches my cheek.

"He kisses my forehead.

"'Good-bye,' he whispers.

"My father is turning away from me. I watch him leave the room. What is happening? I get up and cross the room to the curtain. I peep through the gap. I cannot see clearly, so I rub my eyes.

"The man with a beard is still here. I know him, but I can't remember who he is."

"My mother is now at the door. She is waving good-bye to somebody!

"Wait! It's Father and the man with the beard. Where are they going in the middle of the night?

"My mother is closing the door.

"'Mama?' I call out from where I am standing, partly hidden by the curtain. She turns.

"'Papa, I saw Papa.'

"'Papa is not here.'

"She takes me back to my bed. She hugs me."

My mother and I sat in stunned silence while my father, exhausted, stared blankly into space, seemingly trapped between the past and the present.

My mother, ever practical, rose silently and went into the kitchen. After several moments she returned with a mug of tea for my father. My father gulped at it greedily, as if it were a magic potion that would deliver him with speed and finality to the present.

"I've got to get to Koidanov," my father said.

"As soon as possible," added my mother.

PART III

CHAPTER TWENTY-FIVE
OXFORD

Two weeks after the letter arrived, I found myself waiting with my parents at Melbourne airport for my flight to Oxford to be called.

The plan was for me to organize the journey to Belarus and Latvia, as well, which my father was keen to visit. He had not seen Riga since he'd fled with the Dzenis family in late 1944. My parents would join me in Oxford and then we would make the journey together.

It was torturous to sit opposite them in the airport coffee shop, laughing and joking in spite of the difficulty I had leaving them. I worried that it was the worst possible moment for me to abandon them—for that is how it felt to me—to the ravages of my father's memories.

Nearly thirty hours later, I turned the key in the door to my digs in Oxford. Exhausted, I dumped my bags in the hall, poured myself a glass of water, and sprawled out on the sofa. It was then that I noticed the message light flashing on the answering machine. I had been gone for nearly three months.

I reached across and pushed the button. The machine replayed a dozen or so messages—from friends, the bank, the dentist reminding me of an appointment I'd forgotten in my rushed departure for Australia—nothing of any importance until I came to the final one.

It was my father's voice.

"Mark?" he said. "You're not back yet? Call me when you get in."

My heart skipped a beat. I looked at my watch. It was now 10:00 p.m. in Melbourne. My parents would still be awake. I sighed, picked up the phone, and dialed their number.

My mother answered. I could tell instantly that something was up. Her voice lacked its usual melodic tone. "You got home all right, luv?" she asked.

"No worries, Mum," I replied, then added slightly impatiently, "Dad's called already. Can I speak to him?"

"He's sleeping," she said.

"Okay, I won't disturb him," I said.

"He was so shaken that I had to give him a sedative."

"What's happened?" I said, panicking.

"I shouldn't have said anything. He's fine. You're not to worry yourself. Call him tomorrow, luv."

But I did worry. All afternoon, as I dozed and slowly unpacked, I counted the minutes until it was morning in Melbourne, and I could call my father again. I pictured my mother alone in the house with my sleeping father. There was nobody there to support her. It would not be the last time that I would have a sudden, almost inexpressible realization of how hard all this was for her, and how frequently friends and family would overlook the burden that had been placed on her—the man she had been married to for over forty years was in one sense now a stranger to her.

At eight in the morning, Melbourne time, I called again. The phone had barely rung before my father picked it up. He sounded groggy. He coughed and then began.

"Somebody called," he said. "We'd barely come in the front door after seeing you off when the phone rang.

"I picked it up and at the same time—I don't know why, my intuition, perhaps—I switched on the speakerphone so that your mother could listen in.

"It was a man's voice. I didn't know who he was, but I did recognize the accent—it was Latvian.

"'You were the little boy who was helped by the Latvian soldiers, weren't you?' he asked, without introducing himself.

"'Yes. So the story goes. Who's speaking, please?'

"There was silence at the other end of the line. Then he spoke again.

"'You can call me Daugavas.'

"'How do you know about me?'

"'Many Latvians know about you.' He laughed wryly. 'Recently it's all we talk about. You and Konrad Kalejs. Some say you are destroying the good reputation of our community.'

"'For telling the truth about what happened to me?'

"'I don't wish to argue with you. Before I go any further with this I need your word—this conversation will be confidential.'

"'I cannot give guarantees. I will try, that's all. What does this concern?'

"Suddenly the man seemed nervous and hesitant. I thought he would hang up. I waited patiently, put no pressure on him. My strategy worked. He began to speak of his own volition.

"'Recently I was back in Riga. One night at dinner I began to tell people about a man living in Melbourne—you, and your association with Latvia.

"'They were kind to you, weren't they?' he asked. 'The ones who looked after you.'

"I was embarrassed. 'I guess so,' I replied. 'I have always said that.'

"'When I finished your story,' he said, 'one woman there told me that she'd seen a photo of a young boy soldier standing among Latvian and German soldiers. The photo was in the house of her husband's grandmother in Munich. This woman is the widow of a high-ranking German soldier during the war. Once, when he came back from active duty, he brought this photo. He told her, "This boy, he's a good luck charm!"'

"'It could be me,' I said to the caller. 'So many people wanted to take my photo. Can I see the photograph?' I asked. 'When can I meet you?'

"With that, his mood changed. I sensed his reluctance. I shouldn't have pushed him.

"'I must go,' he said, and abruptly hung up.

"My mind was restless all night. I had to find this man.

"The first thing yesterday morning, the telephone rang again. I recognized his voice immediately.

"'Mr. Daugavas,' I said. I decided to confront him on the spot. I knew that he must've been torn about letting me see the photograph, otherwise why would he have called back. I adopted a reasonable tone. 'Please don't hang up, sir,' I said. 'I understand your predicament and I think you understand mine. I want to see the photo. I have a right to see it.'

"Then there was a long silence at the other end of the line. At first I thought he'd hung up again, but then I heard him sigh heavily.

"'Look. Can't you understand? This is difficult for me. I want to help you, but I don't want to be involved in any trouble.'

"'Why? It's only a photo.'

"'It's a shocking photograph.'

"'I don't understand.'

"'The image is a violent one of you laden with weapons. If people see it, they'll start asking questions. Who are these men with this little boy? What are they doing? What are they thinking? Why is this child in their midst? Are they members of an extermination troop? Now do you see?'

"'This can be just between us.'

"The man seemed to be thinking. Then he spoke. 'I can't take the risk. I'm sorry.'

"'Please, sir, hear me out,' I pleaded. 'It's my past, that photo. Please. I have few photos, so few things from anyone who cared for me at that time. And the soldiers, they did care for me so well, you know, they loved me like their own. They always protected me. Fed me first. Gave me water. We cared for each other. You know what I would do for them? In the summer, on patrol, I would pick strawberries for them. From among the bodies of dead soldiers rotting in the fields. And such delicious straw-berries. So big. I always came back with handfuls and I passed them out. One for each soldier. That was one of my jobs. You see, I was one of them. I cared for them, so why would I betray them? I would be betray-ing myself if I did.' I went on like this—I can't remember every word exactly—trying to convince him.

" 'Let me think about this. I promise I will call you back.'

" 'When?'

" 'Today. Before three. You have my word.'

"He did keep his word. He called back after lunch. He agreed to my request, but only on one condition. I could see the photograph but I couldn't keep it.

"Amazingly, he agreed to meet me that night, as if we were secret agents or something.

"I was flabbergasted. Why let me see it, but not have it? I decided to agree and argue my case when I came face-to-face with him.

"He suggested we meet outside Luna Park, a local amusement park. He knew that it would be closed on an evening midweek and that the area around it would be deserted.

"I went there at the appointed time, and, just as I suspected, there wasn't a soul around. It was a humid summer's night but with rain pour-ing down so heavily I could barely see. I had to keep the wipers on.

"I saw a car pull slowly into the curb. Its headlights blinded me for a moment. Then I saw a tall man get out and head toward the entrance. You remember it, don't you? The giant open mouth illuminated with enormous white teeth.

"I waited to make sure it was him. In my rearview mirror I watched the man pace up and down. Then I got out and went over. I'd never met him before. He didn't say a word to me. He simply removed an envelope from inside his coat and pulled out a photo. Immediately I reached for it, but he stepped back and shook his head.

" 'But I can't let you have it,' he said.

"He held the photo aloft for me to see it. There was enough light from the entrance for me to tell instantly that it was me. I wanted to examine it more closely, but the man kept a firm grip on it. He wouldn't let me touch it at all.

"I don't know—something came over me—I felt the photo belonged to me. It was of me—and this stranger had decided I shouldn't have it.

"I snatched the photo from him. He was shocked; it seemed he never expected that kind of reaction. I was too fast for him. I made for the car as quickly as possible, got in, and locked the door.

"He appeared at the window, breathless with anger. He stood by my car for a while, trying to bargain with me, but I refused point-blank to hand the photo over. Eventually he gave up.

"I watched the taillights of his car disappear into the distance and then headed off in the opposite direction.

"Mum was waiting up for me.

"I got out the photo to show her. It's terrible."

My father described the image to me as best he could.

I could barely believe what I heard and raged inwardly at these men—at those who posed for the photograph and the man who took it.

"Do you recognize any of the men?"

"The man standing beside me with his arm around me. His name, if I remember correctly, was Aizum. Captain Aizum."

I grabbed a pen and made a note of the name.

"Anybody else? Sergeant Kulis?"

"No."

"Lobe?"

"No . . . but that doesn't mean they weren't around. Who knows?"

My father paused.

"You know, I think that this is one of the photos taken on that day I saw the synagogue burned."

"Is there anything visible in the background?" I asked, hoping that there would be something that could identify where it was taken.

"Nothing," my father replied. "Only the side of a train carriage. It's a terrible photo, but I suppose it's better than nothing. A remnant from my past." He laughed bitterly.

For a moment a terrible chill passed through me. But I didn't dare ask my father any more. I would see the photograph in good time.

"One thing is certain, Dad," I said. "You've got to be careful who you show this photo to."

He nodded. "There'd be some who'd use it against me," he said soberly, "no matter what the truth behind the image."

In the weeks following my return to Oxford I set about organizing my parents' journey. I had no idea how long it would take to put everything in order. It was winter now and the weather would be inhospitable for travel. I hoped to be in Belarus and Latvia by April or May, when better weather had arrived.

It was during this period that I arranged to catch up with my acquaintance Elli; I'd kept in touch with her while I was in Australia. I suggested the coffee shop in Blackwell's.

I arrived before her and found a small table by the window overlooking Broad Street.

Suddenly a shadow crossed my table. I looked up to find Elli.

"Dearie," she said. "It's good to see you back." She touched my arm warmly. "I've been worried about you. All the pressure you're under."

"A relief to be in a quieter place for a while," I mumbled. Then I smiled.

"How are your parents these days?"

"They're surviving."

"That sounds grim."

I nodded, playing with my coffee cup.

"If there is anything I can do . . ."

"There is . . ." I decided to tell her about the photograph.

Elli, as usual, proved to be a good listener. When I had finished, she was quiet for several moments. "You don't have a copy of it?" she asked.

"No. My parents will be here in the spring, though. If my father agrees, I'll show it to you."

"Your father should guard it closely. If anybody got their hands on it . . ." She didn't finish her thought.

She looked at her watch. "I must go, dearie," she announced. "Things to do. Let me know if there are any more developments with the photograph." She bent forward and pecked me on the cheek.

I watched Elli as she made her way through the now crowded coffee shop and toward the exit.

Moments later I gazed down the street and noticed her as she hurried across Broad. It hadn't been my intention to spy on her, yet I couldn't help but observe her as she stopped to greet two men who had clearly been waiting for her on the steps in front of the Bodleian Library. They shook hands and all three then headed off in the direction of the High Street, talking animatedly among themselves.

For just an instant, Elli turned her head slightly and glanced back in the direction of Blackwell's wearing a quizzical, slightly suspicious look.

I jerked my face away from the window. I didn't want her to know that I didn't trust her.

Some months later, by early spring of the following year, I turned my attentions to our visit to Belarus and, most important, Koidanov.

I called my father to see if he could cajole Alice into joining us on the trip.

He picked up the phone but was not his usual bright self. His tone was cautious.

"What's wrong?" I asked.

"Nothing."

"You sure?"

He hesitated. "Somebody's been calling . . ."

"Daugavas again?"

"No. They won't identify themselves."

I took a deep breath. "Only one person?" I asked.

"No. Different people."

"What do they want?"

"Just to warn me to keep quiet about the Latvians. That I shouldn't bite the hand that fed me. One told me that consequences will be bad for us, and that the world would judge me as a Nazi. Would I or my family be able to live with that?"

My father sighed wearily. "It's got to the point where your mum won't answer the phone."

"Have you told the police?"

"No. What can they do about it?"

"Put a trace on the calls, for a start."

My father coughed nervously. "It'll be all right . . ."

"You've got to tell them."

"Nobody will harm us."

I argued with my father for several minutes, but the more I did so, the more obstinate he became. Finally, I gave up.

"Whoever they are," he said with firmness, "they'll tire of doing this nonsense."

I hoped he was right.

The next day, in a bizarre synchronicity with events in Melbourne, I, too, began to receive mysterious telephone calls. Whenever I picked up the receiver, however, there were no direct threats at the other end of the line, only silence. This happened about a dozen times; in normal circumstances I would probably not have given these calls too much thought, but now I found them unnerving—I suspected that they might be related to my father's story and to the appearance of the photograph. What did these people want from my father and me?

Matters escalated over the following week. Then, just as the calls stopped, I had a strange encounter in the Bodleian Library.

I was standing in a queue to use a photocopier, absorbed in a book and paying no attention to those around me. Suddenly, I heard a man's voice with an American accent directly behind me.

"The worst time of the day," he said.

"Sorry?" I looked up from my book.

"The queue."

I nodded in a not unfriendly way and returned to my book, but I had the uncanny sensation that the man's eyes were staring into my back.

"Reading history?" I heard him ask.

I turned and nodded once again.

He squinted at the cover of the book. "*Police Brigades in the Second World War*. That's a specialized topic," he said.

"Some independent research," I explained.

"You Belarusian?"

"My father is," I replied.

"A little family history, then?"

"You could say that."

"My family were Jews from the Ukraine. Many died at the hands of the police battalions in operation there."

"I'm sorry to hear that," I said. "My father's family died under similar conditions in Belarus."

"Your father is from Minsk?"

"No. Most likely from a town not far from there. Dzerzhinsk."

"Most likely?"

"It's a long story," I excused myself. I was beginning to feel uncomfortable with his intrusiveness.

"No matter," he answered. "Another time?"

I nodded and turned once again to where I had left off in my book.

Then I heard his voice again and saw his proffered hand in front of me. "Samuel Schwartz," he said.

"Mark Kurzem."

At that moment a copier became free and I dashed for it, relieved to have broken contact.

About thirty minutes later, as I was coming down the stairs in front of the library, someone called my name. It was Samuel Schwartz. He caught up with me.

"Hello!" he said, full of cheer. "We meet again!" He glanced at his watch. "You feel like grabbing a bite to eat?"

I didn't want to, but he caught me off guard. I couldn't think of an excuse quickly enough. "That'd be nice," I replied.

He looked around. "King's Arms?" he suggested.

We crossed to the pub on the opposite corner.

The King's Arms was crawling with students at this hour, but I managed to find a quiet corner while Schwartz fetched drinks.

He found the table and put down two pints of beer, even though I'd asked for a cola. He sat down closely beside me and raised his glass in a toast.

"To poor old Belarus and the Ukraine! So how's the research?" he inquired.

"So-so."

"You're not English, are you?"

"Australian."

"Ah. From Down Under."

"It's all a matter of perspective," I replied.

He laughed.

"And you?"

"The States. New York." He took a sip of his beer. "This topic you're looking at . . ."

"Yes?" I gave him a questioning look.

"The shadow never leaves you, does it? Even if you're from a later generation."

I nodded.

"So how is the situation in Australia with these war criminals?"

I shrugged.

"Australia seems to be full of them," he commented. "Judging by their record to date, the Australian authorities haven't been keen to prosecute. The last wave—the vicious camp guards, the middle-ranking officers, the Balts—were given free entry to Australia and allowed to construct new identities or blatantly flaunt their old ones. The blessing of Australia, its freedom, bearing a poisonous fruit."

"You seem to know a lot about it," I said.

"I follow the news. Besides, these criminals are part of my history," he replied pensively. "I find myself thinking about what I might be able to do in hunting them down. Become a Mossad agent!" He laughed self-mockingly. But I could feel him shrewdly evaluating my reaction.

"Why not try the Wiesenthal Center?" I suggested lamely.

"A tough job. A necessary one, don't you agree?" he said, as if seriously considering my suggestion.

"Of course."

"One is morally obliged to help in any search if one has information to offer." He glanced at me meaningfully.

I understood then where his conversation was headed.

I hadn't been able to place this man but was certain that I'd seen him before. But now it struck me. He was the younger of the two men I'd seen with Elli on the steps outside the Bodleian. I immediately dismissed the thought. "I'm becoming paranoid," I told myself. Whether this was the case or not, I felt uncomfortable in his company.

"Thanks for the beer, Samuel," I said, rising from my seat.

Schwartz was nonplussed but reached out to shake my hand. "I hope we can meet again soon," he said.

"Yes," I said.

What I hoped would be my last glimpse of Schwartz was of him seated, his clasped hands resting on the table, smiling benignly at me.

Three days after this incident, Elli invited me for a dinner at her house. I wanted to steer clear of her, but she insisted and I accepted reluctantly.

"My father will be here as well," she said. "He's just arrived this morning from Israel for the weekend."

As she led me into her dining room that night, I immediately recognized her father as the other man I'd seen with her and Schwartz outside the library days earlier. Over dinner he questioned me vigorously about my father's story, fishing for details, until I felt that I was being interrogated for some hidden purpose. He grew frustrated as I began to resist his probing with vague answers. We had barely finished the meal when I begged off, saying that I had a fierce headache. Rejecting their offers of medication and assistance, I quickly exited and hailed a taxi.

The taxi dropped me in front of my house. I noticed a car parked on the other side of the street, facing into traffic. This was not unusual, but my senses, already on the alert after dinner, registered that the man—it was too dark to notice anything other than that he appeared youngish—behind the steering wheel was closely watching my house.

I noticed that he sat more upright as I made my way along the path to the front door. I let myself in and went upstairs without turning on any lights.

I peered through a crack in the curtains of an upstairs window.

The man strained to look up at the house, and I saw his face at the windshield. It was Samuel Schwartz.

I decided to confront him and headed downstairs. But by the time I had fumbled with the door's inside lock and dashed out onto the street, his car had disappeared.

I never saw Elli's father or Samuel Schwartz again.

I never met with Elli again.

In the days that followed, I would occasionally spot her on the street in the city center, but was careful to avoid her. She called me a few times as well; I remained friendly but distant.

Ellie gradually disappeared completely from my life. I was glad to be free of her. I realized how naive I had been. I knew nothing about her background. I was to learn later that her father had been an investigator for Israeli intelligence. I wondered how much of the intrigue that had developed, and would continue to emerge, had been triggered by my decision to confide in her.

On the same evening of Elli's dinner, long after Schwartz's car had disappeared, my telephone rang.

Before I could even say hello, I heard my father's voice at the other end of the line. "Mark?" he said. "Are you there?"

"This is late to call," I replied.

"The house was broken into last night," my father blurted out immediately. "We'd been out and when we got home we noticed from the car that there was a light on in the bedroom. Your mum was sure we hadn't left it on by mistake. I told her to wait in the car while I unlocked the front door quietly. I opened it just a fraction, and the cats flew out with their tails on end. I got the fright of my life.

"I opened the door farther and called out. There was no reply. I went into the hallway and I could see immediately that somebody had trashed the living room. All our papers and documents were strewn everywhere. The bedroom had been completely ransacked, too. The lock on my wardrobe door was shattered, and all the contents dragged out.

"The strange thing is that nothing of value was taken. Not even our camera, television, or video, or Mum's jewelry. Only our papers had been gone through."

"Did you call the police?"

"Nah . . ."

I'd had this same conversation with my father sometime earlier.

"Whoever it was, they were looking for something but not valuables. Probably the photograph . . ."

I agreed. The culprit would not have known that my father kept any item to do with his identity, including his photographs, in his brown case.

"Still, you need to report it," I insisted.

My father ignored what I had just said. "Look, don't worry about things here," he said. "I'll keep you informed."

With that, he pleaded fatigue and hung up.

Now it seemed that with the appearance of the photograph my parents were in physical danger. Over the last week or so I had come to feel that the task of uncovering my father's past would also involve protecting him—and my mother—from something that I wasn't yet able to clearly identify.

Although I had not seen the photograph, its existence unsettled me more than any other of my father's mementos. How many more images of my father were floating out there in people's wardrobes, cupboards, and photo albums, the secret storehouses of their past?

The question was answered almost before I had formed it.

By the time my mother and father arrived late the following week, another surprise was in store for me.

My father with Sergeant Kulis, tending the floral insignia of the Latvian SS at Volhov, near the Russian front, autumn 1943.

My father with Sergeant Kulis at Volhov, autumn 1943.

My father with other soldiers from his troop, Volhov, 1943.

The mysterious photograph that my father retrieved from Daugavas.

A sympathetic letter from an elderly woman had reached my father the day before he had left for Oxford. It was from Ventspils, a regional city in northwestern Latvia. She made no mention of how some enclosed photos came to be in her possession, only that she felt my father should have them.

He passed me the envelope. It contained a series of three photographs of my father in his SS uniform in the company of his "rescuer," Sergeant Jekabs Kulis. The sergeant and my father were pictured tending what initially seemed to be a small garden plot in a camp. My father told me that it had been taken at the barracks in Velikiye Luki, south of Leningrad. It must have been in the autumn of 1943, before Lobe sent him back to Riga for trying to escape from the front.

"Look," he said, placing the tip of his index finger closer to the flowers. They were arranged to depict the emblem of the Latvian SS.

Troubling as these images were, they did not have as disquieting an effect as the photograph I had been waiting to see: my father posing with pistol and rifle slung over his shoulder in the midst of other members of the Eighteenth Battalion.

Despite the slight physical menace that hovered in the background, I felt optimistic for the first time since my father's visit to Oxford. From nothing at all we'd unearthed a village where my father might have spent the first five years of his life. And we had made first contact with a man, Erick Galperin, who might turn out to be his half brother.

These were joyful discoveries, but they were tinged with sadness—a haunting reminder of what had been lost—brother, sister, mother, father, aunts, grandparents, uncles—everyone who made little Ilya who he was.

CHAPTER TWENTY-SIX
KOIDANOV

Our plane circled above Minsk airport, waiting for permission to land. As we descended, we saw a number of planes dotted around the perimeter of the main runway, many of them rusty and dilapidated, and all partly dismantled for their spare parts.

Erick Galperin was waiting for us in the arrivals terminal. He was modestly dressed in a suit that matched my father's but had seen better days. He stepped forward shyly to greet my father and then presented my mother with flowers. There were numerous introductions to be made. My father introduced me to Erick and his wife, Sonya, who in turn introduced us to their children, Dimitri and Irena, likely my cousins.

Matters grew more confusing as we were then presented with a procession of individuals who all claimed to be distantly related to my father. An elderly woman named Luba, an English teacher from a town near Minsk, introduced herself to my father as "your father's wife's cousin's daughter." My father smiled politely, but there was a glimmer of amusement in his eyes as he leaned across and whispered to me, "God forbid. What have you gotten me into?"

"No," I countered, "this is your family. You got me into this!"

When our entourage finally exited to the forecourt, we were faced with our transportation for the visit: an old blue minibus decorated with polka-dot curtains, plastic flowers, and party lights flashing on and off in what seemed to be a gesture of welcome.

The driver stood proudly next to the rear door and with a wave of his hand beckoned us to climb on board. The interior was also decked out in vivid blue and was smothered in the overpowering scent of air freshener. My mother retched involuntarily.

Seated toward the rear of the van was a young woman in her early twenties who was chewing gum. She was a bottle blond and wore wrap-around dark sunglasses. "Hello," she said in languorous English. "I am Natasha, a friend of Erick's and your interpreter. I've been waiting for you." She peered over the rim of her sunglasses and continued to chew gum as she offered us her hand.

With a slight pop from the exhaust, the bus moved forward jauntily onto the highway to Minsk. The road was deserted for the entire journey, apart from an occasional horse and cart moving slowly along its dusty shoulder. Erick, speaking Russian, pointed out sights to us en route as Natasha, acting as sultry as she could, gave desultory and dubious interpretations of Erick's words. My mother held her hand her hand above her face and rolled her eyes at me. This very serious visit was becoming more surreal by the moment.

As we entered downtown Minsk, we were rescued from Natasha's commentary by the driver, who turned on the sound system. In an instant, the van was transformed into a mobile disco as Russian pop blared out through loudspeakers, as if to announce our arrival to the population of Minsk. Judging from the reactions of people we passed by the side of the street, Minsk knew we were there—pedestrians turned to see where such a racket was coming from, and when they spotted the bus, they pointed at us and burst out laughing.

We eventually stopped in front of a vast, run-down Soviet hotel. A flashing neon sign spelled out HOTEL PLANETA AND CASINO in bright red letters.

"It looks more like a brothel," said my mother.

We checked in, and with Erick's help found our rooms. Our floor was guarded by a large elderly woman, the perfect babushka. Ensconced on a sofa opposite the elevator doors on our floor, she was the first of many such porters we would meet. She gave us an appraising look, nodded dourly, and returned to her knitting.

The next morning I rose early for our journey to Koidanov, which lay about twenty miles to the southwest of Minsk.

I made my way down to the foyer and spotted my father standing at the hotel's panoramic window, gazing at the view of downtown Minsk in the near distance, a scape of low-lying buildings, mostly modern but punctuated by the odd Soviet monument and the occasional prewar construction that had survived the devastation of the German invaders.

Nearby I saw Erick standing with my mother and an attractive, vivacious woman. "I'm Galina," she said. "Your new interpreter." I was surprised. She explained that she was to replace Natasha, our Mata Hari from the previous evening. Natasha had been "fired" and, mysteriously, no explanation was forthcoming. (Later I cornered Galina to find out the reason, and she had merely said the word "vodka" and mimed swilling from a bottle.)

Galina turned out to be an excellent replacement. Quite the opposite of Natasha, she didn't chew gum or wear dark glasses. There was nothing of the vamp about her. She was forthright and spoke flawless and idiomatic English.

As we walked toward the bus, I saw the driver lean into the front cabin and turn on the flashing roof lights. He then looked at us gleefully, giving us a thumbs-up sign and hoping for our approval. We embarked, the engine rattled loudly, and with a few jerks we took off into the traffic.

After ten minutes or so on a narrow highway, we came to a turnoff with a battered sign: DZERZHINSK 14. As we drove through the industrial sprawl on its outskirts, it seemed merely to epitomize a drab, industrial Soviet town. And with its expanse of gray concrete public housing it was clear that Dzerzhinsk had expanded since the war.

"Not far now," Erick declared as we wound our way through streets. Then, without warning, we came upon an enclave of old, colorfully painted wooden houses with carved shuttered windows on half-paved streets. "This neighborhood was the village before the war," Galina translated for Erick.

I glanced at my father: he was staring out of the window pensively, his hand held to his cheek. This gesture was to become habitual during our journey. At other times, however, he would withdraw into himself, holding his hand to his cheek, only to reemerge moments later either claiming or rejecting what he had just seen as part of his own past.

"Dad?" I whispered, lightly touching his arm. I didn't want to startle him.

He didn't respond.

My mother gently grasped his elbow so that he snapped out of his dreamlike state. His eyes were intensely blue and alive with curiosity.

"Do you recognize anything?" my mother asked.

My father shook his head. "Not anything specific, but it all seems very familiar."

Erick leaned across to the driver, shouting instructions for him to pull over. He jumped out of the rear of the minibus and beckoned us all to join him on the deserted street. It was midmorning and the houses were closed up, but when I turned around unexpectedly I saw several curtains twitch. Our arrival had not gone unnoticed.

Erick looked at my father.

"This is the street you grew up on," he said. "October Street."

My father turned slowly in a circle, again lightly touching his cheek. "I just don't know," he said.

Erick grasped my father's hand and led him two houses farther down the street. We followed. "You grew up in this house," Erick stated emphatically, pointing at the house in front of us. There was little to distinguish this house from any of the others in the row.

"Here?" My father was surprised.

Erick nodded his head several times.

My father was silent as he examined the exterior of the house. He approached the front fence and stared even more intently at the building before him.

Erick joined my father. "Your home!" I heard Erick insist.

My father turned to my mother and me. He gave a shrug, looking bewildered, and came over to us.

"I don't remember this place," he said in a dispirited tone.

"Perhaps it's been altered," my mother suggested.

"That's right," I added, trying to sound encouraging.

But my father remained doubtful. "I don't remember," he repeated.

Erick must have sensed the gist of our exchange because he became slightly agitated and began to repeat "your house" over and over. His insistence only confused my father even more so that he retreated into himself, uttering in a low voice, "My home was different. It had a drive down one side where my father had a cart and next to that there was a shed where he worked and the apple tree that I used to climb. I remember that clearly."

His recollection made him more resolute. "No," he said. "This is not the house I grew up in. It's the wrong house."

"Are you absolutely sure, Dad?" I asked.

"Absolutely," he said slowly.

I was disappointed for my father and for all of us, but I admired his faith in his own memories and his refusal to yield to the incredible pressure we all felt to confirm Erick as his half brother.

Everybody remained still, waiting for him to make the next move. My father shook his head and looked away from the source of his disappointment. I watched as he crossed to the other side of the street. With a subtle nod he beckoned me over.

"I must be a Panok after all," he said with finality. "Not a Galperin. I hoped for all our sakes that this would work out. We'll have to start all over again."

I felt grim but my father didn't seem to notice. He was immersed in his own train of thought.

"What can I say to Erick?" he said with compassion in his voice. "He was so happy to find he had a brother. Did you see his face? This will break his heart."

And I had seen my father's face. Despite his reservations, I knew that he, too, had hoped that some of his early childhood might be returned to him.

Something had to be done to salvage the immediate situation. We couldn't simply turn around, get back in the van, and with a brief apology make a quick exit from Belarus.

I returned to Erick, who was still waiting in front of the house. "You grew up here after the war?" I asked through Galina.

"Yes," Erick replied, shifting on the spot and not looking at me. I wondered what the matter was and then immediately reprimanded myself—he must have been as disheartened as my father.

"Your father didn't change houses when he came back from the war?" I persisted.

"No," he retorted, now slightly belligerent and pointing at the house. "He returned to this house where I was born."

"When did your father sell it?"

"In the early seventies, when he got sick. He came to live with us in Minsk until he died."

"Who lives there now?"

"I don't know," Erick replied. The glimmer of a scowl crossed his face. I decided to let the matter drop, partly because my father was now moving slowly along the street, looking in all directions. His expression changed, becoming more alert. He stopped. He had seen something that the rest of us could not.

"Over there seems familiar," he said, pointing farther up the street.

My father headed off toward an intersection, where he again came to a stop. He turned to look at us. "I know this," he said about the intersecting street. "It goes down to the village hall, I am certain of it."

My father smiled broadly. "I remember the hall," he said. "That's where I went to see a film one time, when a traveling show came to town. I went with another boy, my friend. We walked down the hill together, hand in hand. I can't see his face or remember his name. But I do remember that my father tossed me a few coins for an ice cream from the man who stood in front of the hall. That was the first time I ever tasted ice cream."

My father forged ahead. A few yards farther into that street we came to another intersection. My father stopped dead in his tracks. We waited in silence.

"This is the way the soldiers . . ." he said, staring down the path before him. There was no need to complete the sentence. He was visibly shaken, but after several moments he seemed to gather himself. With a wave of his hand, he motioned for us to follow him and set off quickly along the path. We hastened after him.

About two hundred yards farther along, the path opened up into a grassy space about the size of a football field.

"That's where it happened," he said in a low voice.

My father led the way forward, but he had lost his vigor. He walked with trepidation, almost tiptoeing, as if he were creeping up on the scene from over fifty years ago and he did not want the soldiers to notice him.

He turned at one point and summoned us to keep up as if we were reluctant tourists who had suddenly lost their taste for the journey ahead and begun to dawdle.

But there was no going back.

He came to a stop. His eyes were empty, and he had forgotten that we were standing right beside him. He appeared to recognize a topography from the past and began to make comments aloud, as if confirming what he saw to another person.

"Yes," he said. "This is it . . ."

He looked back up the path he had just taken. "It's strange," he said, suddenly becoming aware of us. "I remember being led down that path toward the soldiers. But it was steeper before, so I could see what was happening ahead of us. I was holding my mother's hand and my little brother's as well. But I'm confused. I was with them, but I didn't go to my death with them. Something must have happened to have stopped the executions that day, but for the life of me I have no memory of what it was."

My father turned in all directions.

"Over there," he said, pointing at a track off to the right. "That's the direction I came from when I ran away from home." Then the sequence of events seemed to get more confusing. "It happened during the night after we'd been led down the hill, after my mother had told me that we were all going to die in the morning."

He headed over to the path and began to retrace his steps from the night of his escape. He walked tentatively across the open space as if trying to find his way in the dark.

"Up there," he said, this time pointing off slightly to the left. "That's where I headed—up the hill and into the trees."

We all turned our heads in that direction. There was a hillock with a few trees at its peak.

My father appeared to forget about us once again and strode across to the hill. Though I felt slightly ashamed to do so, I hurried ahead of the others so that I could continue to eavesdrop on his words.

"Not as steep as I remember," he said. "It seemed like a mountain at the time. I climbed as fast as my legs could take me."

My father stopped and stared back down the slope with a frown on his face. But he was unaware of the scene unfolding in front of him: my mother had run out of breath and was now struggling to climb the slope. Fortunately, at that moment I saw Galina and Erick come to my mother's aid, and together they made their way slowly in our direction.

By this point my father had reached the top of the hillock and, hand to cheek, stood very still looking down over the vista below us. He nodded grimly. "Yes," he said. "Yes."

At that moment the others reached us.

"You okay, Mum?" I asked. She nodded, still quite breathless.

"Trees, Erick," my father called out. "Were there more trees here?"

My father hadn't even noticed that my mother had joined him. And for a moment I was annoyed by his lack of regard for her condition.

"Yes," Erick replied. "I used to play up here as a child sometimes. They removed many of the trees years ago."

My father was silent, and we waited for him to speak.

"In the morning I saw the people being led from over there. Near that cottage. I was peering between the trees. They were lined up on that hill as the soldiers pushed and prodded them down in groups," my father said, indicating the path we had taken earlier. "Then I saw my mother and the children and"—my father gasped as if the air had violently been knocked out of him—"the rest of my family were among them, and they were almost there . . . the pit."

My father took a deep breath. "My mother was holding my brother and sister. She looked away from what was going to happen to her and that's when I am sure she saw me up among the trees. For a split second I saw her eyes. She recognized me.

"I am sure that she must have been beside herself with worry when she'd woken in the morning and found me gone. At least she knew I was alive, for what that was worth . . ."

I stared at my father, who seemed to be in a state of shock. "I bit my hand not to cry out," he said in a strangled whisper. I saw him raise his hand and bite it as he had on that day, as if reliving the horrific scene. A trickle of blood dripped down his wrist and onto the cuff of his shirt.

My mother had noticed, too, at the same instant. "Alex!" she cried out, but he didn't hear her.

Panicked, she dashed forward and began to shake him. "Alex!" She was alarmed. "Stop it! Please, stop it, Alex!"

My father returned to us. His face was ashen and he seemed fragile and disoriented. He stared down at his bleeding hand. My mother pulled out her handkerchief and gently bandaged it, while my father stood like a helpless child.

"C'mon, luv, let's get out of here," my mother said, putting her arm in his and moving him away from the edge of the hill. My father didn't resist.

As we made our way down the hill, Erick pointed us in the direction of a simple monument on the right. It was the memorial to "the martyrs of the Koidanov massacre," as he described them. It had obviously been neglected for many years and was partly obscured by the bushes and tall grass.

"This way!" Erick ordered, and, dashing ahead of us, he began to tear away at the foliage. By the time we reached him, he had managed to clear the debris from around the dedication plaque.

Reading aloud, Galina translated it for us: "Here lie sixteen hundred men, women, and children who suffered at the hands of the Fascist invaders."

My father stepped forward with his head bowed. My mother, who stood close behind, passed him three roses that she'd had the foresight to bring with her from the hotel.

We stood quietly as my father placed the roses at the base of the memorial, his mother's gravestone.

As we made our way slowly back from the site of the mass grave, my father stopped and took me to one side. "This is my village," he whispered. "I'm sure of it. But I'm still not certain that I'm a Galperin." Then, leaving me with that thought, he took off in pursuit of the others, who had reached the base of the hill.

We had been so absorbed in our search, we hadn't noticed the sun come out. Although it threw off only the palest spring light, its mere presence alleviated some interior chill. We'd also been oblivious to the attention our visit had attracted.

A few yards away, a number of children had gathered by a bench, staring at us with both shyness and frank curiosity. One of the boys waved to us, indicating that we were welcome to make use of the bench. He wore a cheeky grin, and, as we approached to sit down, he called out to us, "Hello, Mister America."

"Not America," Galina explained. "Australia."

This provoked a wide-eyed response. We must have seemed very exotic. The children began to gather around chanting "kangaroo" at us. My mother burst out laughing with pleasure—she loved being around children—and took a seat on the bench, as did my father and Erick. I remained standing and only half listening to my mother and father as they tried to tell them more about Australia.

I was restless. I looked around and only then noticed that a handful of people had come out onto the front porches of their houses and were observing us silently. From where I was standing they all appeared to be quite elderly, and my immediate thought was whether any of them had witnessed the massacre. I wondered whether they had been the ones my father had remembered standing on their balconies, laughing and chatting as women and children were led to their deaths.

I suggested to Galina that she and I walk past these houses. I was not surprised when a man, no more than seventy years old, called out to us from where he was seated on his front porch. We stopped.

His face was alert with curiosity. He spoke and Galina translated. "What are you doing here?"

"I am trying to find out more about what went on in this square during the war," I said.

"The massacre by the Fascists?" He fixed me with a shrewd, assessing gaze. "Why?" he asked.

"My father's family perished in it," I answered.

"Jews, were they?"

I nodded.

The man gave a low grunt and shifted the blanket that covered his knees.

"I saw it," he said, after a silence of several moments. "I grew up in this house and from here I could see everything. I remember it better than what I ate for lunch today." He chuckled to himself.

"What happened that day?" I asked.

"It began in the middle of the night. We were woken by the sound of men in the square. Father and I went out onto the porch, as did some of our neighbors. Soldiers and a group of men—about twenty or thirty of them—were there. We couldn't understand what was going on. The soldiers were guarding the men who were digging.

"One of the officers caught sight of us and ordered us back indoors, telling us that we'd be put to work digging as well if we didn't disappear.

"The sound of the digging went on till first light. That's when I sneaked a look through the window." He indicated the window behind him. "I couldn't believe my eyes—there was an enormous gaping hole in the earth where the square had been."

The man rose unsteadily to his feet and shuffled to the edge of the veranda and closer to us. Slowly he raised his arm and pointed in the direction of the slope we had descended earlier with my father.

"They came from there," he said. "Women. Children, babies, old people. Jews, they were. Hundreds of them. The queue led all the way back up the hill as far as the eye could see.

"The babies were wailing and many of the children were in tears. Their mothers were trying to calm them, but the soldiers showed no patience. They prodded at the little ones with their bayonets, screaming at them to shut up."

His finger shifted in the direction of where my parents were still

The memorial to the martyrs of Koidanov at the site of the massacre.

seated on the bench. "The soldiers pushed and shoved them down there. And over there, near the memorial, that's where the officers stood. You can see that it's higher than the square, so it gave them a good view over the crowd. They were German; their uniforms were different than those of the soldiers."

The man paused for a moment.

"At the base of the hill, the Jews were put into groups of about ten or twelve. Soldiers forced them to undress and then lined them up in front of the pit. Then another group of soldiers—with rifles—stepped forward.

"I knew by then why the earth had been dug up, and those Jews knew what was going to happen to them. Not a single one of them made any effort to fight back or run away. True, there was nowhere for them to flee in the face of those men and their weapons. But better that than give up the way they did . . .

"The soldiers raised their rifles and fired into the line so that the people fell backward into the hole. Sometimes if a body didn't fall in the right way, a soldier would step forward and kick it the rest of the way in.

"They didn't waste their bullets on the babies or children; they simply used the bayonet. A quick sharp lunge and that was the end of that one."

Throughout his description, the man's voice had remained low-key and the expression on his face blank so that it was impossible to tell how this had affected him.

"This was repeated several times," he continued. "A new group was shot and shoved into the pit. Like clockwork. Even though you could see that many of the soldiers were drunk, they were efficient.

"And all the way up that slope the Jews queued in silence, watching what was happening below—to their friends and neighbors, members of their family—and waiting for their turn."

The man turned away from the open space before him. If it had once been the village square, it was now a derelict place used by children unaware of its poisonous history.

"It was then that the strangest thing happened." His hand trembled as he raised his arm to the sky. "Without any warning at all, I swear, the sky turned black and the heavens opened. Not just rain, but a deluge. A flood of such power.

"In seconds the square turned into a muddy mess. The soldiers and the Jews were drenched and slipping all over the place. The Jews began to panic. I could understand why—I did, too, from the safety of my house. It was mayhem. I could see the officers giving orders for the soldiers to control the crowd.

"And then the thunder began, and bolts of lightning began striking so close to the ground. It was as if God himself had descended and was going to destroy us all." The man crossed himself before continuing.

"Even the soldiers became spooked: some of the firing squad had put down their rifles. They didn't want to continue with the killings. The commanding officer must've made the decision to stop because next thing the Jews were being forced back up the hill and into their houses. Even the ones who were already naked and about to die were forced to dress—they grabbed at any piece of clothing from the pile that had been dumped by the pit from the previous victims—and then ordered up the hill.

"After that I saw the remaining soldiers gather their weapons and packs and head off. They left the pit just as it was: open and piled with bodies, and filling up with water. The rain didn't cease all day, not for a single moment, until nightfall."

In the background was the sound of children laughing and playing in the square.

"When it was completely dark," the man said, "I crept out onto the porch. I stood there for some time. At first I thought it was silent. But soon, I detected the sound of movement coming from the pit.

"I was petrified. I ran back inside and told my father, who gave me a clip around the head for disobeying the soldiers by going outside. He told me that it was the sound of the dead bodies as they shifted around on top of each other. I'd heard groans, too, and told my father that some of the people were still alive. But he only laughed. 'It's just the ghosts departing from their bodies,' he told me. 'Leave them alone or they'll take you with them as well.'

"That put the fear of God into me. I went to my room and closed the curtains, not even having the courage to look out the window anymore.

"The next morning I was woken early by the sounds of gunshots. I parted the curtain a fraction and peered through. It was the same scene as the day before—the killing had begun again. It must've been going on for some time because the hill was by then half-emptied of Jews. I crawled back into my bed and covered my head so I wouldn't hear the cries and wails that had begun to reach my ears.

"As I lay there I wondered what the Jews had done the previous night. I'd dropped off to sleep despite my fear of the ghosts, but they must have been awake all through the night knowing what was going to happen to them in the morning."

The man took another break from what he was saying and this time lit a cigarette.

"Just one more thing," I said.

He looked at me innocently.

"What did you think about what you saw?" I asked.

He shrugged and rubbed the back of his head. I couldn't tell whether it was out of embarrassment. "They say not a single Jew survived," he said with finality.

But he didn't answer my question.

With the clarity of his recollections, this man had unwittingly solved a mystery that had fostered doubt in the Oxford professors: it was possible that my father had begun to make the journey down the slope in the company of his mother, holding his little brother's hand, only to be turned back by the eerie storm before he faced his own death.

That would explain how his mother knew exactly what was in store for herself and her children when the storm was over. She had gathered her young son onto her knee and told him that they would all die the following day, prompting him to flee during the night.

The man had retired to his seat once again and covered his knees with his rug. I thanked him so profusely for speaking with me that he was taken aback.

"Nothing at all," he replied, still smoking.

He hadn't the slightest inkling about the burden he had lifted from me. Even though I had trusted the general sweep of my father's story, the Oxford professors had planted in me a seed of doubt.

Galina and I walked back slowly toward the bench. All around us was silent apart from the laughter of my parents and Erick as they chatted with the children.

Although it could never be proved beyond dispute, two days in Belarus had already reinforced the truth of what my father had claimed. Later, after I had returned to Oxford, I wrote to the professor who had been most insistent that my father had concocted the incident with his mother. I explained to him what I had learned "on the ground" in Koidanov. He never replied.

CHAPTER TWENTY-SEVEN
CONNECTIONS

We were seated in a café not far from the site of the extermination, where Erick had brought us for a lunch of *plov*, a Russian specialty akin to pilaf. "My mother never cooked anything like this," my father said to me, making a sour face. "I'd never have forgotten it." After lunch my father became immersed in conversation with Erick, telling him further details of his story and of his life in Australia.

I'd heard these stories many times and decided to take a walk around the neighborhood. Within minutes I was surprised to find myself back where the visit to Koidanov had begun—on October Street.

To my right I recognized the house that Erick had insisted was my father's. Then I began to make my way along October Street in the opposite direction. I had gone only a short distance when, unable to resist a *plov*-induced torpor, I located a patch of grass by the side of the road and sat down. I let my eyelids droop shut. As they lowered, I could just make out the staring face of a babushka at a window in the house opposite. I raised my head slightly to look, but, caught spying, she snapped the curtains shut.

I must have drifted into a half-sleep momentarily; a sharp cackle and snorts of laughter close to my ear roused me. Still on the ground, I was surrounded by four elderly women, all wider than they were tall, dressed in head scarves and colorful skirts over trousers. The one who'd cackled in my ear gave me a broad, toothless smile, then eyed me suspiciously.

She stretched herself upright and began to chatter with the other ba-bushkas, who shuffled around me on their heavy feet.

Then she spoke. I didn't understand a single word she said.

She spoke again, and I could tell that she was repeating herself. Another joined in, saying the same thing.

Then I recognized one of the half-dozen words I understood in Russian.

"Foreigner?" she asked.

I looked up, shading my eyes against the sun, and nodded my head vigorously. "Yes," I said. "Foreigner."

The women clapped their hands together. "You speak Russian!" one of them exclaimed with delight.

"No," I laughed, waving my hand in front of me. Spurred on by the breakthrough, such as it was, I began to explain in English, "I'm here with my father."

They looked at me blankly.

"He's looking for his village," I went on. "The home he grew up in."

They exchanged glances with each other and then burst into roars of laughter, shaking their heads at me.

"Papa," I said, banging my chest. I was fired up now and tried another strategy. I jumped to my feet and began to mime that I was searching for a house. I held my hand above my eyes, walked over to the fence of a house, and peered intently into its garden. Then, putting on a sad expression, I shook my head, before moving on to the next house and miming the same actions.

The women continued to stare at me, open-jawed, as if I were an alien who had just descended on October Street. I was on the verge of giving up, when all of a sudden one of them caught on.

"House of father?" she asked.

"Yes." I was delighted. "Yes."

The others nodded and made comprehending noises. "October Street?" another chimed in.

"Yes, yes," I repeated.

"Name?" Another Russian word I could understand. The ringleader looked at me shrewdly.

"Which should I try, Galperin or Panok?" I wondered aloud to myself. One of them immediately picked up on what I had just said.

"Galperin?" she asked. "Galperin?"

I nodded. "Galperin house?" I asked, pointing in the direction of the house we had seen that morning.

They shook their heads in unison. One of them pointed in the opposite direction, farther down a section of the street I'd not yet seen. I followed the line of her finger, but I couldn't see where she was pointing. Good-naturedly, she took my hand and led me along the street with the others in tow until, about a dozen houses down, we came to a stop outside a neglected-looking green building.

"Galperin," she said, pointing.

"Galperin?" I asked.

She nodded firmly, folding her arms.

"It might be the house," I thought. There was a driveway that ran alongside the house that matched my father's description. I wanted to know who, if anybody, lived there now. I needed to get a closer look.

I tried to explain this to my companions but failed. Then I remembered Galina. I made a gesture to the women that they should wait for me and, without waiting to check whether they understood or not, dashed off in the direction of the café.

Everybody was just as I had left them. My father was still involved in an intense conversation with Erick, gesticulating dramatically to make his childhood Russian clear.

Neither of them noticed my breathless arrival, and I didn't want to disturb them. Galina was chatting with my mother.

"Can I borrow you for a moment?" I asked Galina.

"Something the matter?" my mother asked, looking up at me.

"Nothing," I replied, not wanting to build up anyone's hope at this stage.

Galina questioned the women while I waited beside her anxiously.

"They insist that this was the Galperin house from before the war until sometime in the seventies," she said excitedly. In her short time with us, Galina had generously become caught up in our search.

"Are they certain about this?" I asked.

Galina turned to the women and asked them again. In response they nodded their heads resolutely.

"Ask them who owns it now."

"A woman from a nearby village," came the reply. One woman was certain that it was a place called Fanipol, about ten miles from Koidanov. She also knew the woman's name.

"Gildenberg," she said. "Dina Gildenberg. She's from one of the old Jew families of Koidanov. She bought the house in . . . when did old Solomon Galperin die? It must have been 1976 . . . no . . . 1975. The son . . . what was his name? Erick, that's right . . . from Minsk, sold it to Dina Gildenberg about ten years ago. The house was deserted for years." Then she added, "She's in Koidanov now. I've seen her. She does casual work in the canning factory up the road from here."

"I want to meet her now," I declared. "Will she be there?"

"Probably. I don't know her," the woman answered.

It seemed typical of village life that the women knew all about Dina but didn't actually know her.

"Where is the factory?" I demanded.

The women volunteered to lead me there. As we made our way to the factory, they remained in high spirits and fired questions at me about who I was. At one point, one of them said, "You're not a Yid, then, are you?" only to be hushed by the others.

I answered their questions as best I could, but all the while I was thinking about Erick. Had he led us to the wrong house? Why?

Galina volunteered to inquire after Dina while I stood in a huddle with the women outside the small factory. As the minutes passed, they became restless. There was a mumbled discussion and suddenly they moved off, giving me a cursory wave. I was startled. I didn't know any of their names. I hadn't even thanked them. But before I could make a move to go after them, they had disappeared into the next street. Just at that moment Galina reappeared at the factory door accompanied by a woman whose appearance surprised me even more than the babushka's hasty departure.

She was stockier than my father, but she had his kind and jolly expression, his rosy, chubby cheeks, and the same intense, watery blue eyes. In the center of her face was the same slightly bulbous putty nose and impish smile. It was her persona, though, the same inflection of shyness in her demeanor, that convinced me that she had to be related to him.

Galina introduced her to me, and she took my hand. Dina had been allowed to leave the production line for a short time and agreed to take us back to the house and let us inspect it.

On the way, Dina volunteered as much information as she knew about the family history on her side. She explained that she was related by marriage to the Galperin family. Her father was Boris Gildenberg, and Boris's younger sister, Hana, had been married to Solomon Galperin. They had lived together in the house on October Street. Dina's aunt was the Hana Galperin Erick had spoken of as my father's mother. Dina and my father were likely first cousins. Confirming the babushka's account, she told us that she had bought the house from Erick, who had made the sale in an effort to raise funds to buy a printing press for his business.

Dina's family had been lucky: they'd escaped the Holocaust. Her father and mother moved to Moscow in the late 1930s and Dina had grown up there. She moved to Belarus in the 1980s, after Solomon had passed away. She'd never met him and knew only that his three children had died along with Hana and other family members in the mass killings. Only Solomon had survived the war, but Dina had no idea how.

It appeared that Erick had not even told Dina of our existence, let alone our visit. She was not aware that another of the Galperins, her cousin—if my father was that—had survived under incredible circumstances and that she was about to meet him.

"Erick Galperin could tell you much more about the history of the family and the house," she said.

I remained silent.

We came to a stop outside the house the babushkas had led me to, number 12, October Street, but I wanted to go no further without my father and mother. Galina set off in a hurry to fetch my parents. I told her to say nothing of our discovery. I wanted my father to reach his own conclusions once he had seen the house.

Meanwhile, Dina led me to the door at the side of the house. She pulled out a large key and was about to place it in the lock. I gestured for her to stop. I was reluctant to enter. If this was my father's home, then he should be the first to enter.

"Father," I uttered, hoping that Dina would understand. She must have, as she agreed to wait.

Before very long the blue bus pulled up near the gate and my father sprang from it followed by my mother, Galina, and Erick. My father immediately began to appraise the house, all the while gripping the picket fence. Behind him stood Erick, looking decidedly apprehensive and shifting from foot to foot. I joined them.

"What do you think, Dad?" I asked.

My father raised his hand to quiet me. "It looks familiar," he said in a low voice. "I remember the door being on the side as it is here, and this is like the drive where my father used to put his horse and cart. But there should have been a shed on that spot," he said, pointing at the neighboring house adjacent to the driveway. My father held his hand to his cheek.

"Why don't we see if the neighbors are in?" I suggested. I knocked on the door while my father waited at my side. Within moments an elderly peasant couple appeared.

"Yes?" The man eyed us suspiciously. Then he suddenly noticed Erick standing quietly in the background.

"Erick, hello!" he called out, becoming more friendly. Erick nodded sheepishly, then looked away.

My father ignored the exchange. "We are trying to find out about the house next door," he explained. "Before the war, was there something built here, next to the drive?"

"There was a small shed. After the war, old Solomon Galperin sold us this piece of land to build on."

My father shifted away from the house and pointed at the earth. "It would have been about here," he said.

"Yes, exactly there."

My father became more animated. He turned and gazed down the rear garden. "The apple tree," he exclaimed. "There it is." He set off down the yard and we followed behind. He stopped below the tree.

"This could be the tree," my father said, looking at each of us. He wore a look of startled pleasure. "I remember picking apples for my mother. I'd toss them down to her until her apron was overflowing and she'd cry out, 'Enough, no more!'"

It was then that I noticed Dina standing shyly halfway between the house and the apple tree. In all the excitement I had forgotten to explain my father's visit to her. They had exchanged polite nods but remained unaware of exactly who the other was.

"Dad!" I called out, joining Dina.

My father walked back to us and stood awkwardly, smiling and clutching his case.

"Have you heard the name Ilya Galperin?" I asked Dina.

"No . . ." she replied slowly. "Is he a member of Erick's family?"

"He was one of Solomon and Hana's children," I said. "Their eldest boy."

"One of those who perished—" Dina began to say.

"No," my father interrupted. "He might be alive. I might be Ilya."

Dina looked bewildered by my father's declaration, and he tried to explain why he had come to Koidanov. She looked from my father to me and then to Erick, who had joined us. "He is Ilya," Erick said, raising his arm slightly as if introducing my father on stage.

Dina and Erick exchanged words in a language that was not Russian—perhaps it was a Belarusian dialect—but it was obvious that there was tension between them, perhaps because Erick had not told her anything about us beforehand.

I stepped in. "May we see inside the house?" I asked Dina.

My father's orignal home at 12 October Street in Koidanov.

The door squeaked open on its rusting hinges.

I followed behind my father and mother as they tentatively entered the run-down kitchen, which appeared not even to have running water.

"When I bought this house it was deserted," Dina said self-consciously, "and in even worse condition than it is now."

We moved deeper into the house, which consisted of two other rooms. Both were bare of furnishings apart from a solitary chair and a small divan. My father looked around.

"Do you remember this room?" I asked.

"This might have been where I slept . . ." He shifted the chair from its position by the window and stood where it had been.

"The bed would've been here," he said. "I was lying with my head at this end on the night my father said good-bye to me. The dividing curtain must have been over there. Later, I would've seen him leave that way, over there, through the door." My father pointed directly at the main door we'd just entered through, visible in the kitchen on the far side of the house. He stared up at the ceiling.

"My father's feet would've been dangling just over there."

I went over to inspect the ceiling. There was evidence of a trapdoor to the roof space that had been boarded up. My father joined me to inspect it. He noticed something else.

"Look," he said, pointing off to the right. There was a row of about a dozen rusted hooks that had been nailed into a ceiling beam. "Yes." My father nodded. "They could've been used to hang a curtain."

"And when I came to the curtain to eavesdrop on my parents, they were sitting at a table there." My father pointed in the direction of the kitchen.

Dina, who had been watching and listening intently to my father, added that in fact there had been a table there when she'd moved into the house.

"Isn't that correct?" she said, turning to Erick, who'd been strangely silent.

"Yes," he replied uncomfortably.

It seemed as if the layout of the house coincided with my father's memories.

"So *this* was the Galperin house," he said. As if reading my mind at that moment, I heard my father's voice. "From before the war."

"Yes," Erick said.

"I grew up here?"

"Yes."

"I have another memory," my father said, "of a soldier coming into this room. Not a Nazi. A friendly one." My father squinted, trying to remember more. "He was visiting a lady, not my mother, but another who lived with us, I think."

"That must have been your aunt Sonya, Solomon's sister," Erick replied. "She did live here. She died with the rest of the family. She was engaged to a Russian soldier who was sent to the front. Nobody knew what became of him. He never came looking for Sonya after the war. He must have perished, too."

"Can you think of anything else about the history of the house or the family?" I asked.

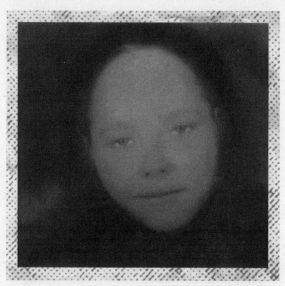

A likely image of Hana Galperin, my father's mother, found in a
dusty bag of photographs in the old family home in Koidanov.

Erick shook his head, as did Dina, but suddenly her expression
changed. "One moment. There is something . . ."

Dina crossed to the divan and began to rummage underneath it. "I
forgot. Last year, some of the floor had to be replaced. The carpenter
found it hidden there. I meant to tell you, Erick. Sorry, I forgot."

We waited expectantly. She rose with something in her hand.
"These."

She dusted off a plastic bag and held it aloft. "Old photos," she declared. "I don't know who the people are. You are welcome to look."

I reached for the bag and sat down on the one chair in the room,
removing a handful of photos. I flipped slowly through faded pictures of
individual faces and family group portraits. It was difficult to say when
these had been taken, but they likely predated the war. Judging by their
garb, some of the people were Jewish. One particular photograph of a
young woman gave me pause. Smiling confidently at the camera, she was
in her early twenties and had an attractive and open face. She was dressed
up in her finest and may have been off to a special occasion. I had no idea

Father and son outside the family home in Koidanov, 1998.

who she was and passed the photograph to my father. He shook his head.

I returned the photographs to the bag and removed another handful, which I began to go through before passing them on to my father. Suddenly I stopped, transfixed. The photograph I held had been partly torn so that its top right corner was missing, but one side of the face of another young woman was still clearly visible.

"It's Krystal," I gasped. Whoever this woman staring intently into the camera was, she was identical to my niece, my brother Andrew's daughter.

My father reached across for the photograph. I was still dazed but I heard him say, "Oh my God," and then pass it to my mother, who similarly exclaimed, wanting to know what a photograph of her teenage granddaughter was doing among these faces from the past.

We were silent, overwhelmed by what we'd just seen.

My mother spoke first, clearing her throat. "The eyes," she said. "And the shape of the face. She's so like Krystal, isn't she?"

"Uncanny," my father replied.

"She must be related to us somehow," I said. "Who is she?" I passed the photograph to Erick. He examined it closely.

"It might be Hana, your mother," he replied. "But I'm not certain. I only saw one photograph of her one time." Erick returned the picture to my father.

"Do you remember this face?" my mother asked gently, looking over her husband's shoulder.

"No," he answered. "But it's so like Krystal, it must be someone close to me. My mother? I must be Ilya Galperin. I believe it." He shook his head.

We were all infected by his sense of astonishment. How could a man with only those two mysterious words—"Panok" and "Koidanov"—have found his way home nearly sixty years later to the room where he had slept as a child in the company of his baby sister and younger brother, to the place where he had been nurtured by his mother and father before the Nazis tore them apart?

I followed my father and the others as they made their way back up the driveway toward the blue bus. I stared at my father's back. He was hunched forward, carrying the bag of photographs that Dina had given to him as a gift. Such a gift. He was still shaking his head in amazement.

CHAPTER TWENTY-EIGHT
SOLOMON AND VOLODYA

I t was late afternoon, but the day wasn't over for us. Erick wanted us to meet an old, dear friend of Solomon's. He'd been sullen since we'd discovered Solomon and Hana's house.

The bus rattled to a halt outside a run-down cottage: paint was peeling from its walls and the shutters on the windows swung loosely on their hinges. Erick, who had been riding up front with the driver, turned to look at us.

"We are at the house of Volodya Katz," he said. "My father's best friend from before the war up until he died." Erick was the first out of the bus and waited for us to join him. "I'm sorry," he said, "but Volodya can only meet Alex and Mark, and, of course, Galina to translate."

"Why can't Patricia come?" my father protested.

"Volodya is uncomfortable with having too many people in his humble surroundings," Erick explained.

"Don't worry," my mother said. "I can take a nap while you're gone."

We passed through a gap in the fence where a gate had once been and made our way along a path to the house. Before we'd even reached the front door, it opened, and a very elderly woman appeared on the veranda. Beside her, holding her hand, was an equally aged man with startling blue eyes that seemed to look through us. He raised his hand in the air and called out, "Shalom! Ilya Solomonovich!"

"Shalom!" my father responded.

We climbed the steps up to the veranda, where Volodya stood with his arms outstretched. He embraced my father awkwardly. It was then that I realized he was blind.

"Ilya Solomonovich." Volodya wept at the words. "Ilya Solomonovich."

"Yes, yes, that's me," my father answered slightly self-consciously. It would take some time for "Ilya Galperin" to sit comfortably with him. "This is my son Mark," he said quickly.

Volodya beckoned me toward him. He gripped me strongly by my shoulders and appeared to take my measure intuitively.

"My wife, Anya," Volodya said as the woman behind him stepped forward and greeted each of us. Although she was well into her eighties, one could tell that she was a woman of character. She still had piercing and decisive eyes—she must have been handsome and charismatic as a young woman. She took my father by one hand and Volodya by the other and guided them into the house while we followed behind.

The room was dark and sparsely furnished with a few shabby pieces. There didn't seem to be any heating apart from a small brick stove. The floor covering was pitted and buckled linoleum. The couple seemed to live only in this room, and in the far corner there were two bunk beds made out of wooden planks with thin blankets strewn over them. The table had been set for a modest tea, which Anya served while Volodya began to speak.

"I could not believe my ears," he said, shaking his head, "when Erick told me that Solomon's boy had been found alive. In Australia!"

My father smiled. "You knew my father well?" he asked.

"Your father and I were good friends all our lives. We were the same age. We grew up together in this village. Even after your father married Hana, and I, Anya, we remained close. We were always at their house on October Street."

Anya nodded. "Your mother was an excellent cook," she said. "She could make a feast out of nothing."

"What was my mother like?" my father asked.

"She was very gentle," Anya said, wiping her hands on her apron.

"She was young. She must have married your father when she was about sixteen. That was the custom in those days. Solomon was older than her—he must have been about twenty-one. They were a lovely couple and even though a matchmaker had been involved, they cared for each other. You could see it in the way they were when they were together."

My father leaned forward, hanging on Anya's every word.

"She showered so much love on you and your brother and sister."

"Do you remember me?" my father asked.

"Of course I do," Anya replied. "I used to nurse you when you were a baby. When you got older you loved to sit on my lap. Not as much as you loved to sit on your aunt Sonya's. You were the apple of her eye. She was your father's sister. A real beauty. She lived with your family. Your mother and Sonya were great friends. They'd known each other all their brief lives, too. She'd been planning to get married to a Russian soldier—"

My father interrupted, exclaiming, "I mentioned that before. I have a memory of a man in a uniform."

"Sergei was his name," Anya said. "He was very quick-witted and charming. He'd make us all laugh when he was there. Do you remember Aunt Sonya?"

My father shook his head.

"You don't remember her singing to you?"

"Not at all."

Anya paused. She'd noticed my father's mood darken at her last comment. "As you got older you didn't want to sit on my knee anymore. You'd wriggle away from me and stand with your hands on your hips, telling me that you had business in the village. You'd make all of us laugh out loud with your antics. You were quite the man about town. Everybody in the village knew you. You'd talk to anyone—the policeman, the baker, anyone. You'd have a word for them all. You were a good boy. You had a kind nature. You were always considerate. Helping the old people in the village, chatting away to them."

My father shook his head, laughing. He was both moved and embarrassed. "I had no idea I was such an angel." He feigned surprise.

"Oh, but you weren't," Anya joked. "You were a rascal, too, especially when you were out and about with one of those boys. What was their name?"

She paused.

"Panok," she said, clapping her hands together. "Now those boys were trouble. Always up to mischief and trying to involve you."

"Panok!" my father exclaimed, almost jumping out of his chair with excitement.

"There was one your age. The pair of you were inseparable. You'd have your arms around each other's shoulders as you walked around the village. You both loved playing in the apple tree behind your house."

"That's right," my father said. His face was bright red and his blue eyes shone with pleasure and emotion. "We used to play pirates in the apple tree. One of us would climb up to the top and act as a lookout and report on the pirates about to invade our village."

My father turned to look at me. "So that was the answer all along," he said. "Panok was my best friend." My father touched Volodya's arm.

"Tell me, do you know what became of him?"

"He perished that day," Volodya replied. "With the rest of his family."

My father sank back into his seat, defeated. "And none of them survived?" he said.

Volodya shook his head.

The mystery of Panok had been solved, and although he didn't remember it, I realized that my father had likely witnessed the extermination of his dear friend, also only five, that day.

Anya poured more coffee.

After some time my father spoke again.

"Do you remember my birthday?" he asked.

"It may have been late in 1935," Anya answered. "But I can't say for certain."

"What about my little brother and sister, do you remember them?"

"Very little. By that time, I was spending more time in Leningrad with my sister, who was unwell. I returned to the village occasionally, but there were few chances to meet with Solomon and Hana."

"Do you remember?" Anya asked her husband.

"The little girl . . . no. But the boy was perhaps called David. You were definitely Ilya. Named after your grandfather, who was also Ilya. A tradition among us Jews."

I looked at Volodya and noticed that there were tears in his eyes.

"I miss our village," he said. "It was a true shtetl. Of course, there were the usual fallings-out and scandals, but people looked after each other. That's all gone now."

Volodya wiped his cheeks. "When I finally reached home after the war I was told that every single Jewish soul had perished." His large, bearlike hand reached for Anya's.

"We didn't even know that each other had survived then," Anya said.

Volodya nodded grimly. "I'd made my way through the forests to the northeast of Belarus," he said, "and when I got back the village was almost deserted. Fortunately this place was still standing, but it was in bad condition. I set about repairing it and, one day, when I was on the roof, I saw Anya coming along the path. I rubbed my eyes to make sure I wasn't dreaming. Anya had survived."

"You are both survivors," my father said.

"We were fortunate," Volodya said. "Anya was in Leningrad with her sister when Belarus was invaded. She stayed there and later joined the partisans."

"And what about you?" my father asked Volodya.

"I joined the partisans, too. Outside Mogilev in the northeast of Belarus."

"And my father?"

"Your father was a survivor, too."

"My mother told me that my father was dead. Why would she have done that?"

"So that you wouldn't have given the game away," Volodya replied.

My father gave him a puzzled look, forgetting that the man was blind.

Solomon and his friend Volodya, with whom he escaped
from Koidanov in 1941.

"We—your father and I—didn't want anybody, including you, to
know where we were hiding," Volodya said.

"I don't understand," my father said.

"Let me start at the beginning," Volodya said. "The Fascists invaded
our country in 1941. There'd been scraps of news and rumors that the
Nazis were rounding up the men and boys from the villages and taking
them away. We knew what that meant—it was going to be like the old
days of the pogroms. None of the Jews in the village knew what to make
of it. But we were sure that the elderly, the women, and the children
would be safe. We knew that if the Nazis came into Koidanov we'd be
done for. Some of the other men in the village were also making plans to
get away before the Fascists arrived. There was a lot of talk about joining
the partisans that were forming in the forests everywhere throughout

Belarus. A few men talked about heading farther east away from the invaders.

"In late summer of 1941," Volodya recalled, "I visited your parents to discuss the situation. I put it to Solomon that we, too, should think about escaping. He was reluctant.

"'And my family?' your father said. 'My children? What about them?'

"I had to convince him of the danger to both of us. 'The Germans aren't coming for the women and children,' I told your father. 'They'll be safe if they keep to themselves.' Your father knew the history of the pogroms, after all. But he couldn't be convinced that this was the best course of action.

"I had another idea. Anya was already in Leningrad with her sister. I told Solomon and Hana that I'd hide in the roof of my house but spread the word that I'd joined the partisans.

"'Ridiculous!' Solomon said. 'How will you survive up there?'

"'I'll store food and water with me and anything else, then I'll wait until the middle of the night,' I told Solomon.

"Suddenly we heard a noise and jumped up. Somebody had been listening to our plans. Do you know who it was?"

My father shook his head.

"You." Volodya laughed. "You'd been eavesdropping from behind the curtain.

"Your mother ordered you back to bed, but you didn't want to go. You were stubborn, that's for sure."

"I remember a scene like that. The talk had woken me up. Wait!" My father stopped abruptly. "Did you have a beard?"

"That's right!" Volodya burst out laughing. "Like this," he added, indicating its large bushy shape. "What a memory you have!

"Eventually Solomon came around to the idea on the condition that we hid in the roof of twelve October Street instead. That way he could keep an eye on his family. Hana was keen on that—she could fetch anything we needed and let us know when it was safe to come down.

"'If events do not go to plan,' Solomon said, 'I'll escape—take the family—in the middle of the night.'

"We had to be certain that nobody—not you, not even the neighbors—knew where we were. Hana would tell the neighbors that her husband had fled during the night to join the partisans and she had no idea if and when he'd return.

"'We'll have to keep it from Ilya,' Solomon said. 'He doesn't know how to keep a secret. We must tell him that I am gone.' It hurt your father deeply to have to say that."

"My mother told me that my father was dead," my father said. He looked perplexed. "I'm sure of it."

"You were only a child. Gone must have seemed like dead in those days," said Anya.

"We decided we would put the plan into action at the right moment," Volodya continued. "It was another two months, October 1941, before we did so. The news had reached us that the Fascists were in the region of Koidanov. The remaining able-bodied men began to flee, and the streets became more deserted day after day. By the middle of the month, Solomon and I were living in the roof.

"Less than a week later, late one night, Hana told us she'd heard the Fascists would arrive within the next few hours.

"Solomon and I had had a lot of time to think up in the roof. We weren't as well protected as we should've been, so we'd decided to escape and hide out deep in the forest for a few days, until the Fascists had passed. Your mother and Sonya agreed with us.

"One night, when the children were fast asleep, Solomon and I let ourselves down. Your father wanted to see you before we left. He went quietly to your bed and kissed you. You stirred for a moment, calling out, 'Papa.'

"I remember," my father said. "He said good-bye, didn't he?"

"Exactly as you say," Volodya answered. "Then we made ready to leave. Hana had organized a bag for each of us—filled with food that she'd prepared. I bid my farewell to your dear mother and your aunt Sonya.

" 'Come back to us,' Hana whispered.

"We promised we would, but in truth we weren't confident. We opened the door just enough to slip through. The last thing we saw were Hana's and Sonya's faces, peering at us with worried expressions. Solomon raised his cap to them and whispered 'farewell' one final time. The door closed."

"I saw you leave," my father said somberly. "I'd woken again. I called to my mother and told her, but she said that I'd been dreaming. That Papa had died."

Everybody at the table was silent.

"The night was cloudy, which gave us some cover as we left Koidanov," Volodya continued. "But your father was still torn: no sooner were we on the outskirts of the forest than he wanted to return to Koidanov. In the end I talked him out of it.

"Over the two days that followed we trudged on. Each night we took a few hours' sleep while the other kept watch. On the third day disaster struck. We'd been going in circles and had ended up within minutes of Koidanov again. We huddled together for some time and then, when it was safe, we headed back into the forest.

"We'd only been on the move a short while when we heard the sound of repeated gunshots in the distance. Solomon stood upright, frozen to the spot.

" 'Get down!' I shouted at him. 'In God's name, what are you doing?'

" 'I'm going back!' he cried. 'There's something wrong.'

"I grabbed your father by the arm but he shook me off.

" 'My family is there!' he said.

"Solomon understood that I loved your family, too. But I knew that we could not stop whatever was happening back in Koidanov. 'What good would it do if we were caught?' I argued with him. 'We must move forward, wherever that is.'

"Solomon went mad. He gripped his head and wailed for what seemed like an eternity. I didn't know how to help him. Suddenly everything went quiet, and a terrible rain began. We were drenched and had to huddle together. It didn't stop all day. By the evening we had to head off—it was too risky.

"'All right,' your father said. 'What are we waiting for?' He looked defeated. We headed back into the forest."

The room was deadly quiet. My father stared at his hands resting on the table.

"You know I was there that day?" he said.

"Where?"

"In the village. I saw what happened."

Both Volodya and Anya seemed too overcome to speak.

"I saw it all. My own family. The others. The killings went on for two days."

"I cannot imagine," Anya said softly. "Our grandson is nine years old. Even a child of that age could not cope. Not even an adult . . . do you want to tell more of this?"

"I, too, ended up in the forest outside Koidanov on the day of the exterminations," my father said. "What if you and my father had passed within reach of me with no idea I was there?"

Anya touched my father's hand. "We need brandy," she said.

The fortifying liquor seemed to revive my father. "Tell me more about what happened to my father and you," he said to Volodya.

"We were tired and hungry but kept pushing ourselves in the direction of Mogilev in the northeast," Volodya said. "Sometimes a farmer shared his food or gave us shelter, but we never stayed more than a single night. We couldn't put anybody else in danger. Germans and Latvian and Lithuanian police battalions were on patrol everywhere.

"We made it to the outskirts of Mogilev. Solomon knew there was a risk, but he wanted to get into the town to find out if there was any word of life back in Koidanov. I tried to stop him, but he wouldn't listen.

"That morning he set off for town. I agreed to wait for him until the next morning. If he didn't return by then, I wasn't to wait any longer. The following day came and there was no sign of him. I decided to wait a further night, but as another day dawned, I assumed that he'd been captured, that his fate was sealed. I never thought I would see your father again. Eventually I met up with a group of partisans. I fought with them in the forests, attacking trains, until the war ended.

"You're kidding!" my father said. "I used to guard the supply trains. The soldiers would hoist me up onto the carriage roofs, where they'd make me shoot into the air with a rifle to frighten off the partisans."

Volodya shook his head in disbelief. "Imagine if I'd been shooting at you," he said.

"Thankfully you missed." My father laughed darkly. "Later I was sent to Riga and, after a few happy days there, it was decided that I should again join the soldiers. This time they took me to the Russian front. It was terrible. The humidity was unbearable. And the mosquitoes at night were the worst. We slept in dugouts that were always full of water."

"When was this?" Anya asked, sitting up in her chair.

"The summer of 1943."

"Where exactly were you?" Anya asked.

"The Volhov swamps," my father said, "south of Leningrad."

"This is beyond belief!" Anya interrupted. "I was in the Volhov swamps with the partisans at the same time as you." She rose and crossed to a shelf. "See this," she said, indicating a framed certificate there.

My father and I joined Anya and examined her award.

"For bravery in the war. From Stalin, no less. Before he decided Jewish partisans needed punishment and not reward."

My father's eyes then moved to a photograph perched on the shelf.

"That's me," Anya said. "Taken during the war."

He picked it up. Suddenly he gave a very slight start that nobody else seemed to notice. His face went pale. "You were beautiful," he said.

Anya laughed, pleased. We returned to our seats and my father continued with his story.

The late afternoon wore on. My father and Volodya jumped from one topic to another as my father devoured what Volodya knew. But there was still more that my father wanted to hear about his father's survival.

"Early one morning," Volodya began, "there was a loud knocking at the door. When I opened it, before me was Solomon, disheveled, dressed in an SS overcoat, haggard but smiling. I couldn't believe my eyes.

"He had the hunger of a bear. I let him gulp down the food without interruption until he could eat no more. Your father told me that after we'd separated, he had in fact made it into Mogilev. But almost as soon as he entered the town he was stopped by a policeman wanting to see his papers. He had none, of course, and was arrested. At first he worked in a number of labor camps, until finally he was delivered to Auschwitz. He survived there for over two years. You know what saved him? His skill with leather. He looked after the guards' boots, and for that they kept him alive.

"Much later he was transported to Dachau. He told me he wouldn't have survived there for long. The conditions were even worse than in Auschwitz—but liberation turned out to be only months away. That must've been around the end of April in 1945.

"The Allies even gave him the chance to emigrate to America. But he wanted to return to Koidanov to see if his family was still here. Your father then made a journey back from hell. He walked all the way across Europe from Dachau concentration camp in Germany.

"When he'd entered Koidanov, only minutes earlier, he'd found his house deserted. He decided then to find me. I had to confirm the awful truth about his family: that all had perished, even you.

"Solomon was exhausted beyond belief, but still he insisted on seeing the mass grave. He went by himself. It was many hours before he returned. For some days after that he never said a word. And then his silence broke, and Solomon returned to us, changed—we all were—but stronger.

"He began a new life, but he never forgot his first family."

Anya reached across and gently took my father's hand. "Try not to despair," she said. "He never forgot you, his little Ilya. What a happy, friendly, and good boy you were. You have the same feeling as Solomon."

"My only inheritance," my father said sadly.

"No!" Anya sprang to life. "You have more than that! Your family were good people. You carry that goodness in you. The Nazis took you, but they never touched your goodness. I can see that. Don't ever forget it—you must always keep it close to you."

My father shifted in his seat, uncomfortable with the vehemence of Anya's emotion. He signaled to me with his eyes that he wanted to leave. He sighed loudly and looked at his watch.

"We've been here over three hours," he said, feigning surprise. "We should make a move. Mum'll be wild."

We made our farewells. Volodya and Anya remained on the veranda, vulnerable and frail, waving as we passed through the gap in the broken fence. I wondered whether we would ever see either of them again. As it turned out, we did not. They both died within months of each other before we had the chance to visit again.

The following evening, our last in Minsk, we found ourselves in Erick's modest apartment in one of the city's inner suburbs. The room was dominated by a very large table laden with food and drink prepared by Erick's delightful wife, Sonya.

At one end of the table, Erick showed my father the few photographs he had of Solomon during the postwar years until his death.

"If only I'd spoken sooner," my father said. "We might have found each other."

"You weren't to know," Erick replied.

"I thought everyone was dead," my father continued grimly. "I had nobody to look for. And nobody was looking for me. I was dead to this world."

"Even if you had spoken, it would have been impossible to find anybody here," Erick added. "Can you imagine what Belarus was like under the Soviet system?"

Later, as the evening drew to a close, my father tapped on the side of his glass and rose. All filled their glasses and then quietened down.

My father held his glass high. "I am not a very good toast-giver," he joked. "I just want to say that it's been a long way home, but it has been worth it. We have found each other now."

My father united with Erick Galperin and his family in 1998.

We raised our glasses in response.

"To the brothers!"

The following morning we waited in the departure lounge for our flight to Riga. My father leaned forward, his hands clasped together. "How could Erick have been confused about the house he grew up in?" my father asked me.

I shrugged impatiently.

I had a number of explanations in my mind but decided to keep them to myself. Talking about them would not move us further on our journey. Initially I had been simply grateful that other evidence—the mass grave, the memories of Volodya and Anya—had been enough to persuade my father that he'd found the right village. The subsequent last-minute discovery of his original home, of which he'd retained memories, had been beyond all our expectations.

The boarding of the flight to Riga was announced, and the three of us made our way wearily to the departure gate.

I quietly observed the profiles of my mother and father as they rested in their seats across the aisle from me. My father must have sensed my gaze because suddenly he opened one eye and, without looking at me, asked, "When do we get in, Marky?"

"Not long now!" I replied. "Some water, Dad?"

"I'll come with you," he said, following me to the rear of the plane. We stood together at the water fountain.

"Will you change your name, Dad?" I ventured.

My father raised his eyes to heaven. "God forbid," he chuckled. "To Ilya Solomonovich Galperin? What a mouthful!"

I had something else on my mind. "Dad," I ventured, "what was it that bothered you when you looked at Anya's photograph on the shelf?"

"What do you mean?"

"I saw your reaction," I persisted.

My father didn't respond immediately. He sipped on his water, reflecting on my question. Then he spoke.

"Do you remember when I was in Volhov, hiding in the tree, when the partisans passed below me?" he said.

I nodded.

"And I caught a glimpse of one of the women and thought I recognized her . . . Judging from the photograph I saw of her in Koidanov, I now believe that woman was Anya."

With that my father returned to his seat.

Moments later, the voice of a stewardess announced our descent into Riga.

CHAPTER TWENTY-NINE
RIGA

We made our way through passport control at Riga's gleaming new international airport, a stylish edifice of glass, Baltic pine, and concrete. While Belarus had paid a high price for its struggle against Nazism, Latvia, which had welcomed its Nazi occupiers, had now begun to prosper.

In the taxi on the way to our hotel in the old quarter of Riga, we saw that the landscape was dominated by enormous billboards advertising Vodafone, Mercedes-Benz, and Kylie Minogue.

"Unbelievable," I heard my father say. He had always described Latvia as gray and cold—a place for dour, Nordic-looking people whose forests might be inhabited by elves and trolls and woodsmen. Latvia, I thought, might prefer it if we were to go away, leaving its past undisturbed so it could get on with its bright new future.

I woke at dawn and decided to go for a walk in the old town. I dressed quietly and slipped out onto the damp cobbled streets that reeked of powerful antiseptic. I wandered through the narrow lanes and could see now that I'd misjudged the affluence of the city. In this quarter there were fewer signs of gentrification: for every renovated shop front there was also a run-down or abandoned building.

It was now daylight and there were more people on the street. I turned into a broad square that had a fountain in its center. I perched on its edge, taking in the buildings that formed the perimeter of the square. Opposite me was a relatively new building, the Museum of the Occupation of Latvia.

In my research of Latvian wartime history and its postwar dealings with its past, I had soon come across references to the museum. According to one report, the site of the museum was originally occupied by a museum of Jewish history in Latvia. The Jewish museum had been evicted from the site and shunted into a single room in a backstreet of the old town. The author argued that this incident symbolized the way the Latvians handled their wartime history: replacing one of the most savage aspects of their recent past with a "cleansed" version.

Indeed, opinions on Latvia's "complicity" during its period of so-called occupation remain divided. According to some historians, Latvia was not "occupied." Many Latvians had "welcomed" their Nazi visitors, whom they saw as liberators from Soviet oppression. But there was more than political expediency behind this attitude. Some historians argue that Latvia adopted the Nazis' ethos enthusiastically because of its native, often virulent anti-Semitism.

I looked at my watch. It was almost eight o'clock. I hurried back to the hotel.

My father and I had lots of territory to cover on that first day. He wanted to find the apartment on Valdemara Street, where he had lived with the Dzenis family, and the Laima chocolate factory.

My mother pleaded off, saying that she was content to rest for a while, but I could detect disappointment in her voice. I knew that she felt her exhaustion was disloyal to my father.

We hailed a taxi outside our hotel. "Valdemara iela," my father told the driver, without giving a house number.

"Don't you remember the exact address?" I asked.

"No. But I would remember the building instantly. Mirdza said that it was number ninety-nine. Wherever it is, I'll find it."

"It's that one," he said, nodding at a building diagonally across from where we were standing. We crossed the street and stood before the brick-and-concrete apartment block.

"It's not number ninety-nine," I said.

"But I'm certain this is the one." My father lingered in front of the building.

"Number ninety-nine must be around here somewhere," I said. "Come on."

We began to make our way slowly along Valdemara iela. My father seemed perplexed and he dawdled, reluctant to move on. He had taken no more than a dozen or so steps when he stopped abruptly.

"No," he said firmly. "Mirdza must've got it wrong."

Without waiting for me, he strode back toward the building we'd just left. I caught up with him outside its entrance. "This is it," he insisted. "Flags flew on either side of the front doors. On one side there was the Nazi flag, on the other the Latvian flag."

I walked up to the building's facade and examined it. Indeed, there were two metal cups embedded in the brickwork that might have functioned as flagpole holders. I called my father over to see.

He only nodded a response, then backed away from the building in order to get a view of its upper stories. "We lived up there on the top floor. That was my bedroom window," he said, pointing.

I walked up to the glass doors on the ground floor and strained to get a look inside, but the lobby was dark.

"Come on," my father said, brushing past me and pushing open the door. He stepped in ahead of me. The deserted foyer reeked of cat urine.

"The foyer is exactly as I remember it," my father said quietly. "Of course, it was in better condition back then." He pointed to the center of the room. "There was a stand there with fresh flowers in a vase. It was changed every day by the elderly caretaker. Mrs. Impuls was her name. I used to love coming down in the morning when Uncle and I were off to work. As we went downstairs and got to about there"—my father pointed to the last of the steps—"I'd close my eyes for just a second and breathe in the smell of the flowers."

My father gazed up into the darkened stairwell and began to climb the stairs. I could sense his mounting excitement as we reached the third floor. Before we'd even reached the landing, he turned to me, his face beaming, and pointed up at a door on the left.

He knocked but there was no reply. He knocked again and waited. After several moments he reached for the doorknob and began twisting it frantically. The door was locked. He hammered loudly on the door, abandoning all restraint.

"If only I could get inside," he said. He thought for a moment. "I know," he said, crossing the landing to another door and knocking loudly. "Hello!" he called out. "Anybody home?"

"The building is uninhabited, Dad."

He ignored me and continued to bang on the door. Eventually he gave up, and in an uncharacteristic gesture of disappointment, he remained motionless for some time with his head resting against the door.

Later that morning we stood opposite a famous landmark to Latvian independence on Brivibas iela.

"I want to show you something," my father said. "It's this way." Once on the street, he picked up speed. Then abruptly he stopped. "Look!" he said, indicating with a nod of his head.

In the near distance was a small art deco clock tower. Its face was illuminated, as was lettering down the side of the tower that spelled out LAIMA.

My father reached the tower and gazed up at it. "Laima, laima," he said affectionately. "This was a famous meeting spot for everyone in Riga. 'I'll meet you at the Laima clock,' they'd say."

"What does *laima* mean?" I asked.

" 'Luck,' " he answered wryly.

My father looked around in all directions. "Let's get to Laima Chocolates," he said, taking off up the street.

My father stopped at a street corner and waved back at me. "Quickly!" he called out, attracting the attention of passersby. "It's down here. Miera iela. Peace Street." Then he hurried on.

I caught up with him farther down Miera iela, where he'd suddenly stopped. Transfixed by the building opposite him, he didn't appear to notice me. It was a factory, and perched on its rooftop was an enormous sign: LAIMA. My father had found it without a moment's hesitation.

"It's been over fifty years," he said pensively, "but it's as if it were yesterday. See over there!" My father pointed across at the entrance, a wooden door adjacent to a row of dusty display windows.

"That's where Uncle was waiting for me when I met him for the first time. I can see him now stepping out of the shadow of the wall and onto the pavement with his hand extended."

My father continued to reminisce in a hushed tone about his time at Laima. I glanced at him and saw that he was looking in all directions as he spoke, as if he were frightened about being overheard. He seemed acutely conscious of the fact that he'd been in the company of Dzenis and Lobe.

"Are you okay?" I asked, giving him a curious look.

"Let's go around the back," he said. In a flash, he disappeared around the corner of the building, and I found him in front of a tall steel gate topped with barbed wire. He leaned his back against the gate. I was certain he was remembering the deportations from the yard.

"You know now what was going on in there?" I asked him gently, sure of what his answer would be.

His nod was almost imperceptible, as was his simple yes. "Those people were Jews transported to an unknown destination where their fate was more or less sealed."

"Did you understand at that time what was going on, Dad?"

"No," he answered firmly. "I must've been only eight years old when this occurred. I'm not trying to excuse myself. I sensed that something was up, but I couldn't put my finger on it. It was only later that night when I was alone in my room that it clicked. But then I told myself that Uncle would not let that sort of thing happen. He was a decent man, a

fair man. Even now I cannot accept that. I believe he was forced to cooperate. Like me. Did I do wrong to pass chocolates to those poor
people?"

We were both silent now. My father pressed his back against the
gate as if he could block the passage of the trucks and their unfortunate
passengers. Then all of a sudden he bolted, fleeing in the direction he
had come, without a final glance at Laima. I chased after him, calling out
for him to wait, but he was already some way down Miera iela.

He maintained his frantic pace, keeping his head down as he passed
Annas iela, where the Latvian SS quarters that he'd watched when distracted from his studies in Dzenis's office had been located. Annas Street,
such a sweet name for a street of such poison.

I caught up with my father just as he reached the far end of Miera
iela. "What's going on?" I asked.

He fought to regain control of his breathing. I waited until he was
ready to speak.

"It's harder than I thought," he said, looking around and avoiding
eye contact with me.

I sensed that he was embarrassed by the intensity of his response to
seeing Laima again.

"My past is coming back too quickly," he said in a low voice. "It's
good to find things, but bad to remember. Maybe that's what it is."

I guided my father back to the hotel for some rest.

CHAPTER THIRTY
CARNIKAVA

The following morning my father and I stood on the concourse at the Riga railway station. "This is where I always arrived when I came to Riga," my father said, "and that's where the limousine was waiting the time Kulis took me to Uncle."

He pointed at the entrance that we had just passed through. "I marched across here ahead of Kulis as if I were in command. People passing by stopped and stared at me, a boy of no more than seven or eight by that time, in my uniform with jodhpurs and knee-high polished boots. Some civilians even applauded me and, of course, soldiers on the concourse saluted me." My father beamed broadly to himself, caught up in his recollection.

Suddenly he snapped out of it. "Come on," he said. "We've got to find the train."

The train would take us to Carnikava, where we hoped to find the Dzenises' dacha, or holiday house, still standing. My father had only his memory to go by.

"Once we're on the platform of Carnikava station," he said confidently, "I'll know the way like the back of my hand. After all, Auntie and I would make the journey from Riga almost every weekend when I was with the Dzenis family."

While my father went to find out train times and buy our tickets, I waited on the concourse. It was nothing like the gleaming airport, its drabness alleviated only by a solitary flower stall. My father soon reappeared waving two tickets in the air. "I got them *so* cheap," he said proudly, as if he'd been involved in barter for them. The express was a series of dilapidated carriages drawn by an ancient engine, which at that moment let out a whistle to indicate its imminent departure. The train began to groan and move slowly forward.

"Hurry," my father shouted above the din. He grabbed me by the arm and dragged me on board.

I had dozed off and, on waking, found myself confused about where I was. I caught sight of my father's face reflected in the windowpane of the train car. Whatever he was looking at, judging by the delicate and considered smile on his face, it seemed to give him much pleasure. Suddenly the reflection of his eyes met mine and instantly I sensed his shyness at having been observed unawares. He gave me a comical and slightly wry look, but it was as if a veil had suddenly descended over his true mood.

The couple of hours spent in the train en route to Carnikava were a welcome respite from the hectic schedule of our journey across Europe thus far. I was exhausted and must have have dozed off a second time, for the next thing I recalled hearing at the edge of my consciousness was "Carnikava" over and over. It turned out to be the conductor's voice echoing loudly over the loudspeaker. It brought me to with a start. My father was already preparing to leave the carriage. He climbed across me and began to make his way down the aisle.

After the train ground to a stop, I joined my father on the deserted platform. Nobody else had disembarked.

"So what do we do now?" I asked, watching the rear of the train as it pulled away. "Find somebody who can give us directions to the house?"

"What on earth for?" My father was astounded by my suggestion. "I can remember the way." With that, he tightened his grip on his case and strode confidently toward the station exit.

I hovered beside my father and quietly watched as, hand held to cheek, he turned in all directions, getting his bearings. Suddenly a cloud seemed to lift as his face broke into a broad smile.

"This was the shortcut we always took," he declared and strode down a narrow track barely discernible in the tall grass. I hurried after him as he disappeared from sight. Less than a minute later, on a bend in the path, my father stopped.

"Lost your way already?" I asked.

"Of course not!" he said dismissively. "Somewhere around here we should come to a fork in the path that joins up again farther on. Auntie and I would each take a different path and race to see who'd get to the other end first. Auntie would take off her shoes and count down, 'Three, two, one!' Then she'd make a great show of waiting before whispering 'Go!' and off I'd run.

"I always got there ahead of Auntie, who'd arrive breathless from running and laughing. We'd both sit in the grass, trying to get our breath back. Then Auntie would present me with a sweet or a chocolate, usually from Laima. 'To the champion, Corporal Uldis Kurzemnieks,' she'd declare seriously."

"So even Auntie thought of you as a soldier?" I asked.

My father thought for several moments. "Yes and no," he said. "She was always respectful. She didn't make fun of me being a soldier like some people did. As if I were an oddity, like a toy soldier."

"A small boy in an SS uniform would strike most people as pretty odd," I said. "Didn't you feel strange yourself?"

"I knew it was an SS uniform, but I didn't understand what that meant. I simply thought of it as a soldier's uniform and I was proud of that. But going back to Auntie, I know she also didn't like me in the uniform. On a couple of occasions I overheard her and Uncle discussing it. Auntie said that it wasn't right for a child to wear such a hideous outfit. She said I should be allowed to be a child. I remember from the sound of Uncle's voice that he seemed to agree with her, but he warned her not to say such things in front of other people."

My father moved on. Not fifty yards ahead he came to an abrupt halt and turned to look at me. "I told you it was here," he called out excitedly.

The main path led directly ahead, but branching off to the left was a narrow trail overgrown with grass and weeds and barely visible. It looked as if nobody had used it since my father as a young boy.

"Do you want to race me now, Dad?" I joked. In fact, I was half-serious about my suggestion. I sensed within my father the exuberance of the young boy as he raced along the path, and I was keen to share this happy experience with him. He laughed gleefully but then gently dismissed my idea, saying, "Nah. Too old for that now, son."

We found the point where the two paths rejoined, just as he had predicted. He smiled proudly at me, seeming to want recognition or even approval for the veracity of his memory. I did not hesitate.

"Your memory . . ." I said, shaking my head in amazement. My father had kept this path somewhere in his mind for over fifty years.

He strode away into the waist-high grass. A short distance on, he pointed off to the left. "Beyond that field," he said, "is a stream where Auntie sometimes let me play. Carnikava is close now."

He headed off to the right, with me trailing behind, until finally we came out onto an unpaved road. "The house is over there," my father said, "behind those trees." We passed several seemingly deserted houses and entered a wood.

Through the thin wall of trees, a house, a square two-story edifice guarded by iron gates and a stone wall, came into view. "Carnikava!" my father exclaimed. He moved forward and rattled the gates. "Locked!" He looked crestfallen.

My father was still gripping the bars when suddenly we were startled by a voice from behind us. We both spun around at the same time. An elderly man in overalls stood before us. As tiny as a dwarf, he was bald and had no teeth, judging by his toothless smile.

"What do you want here?" he demanded, a touch imperiously.

"We've come from Australia," my father replied, in his friendly, casual way.

"Is that so?" The man was unimpressed.

"Did you know the people who lived here during the war?" my father asked.

The old man eyed us both suspiciously for a moment before deciding to continue to speak to us. "Only by sight. From Riga, they were. There were three daughters—didn't see much of them. Then the war came . . ."

"There were no other children?"

The man shook his head. Then something occurred to him. "No, I'm wrong," he said. "There was a boy who suddenly appeared in their midst during the war." The old man laughed to himself.

"He was quite a sight, getting about in a soldier's uniform. An SS uniform, in fact. The family must have had some important connections because many of their guests, too, were officers from the SS, coming and going in their fancy cars. I've no idea what became of them, though."

"They emigrated to Australia," my father replied.

"That so?" the man said warily. "You knew the family?"

My father nodded and then began to pace up and down in front of

The Dzenises' holiday home in Carnikava, outside Riga, where my father spent some happy days in 1943.

the barred gates like a caged tiger, staring in at the house. "Who owns the place now?" he asked.

"No idea. It's been empty for years."

"How can we get in?" My father looked at the man with a pleading expression.

The man rubbed the back of his neck and then walked away from us, indicating that we should follow him. About fifty yards along the stone wall, we came to a narrow section of the fence that had collapsed.

"Welcome to Carnikava!" the old chap cackled.

My father and I climbed through, gingerly navigating the pile of broken rocks. My father glanced at me and then called back to the man, "Thank you, sir!"

"For what?" I frowned.

"Not quite sure yet," he answered.

The house loomed before us like an enormous frog.

"How did Uncle get this place?" I asked.

"From Lacplesis. A reward for bravery. For fighting for Latvian independence against the Bolsheviks, the Soviet occupiers." But my father wasn't even remotely interested, at this moment, in the history of Latvia.

I remained at some distance from the house and let my father approach it by himself. He circled it cautiously, as if at any moment it might lash out and snatch him in its jaws. When my father finally reached its facade, he tentatively stretched out his arm until it came to rest on the wall. He stood there silently for several moments, as if communing with the entire house. Then he began to move, one hand still touching the wall of the house, as if he were somehow placating it so that he could safely close in on his memories.

Farther along he came to a window placed high in the wall. He pulled a handkerchief from his trouser pocket and began to rub vigorously at the pane, but he was unable to break up the thick, encrusted dirt. Annoyed, he turned his back on the house and walked away from it.

As he approached me, it was not difficult to see the mixture of anxiety and impatience contorting his features. "How could they let the place get so run-down!" he exclaimed to himself in a disgusted tone. With an almost childlike directness, he added petulantly, "I want to get inside. Where'd that old guy get to? He might be able to show us a secret way."

The man had disappeared as suddenly as he had first appeared. My father scratched his head, looking in all directions before giving me a bewildered shrug and joining me where I'd now positioned myself—on the steps in front of the building's entrance.

"They used to lock me inside sometimes," he reminisced. "It was my fault. I'd be rebellious and try to run away, but I'd never get any farther than the beach down that track over there." He pointed to a path that ran alongside the property.

"I loved the seashore," my father said, "as long as I didn't have to go in the water. As I said before, the first time I ever saw the sea was at Carnikava, and I was awed by its power.

"I'd practice doing handstands in the sand," he said, taking a seat beside me on the steps. "Most of all I loved walking along the beach hunting for amber. It used to wash up on the Baltic shoreline like common seashells. I'd collect it in my pockets and, before I'd head back to Carnikava, I'd divide it up: half in one pocket for Auntie and the other half I'd wrap in my hankie and hide in my other pocket. That half was for my escape. I figured that if I ever got away from the Latvians, I'd have to bribe people—the police and ships' captains and the like—to get me to another country. I always hoped it was America, even though I didn't know where America was. I just thought of it as paradise—sunny and warm with happy, smiling people in nice clothes."

My father looked around for several moments before he spoke again. "Remember me telling you about the film they made about me?" he said.

I nodded.

"This is the very spot where they filmed me," he said, "playing blindman's bluff with the other children."

My father pulled his brown case onto his lap. He clicked open the lock. This time there was no secretiveness, no holding the lid in a partly opened position so that nobody but himself could see inside. His hands fumbled in the morass of papers and photographs, and he drew out a tatty, yellowed scrap of paper. It was not even a full sheet, and its edges indicated that it had been roughly torn by hand.

"Look!" my father commanded, passing across the scrap.

It was a newspaper article. I handled the fragile page gently: it seemed as though it might suddenly disintegrate. In the center of the sheet was an image I recognized. It was my father in uniform, reading a map.

When telling us stories as children, my father had held it up a number of times, as a prop to whatever he was recounting. But it had always remained firmly in his grip and only ever briefly revealed. This was the first opportunity I'd ever had to scrutinize the photo at some length, and I could now discern that he was actually in military uniform. It occurred

A photo taken during the filming of the Latvian propaganda newsreel in which my father appeared in 1943.

to me how deftly he had always handled this picture—he had positioned his thumb or one of his fingers over any sign that would give away the truth about his uniform. I was unsettled by the effort he had made to keep the truth from our family.

"I am certain that this photo is a still taken on the day the film was made here," he said.

"What newspaper is this from?" I asked.

"It's from the *Eagle*, a paper in Riga," my father replied. "It was taken in 1943."

My father looked around again. "Over there," he said, pointing to a small clump of trees about twenty yards from us. "That's where it was taken.

"I recall some things from the day of filming," he said reflectively. "Various people arrived throughout the afternoon. A group of kids about my age appeared on a bus. Later Lobe arrived with an entourage of officers who inspected the grounds of Carnikava.

"Lobe insisted to Auntie that I get back into my uniform. You see, Carnikava was the only place that I was willing to take off my uniform: in the summer I'd spend all day at the seashore and virtually lived in my swimming trunks.

"We were up at around dawn the next morning. I was still sleepy but Auntie dressed me in my uniform, smoothed my hair, and took me down to a room where a crew member was making the other children ready for the film.

"One group of girls were already dressed in folk costumes, and their hair had been plaited with colorful ribbons. They were being looked after by a lady in a white uniform who was giving them bowls of ice cream. At that hour! When she saw me, she came over and offered me a bowl as well. I couldn't believe it! I thought, 'This is going to be a great day.'

"Then another woman came up to me and began to straighten my uniform. I wriggled about, trying to enjoy my ice cream. 'Be still!' she said impatiently. 'Don't forget you are a soldier! We must make you handsome for the film.'

"Then she tried to apply makeup. I squirmed at that and screwed up my face. 'Soldiers do not use this!' I stamped my foot. 'It's for ladies.'

"This only caused everybody in the room to laugh at me.

"'Shush, you,' she said playfully, planting a kiss on my forehead. I could feel my face turn hot and red with outrage. 'You don't like my kisses?' she exclaimed. Fortunately for me, somebody interrupted us. They were ready to film me.

"Outside in the morning sunshine the crew was waiting with a camera. The girls rolled their eyes and began giggling when they saw me. Everything had been planned, down to the last detail. The director organized our positions around a maypole, telling us to join hands to rehearse our dance."

"A maypole dance?" I laughed. I simply could not imagine my father dancing.

"I know," he said, shaking his head in disbelief. "And those girls I had to dance with. They were real little Aryan maidens with terrible, fierce tempers." My father screwed up his face as if he were being asked to dance with them this instant.

"One girl complained that she didn't want to be next to me: 'the little nuisance,' she called me. 'I'm not holding hands with any of these awful girls,' I said arrogantly. That started the girls off again. 'You're not even a real Latvian!' one of them said to me.

"I pinched her"—my father chuckled loudly—"and all hell broke loose. The commander gave me a harsh warning. I settled down quickly.

"After that, I can only recall bits and pieces, because the fun had gone. It was work and, with Commander Lobe hovering threateningly in the background, I just did what I was told.

"They filmed us eating lunch. The girls tormented me again, this time because I couldn't use a knife and fork properly. I showed them up later, though, when we had to change to our swimming trunks and play on the beach. I could run faster than any of them, and I was the only one who could do handstands."

My father and I both laughed, but then his mood altered. "Imagine if we found the film," he said pensively. Without another word, he rose and made his way down the steps. He walked directly toward a small copse that had been planted in a semicircle with the opening facing toward the house. Before he actually reached it, he stopped and nodded his head as if confirming something to himself. Then he headed to one particular tree. He beckoned me with a wave of his hand.

By the time I reached him he was crouched at the base of the tree and patting the grass all around him. "Help me up. I'm looking for treasure," he said with disarming simplicity.

"Treasure," I repeated. "What treasure?"

"Buried treasure that Uncle left behind when we fled Latvia."

My father registered my look of disbelief. "No," he protested, "I'm serious. It was in the summer of 1944. He and Auntie had taken me to Carnikava by car for the weekend. Uncle must have sensed that the writing was on the wall for Germany and Latvia, and he began to make plans for our departure.

" 'This might be our last visit here,' Uncle explained. 'We will have to leave many belongings behind. Collect a few of your things that will fit in your case.' That's the case I'm holding now. Uncle bought it for me in Riga.

"That first night in Carnikava I was asleep when something woke me. As I came to, I heard a noise coming from outside my bedroom window. I didn't know what to do. In truth, I'd gotten used to the good life—being safe from the elements—and I thought it might be wolves. But as I sat there on the edge of my bed, I soon realized that it wasn't wolves; it was a digging sound.

"I went over to the window and peeked from behind the curtain. There was enough moonlight that I could just make out the garden. By these trees—literally where we are standing now—I could see two figures moving about. As my eyes got used to the darkness, I saw that it was Auntie and Uncle. Auntie was holding a small lamp close to Uncle, who was digging up the soil. I noticed that Uncle had two small sacks at his feet, which he then placed into the hole he'd created.

"I have no inkling as to why, but at that moment Uncle looked up at my window. I backed away quickly, but I was sure that he'd caught a glimpse of me. I pressed myself against the wall, worried because I knew that I'd just witnessed something that I shouldn't have. I crept back into bed and drew the covers up so that only my eyes and the top of my head were visible. I couldn't sleep. I lay there worried that Uncle would be fierce with me the next morning.

"Downstairs I heard the sound of a door closing and then footsteps as Auntie and Uncle made their way upstairs. They passed by my door, but moments later I heard one set of footsteps return and stop outside. I could tell that they were Uncle's. I held my breath, waiting for the handle to turn, but he seemed to think better of it and moved on.

"Early the next morning I woke with a start. There was a shadow over me. I let out an unholy scream and tried to spring out of bed. Whoever it was put his hand over my mouth and held me down on the bed. Then I saw that it was Uncle. He put one finger to his lips indicating that I should be quiet, and then he sat down on the edge of the bed. He spoke in a whisper, explaining what he and Auntie had been doing the night before: he had some gold and silver that he couldn't take with him.

"'You must promise to keep it our secret,' he said solemnly. 'It's yours. If Auntie and I never return, it's yours. After all this mess is over, come back and get it.' Then he rose wearily from the bed. 'Get dressed,' he said, 'and go down for breakfast.'

"At the door he stopped and turned. 'Don't forget,' he said. 'It's our secret.' With that he was gone.

"I think it's still here." My father frowned intently at the ground. "Nothing seems to have been disturbed."

"Uncle didn't come back for it?"

My father shook his head. "No, he never returned to Latvia. And he never once mentioned the hidden treasure to me again. Not even after we'd emigrated to Australia."

"He must have told someone else about it," I suggested. "And they've collected it."

"Who would he tell?" my father responded as if my idea were absurd.

"His daughters or grandchildren, perhaps?"

"No." My father shook his head vigorously. "We would've known about that, one way or another. The loot should still be here, below our feet."

"What happens now?" I asked. "Do you want to look for it?"

"What, with our bare hands? Don't be stupid. Perhaps we'll come back another time," my father added.

"When?"

My father tried to shrug me off. He began to walk away from me toward the hole in the fence we had climbed through.

"When are we going to get another chance to go back for it?" I called after him.

"Look," he said, turning back to me. "I don't want their gold and silver. It's not mine."

"Uncle said you should have it."

"Leave well enough alone, son," he replied irritably.

"Why don't you want it?" I persisted.

My father turned to face me. "Because that would mean they'd bought me," he spat out, incensed. He looked at his watch. "If we don't hurry, we'll miss the train back to Riga."

Without waiting for me, he strode to the gap in the fence and onto the unpaved road, where for one moment, he faltered. He seemed to be torn between continuing on his way and turning for one final glance at the house that had now taken on a malevolent presence: my father had been used as a propaganda tool—a little mascot for the Reich and its poisonous ambitions.

He did not turn around. Instead, together we began to retrace our steps back to the train station. He quickened his pace, as if in flight, now from Carnikava.

By the time we reached the station, my father's mood was calmer and more pensive.

"Who would have thought we'd find Carnikava again?" I ventured, hoping that he'd confide his feelings to me. "Greater chance of winning the lottery . . ."

"Carnikava was no prize," he snapped harshly at me.

I was shocked. I could tell that my father instantly regretted his tone with me.

"Too many memories there," he said. "Memories and ghosts."

"You don't believe in ghosts!" I joked, hoping to return him to a better mood.

"After seeing Carnikava I do," he hit back. "The place is full of them."

The train to Riga pulled in, and soon we were safely ensconced in a carriage, heading away from Carnikava. He would likely never see his refuge by the sea again. He seemed relieved.

CHAPTER THIRTY-ONE
THE FILM

In the months since his astonishing revelations in our kitchen, I had contacted various film archives in Russia, Germany, Latvia, and elsewhere. In my communications I'd described the bare details of the film that he had given me.

Nothing had come of the search. None of the organizations had had the film in their archives. At the time I'd kept it from him because I wanted to surprise him if I found it. I didn't want to get his hopes up unnecessarily.

The Latvia State Archive for Audiovisual Document was among those that had responded in the negative, but now that I was actually in Latvia I decided to approach it again. Having just been to Carnikava, I knew how meaningful it would be not just for my father but for all of us to see the film.

We returned to the hotel from Carnikava just before three and went our separate ways. My father was keen to return to his room and check on my mother. I went to my room and placed the call to the archive immediately. After a brief reminder, Miss Slavits, my contact there, recalled my unusual request. I described to her the new information I'd gotten from my father that day. I skirted around the issue of my father's SS uniform. I was still uncertain about the depth of Latvian nationalism, particularly in a government institution, and had no idea whether Miss

Slavits would willingly locate a film if she knew its potential for controversy. My parents' experiences in Melbourne had taught me that some
Latvians did not take kindly to my father's story. As it turned out, Miss
Slavits was willing to assist me provided I could pay the archive for its
time. She'd warned me that closing time was 5:00 p.m., and it was already well past three o'clock. We were due to leave Riga for London
early the next morning, so this would be my only opportunity. I put on
my jacket and left the hotel.

The taxi took me to the outskirts of the city, where it stopped outside a
building. I hurriedly paid and made my way to the entrance. I cursed. It
was a department store. Anxiously I hailed another taxi and frantically
stabbed at the paper on which the address Miss Slavits had dictated to me
was written.

"Yes, yes." He took off wildly into the traffic.

I looked at my watch. It was now nearly four. I urged the driver to
hurry. He floored the accelerator, and the car surged forward as if it were
about to take off into the air.

Within minutes the taxi screeched to a dramatic stop outside a drab
concrete building. A sign on the facade indicated that this was the archive. I sprinted up the steps that led to the entrance.

I quickly glanced again at my watch: 4:15. I tried the door but it was
locked. I pushed my face flat against the glass and peered inside. At first
glance, the dark, vast, cavernous space appeared to be deserted. However, as my eyes grew accustomed to the dim lighting, I could just make
out a bulky silhouette at a desk. It stirred slightly, giving me a start.

I tried the door again. The creature inside did not react. I tapped on
the glass.

I hammered on the glass with my fist, and the silhouette rose slowly
from behind the desk and moved laboriously toward me. I could see now
that the person was extremely squat, as wide as he or she was tall. This
impression did not alter as the figure reached the other side of the glass
barrier. Now I could see, however, that it was an elderly woman, dressed

in a paramilitary uniform. It was her turn to push her face up against the glass pane and to scrutinize me with her filmy eyes.

"Miss Slavits," I shouted, my face close to hers.

She showed no immediate sign of letting me in. Her eyes sharpened as she appraised me. After several moments she seemed satisfied and opened the door. She began to shuffle slowly back to her desk, indicating that I should follow her, which I did. The guard eased herself back into her chair.

"Miss Slavits," I repeated.

Without even the slightest glance in my direction, she thrust the visitors' book and pen under my nose. After a bored, cursory glance at my signature and without looking up, she pointed her finger at a door on the far side of the room. I entered a darkened corridor, where I was greeted by a captivating young woman.

"Mr. Kurzem?" she said. Miss Slavits's English was gentle and melodic. "My office is this way."

We made our way through a maze of dark corridors. As we did so, Miss Slavits told me about three reels of film she'd unearthed since we spoke. "They were in a dust-covered shoe box at the back of a filing cabinet," she explained, slightly embarrassed. "They may have been there for decades. I'm sorry that I did not find them earlier. I haven't seen them yet, and there is no description of the contents except for the words 'Latvian countryside.' That could mean anything, but it may be worth looking." She gave me a sympathetic smile.

"Can we view the footage now?" I asked. In truth I didn't hold out much hope that I would find my father's film. I imagined that much of Latvia's infrastructure had been destroyed by the Nazis as they retreated.

"Certainly," she replied and led me to a neighboring viewing room.

It took several seconds for my eyes to adjust to the brightness of the fluorescent lights. We both donned bright pink dust coats in a limp gesture toward film preservation and sat down before an archaic Steenbeck footage machine.

"I should warn you that the condition of the films may be very poor," she said, gingerly removing the first reel from the box.

She gently loaded the spool onto the machine and began to pump a pedal so that the film jerked along frame by frame. For a moment I stared at a blank screen before black-and-white images appeared. The reel's quality had deteriorated considerably, so that I could barely make out the images of soldiers marching across a field. The commentary in German, which seemed to be describing the experiences of German soldiers in Latvia, was largely drowned out by the crackle of static.

Miss Slavits let the reel run to its end to be certain. I shook my head. "The next one?" Miss Slavits asked. I nodded.

The second reel, too, contained images of German soldiers on patrol in the Latvian countryside. I watched it through to the end. By then a cloud of disappointment had descended upon me. I sat in silence as Miss Slavits loaded the final reel.

The first images that appeared on screen seemed to be much the same as those on the previous reels—German soldiers marching. I didn't see the point of sitting through more of the same thing. Filled with gloom, I rose and, without waiting for Miss Slavits to turn off the machine, began to remove my dust coat. At that precise moment, with my back to the screen, I heard the words of the German narrator: "And now we are outside Riga." I spun around to face the screen and snapped at Miss Slavits to let the reel continue. She was taken aback but managed to reverse the footage several frames to where the commentary had begun.

This time I saw the images that had accompanied the words. There was Carnikava, shot from its front gate, where my father and I had stood only hours before. It was in much better condition and bathed in sunshine, not a bit ominous.

As the German narration continued, accompanied by happy children's music in the background, the camera cut to a close-up of the steps leading up to the front door. As the voice began to describe the presence of a young soldier at Carnikava, the doors to the house burst open and a throng of children dashed down the steps and into the sunshine. Among them was a boy, no more than eight or nine years old, in uniform. My breath stopped for an instant. I recognized his face immediately. It was my father. He bore a remarkable resemblance to my nephew James: an identical smile and a double cowlick of hair framing his face.

"It's him . . . my father," I said in a hoarse tone.

Miss Slavits stopped the projector. "You must sit down," she said, giving me a concerned look.

"I'm fine," I protested, taking a deep breath and easing myself back into my chair. "I don't want to see any more. My father should see it first. Can I bring him?"

"Now?"

"Of course."

"We are closing very soon," she said, looking at her watch. "I'm sorry. Tomorrow?"

"We're leaving first thing in the morning," I explained. "Back to London."

Miss Slavits was silent for a moment. Then she spoke. "From what I have just seen," she said slowly, "your father was a very special boy."

I was unsure of the inflection in her voice, so I shrugged. "My father can come now?" I asked in a bewildered voice, pushing my case.

Miss Slavits considered my request for several moments. Then she nodded her head sympathetically.

"Can I use your telephone?"

"From my office," she answered. "This way, please."

The telephone rang in my parents' hotel room. Before I had even begun to explain, my father started in on me. "I've been knocking on your door for the last hour. We've been worried sick," he said, alarmed. "Where are you?"

I cut him off. "Can Mum hold the fort there?"

"What's up?"

"Listen! I want you to write down this address and get here as soon as you can."

"I'm just relaxing with a cup of tea—" my father started to grumble.

"Don't argue, Dad," I said irritably.

"First tell me what's going on," he said.

I ignored his demand. "Get a taxi!" I insisted.

"I'm on my way," he said. The line clicked as my father hung up.

I turned to Miss Slavits. "My father will be here very soon," I promised her.

I waited in the dark entrance hall. My footsteps echoed as I paced back and forth near the glass doors. About twenty minutes later a taxi swung into the driveway. I watched as my father got out of the car looking disoriented. As he moved toward the entrance he noticed me on the other side of the glass door. I held it open for him.

"Where are we? Stalin's tomb?" he joked.

"Just follow me, Dad." I led my father to the projection room where Miss Slavits was waiting for us. I introduced them.

"You must be very excited," Miss Slavits said, unaware that I'd revealed nothing to my father. Suddenly it dawned on him. "You've found the film?" he exclaimed, his eyes bright with excitement.

Before I could respond, Miss Slavits cut in. "One moment. You must wear a jacket," she remembered, going to the closet. When Miss Slavits reappeared with another pink dust coat, I led my father over to the projector and positioned his chair directly in front of the screen. With a nod I indicated that she should restart the machine.

I could just make out my father's features in the glare of the screen. He was spellbound. I turned my attention back to the footage and watched my father march across the lawn in front of the holiday house with the other children following behind—a Jewish boy-soldier with a group of Aryan children under his command—as the narrator's voice barks out in German the story of the "boy in uniform," "the child found by the Latvian SS legion who rescued him from the dangers of the front."

Then the footage jumps abruptly to a new scene. My father is now blindfolded and surrounded by the other children: the stooge in a game of blindman's bluff. The boy is spun around and around and then left staggering and groping as he tries to catch the perpetrators. And then I noticed something even more unnerving—on the perimeter of the circle of children, I momentarily caught sight of Jekabs Dzenis smiling benignly at them.

The scene shifts to the seaside, where all the bright, happy Aryan children in their swimming costumes frolic on the beach as if in some Germanic naturist ritual. Among them is my father, bare-chested like the others, doing handstands on the sand. The screen gives another hiccup and reveals an image of the children at dinnertime. The camera focuses on my father, who struggles to use his knife and fork properly. But the camera does not linger there for very long: soon it is bedtime, and as lullaby music plays in the background, the face of a sleepy kitten appears on-screen. A nurse then appears and tucks in the sleepy little children. The narrator informs us that all is well in the world for them.

The footage ended abruptly, and the screen went blank. "That is all. Just over two minutes of footage," I heard Miss Slavits say.

I continued to stare ahead, relieved that she'd not yet turned on the lights. What had just been revealed to me seemed somehow too

A still from the propaganda film.

intimate, and I was reluctant to engage with my father. Then I heard Miss Slavits ask him if he wanted to view it again. Out of the corner of my eye I saw my father nod his head vigorously.

Miss Slavits rewound the film, and then suddenly we found ourselves back in Carnikava, my father springing down the stairs with his Aryan playmates. When the footage came to an end again, we remained seated in the darkness. Nobody said a word. Miss Slavits spoke first. "What do you think?" she asked gently.

My father was overcome with emotion and unable to utter a word. I heard him blow his nose. Then he said, "Who would have believed it?"

After that he lapsed into silence again.

We took leave of Miss Slavits outside the archive. Once our taxi was on the main road heading toward the center of Riga, my father leaned back in his seat. He was exhausted, but his body seemed electrified by what he'd just seen.

"It was as I told you, wasn't it?" he said. "Only a shame that more footage did not survive. Still, there was enough to prove I wasn't lying." My father closed his eyes. I wondered whether he was sleeping or replaying the footage in his mind's eye.

I let him be and gazed out the window as the taxi made its way past the Freedom Monument on Brivibas iela. What a mockery the film made of Latvia's flirtation with Nazism. They'd made a Jewish boy into a symbol of racial purity.

I was roused from my thoughts by the sound of my father shouting frantically to the driver to stop. His eyes were bulbous and panicked, as if he were suffocating. The car screeched to a halt, and my father sprang out and onto the sidewalk. Shocked, I followed him, tossing money for the fare to the driver.

On the sidewalk I gripped my father by the arm and shook him until he gasped as if breath had been knocked violently into him. He jerked away from me. Passersby stared at us.

"Dad! Are you all right?" I cried out. "Speak to me."

My father gave a weak nod. He looked around but seemed unable to take in his surroundings.

"Let's find somewhere to sit down," I suggested.

On the opposite corner of an intersection I spied a brightly painted café. We crossed over to it. Neither of us could have been more surprised at what we found—it was a Jewish café with a large blue Star of David painted on its window. An eager waiter greeted us and guided us to a table by the window.

The café was empty and had a forlorn atmosphere that was somehow accentuated rather than diminished by its bright blue and yellow interior and the artificial grapevine suspended from its ceiling.

The menu listed my father's favorite foods—blinis, latkes, and, most loved of all, cabbage rolls. "Have something to eat," I suggested. "It'll give you some strength."

My father shook his head. "A cup of tea will be fine."

The waiter had been hovering expectantly.

"Two teas, please," my father said.

"Nothing to eat?"

"No."

The waiter's face dropped. As he went to fetch our tea, he snapped his fingers grandly in the air, and from out of nowhere there appeared a violinist who wouldn't have been out of place in a production of *Fiddler on the Roof*. The man looked embarrassed as he burst into a lively tune.

"That music is giving me a headache," my father said tetchily.

The waiter returned with our tea and my father greedily snatched at his cup. He quickly stirred in three teaspoons of sugar and then took a sip. "Not enough sugar!" he exclaimed, making a sour face. My father had always had an exceptional sweet tooth. I watched him add yet more sugar. He took another sip.

"Better?" I asked.

"So-so," he replied.

My father now seemed less restless, almost contemplative, with his hands loosely clasped in front of him. He looked around him. "It's harder than I thought," he said, avoiding eye contact. "I didn't do anything wrong," he said, looking at me for reassurance. "But I feel guilty that I ended up on the wrong side with the people who were doing evil to others."

"You're not guilty of anything," I insisted, but my words fell on deaf ears.

"Why did they keep me alive?" he said to himself.

"They used you, Dad," I said, my anger toward these men growing. "They exploited you for their own purposes. You were a good-luck charm"—I searched for other words—"a prisoner of war."

A knot of confused feelings had began to unravel, and he spoke: "I *was* a prisoner . . . a frightened child . . . but nobody could see the bars around me, except perhaps Commander Lobe. He must've known what he was putting me through.

"I was a pet that was being trained. There was nothing I could do to change my situation. All the time everybody reminded me of how lucky I was to be alive, and how grateful I should be to Latvia. I always had to show my gratitude to them. I had to do the right thing for them. I always made sure that everybody was happy and pleased with me. What would have happened if I'd disobeyed them? But inside I didn't accept it. I knew that I was not one of them, and I never would be." Exhausted, my father fell silent.

The Latvian soldiers had "rescued" him from the forest, but they'd stolen him from himself. I thought back to the film and its background of happy children's music suggesting the life of a mascot was nothing but an innocent game, while offscreen he was constantly terrorized by the threat of death.

My father rose suddenly, telling me to take care of the bill. It seemed that he'd had enough.

EPILOGUE

Following my parents' return to Australia I spoke to them regularly by telephone. As far as I could gather, they had slipped back into their normal routine.

On one occasion when I spoke with my father, he told me how pleased he was to be home.

"You don't think of Belarus as home?" I asked.

"Of course not!" he replied somewhat indignantly. "I'm an Aussie."

With surprising candor he expressed gratitude for his life in Australia, telling me that his early vagabond days there—as an elephant boy and a roustabout in a traveling circus, as well as his itinerant existence in the remote outback—had helped him to bury and forget his past. And in spite of his own intensity, or perhaps because of it, my father enjoyed the laid-back ethos of "she'll be right, mate" prized by so many Australians.

Back in Oxford, as I absorbed the experiences of the past months, I found I had further questions about my father's story as well as recent events. But while I spent hours in pursuit of answers I became increasingly frustrated by dead ends.

Not long after his return to Melbourne, my father received a letter from Erick Galperin informing him that Anya Katz had died after a short illness and that Volodya, blind and not able to fully care for himself, had been admitted to a state-care facility, where he died some months later.

As far as I knew, there were no other witnesses who could cast more light on my father's story, and without the elderly couple's reminiscences my desire to learn more about my father's early life and that of his parents was thwarted. Erick continued to claim he knew little of his family's history.

My research into my father's life in Riga and on patrol with the soldiers proved equally frustrating.

Though I had my own intuitions, there was so much I wanted to ask Jekabs Dzenis and the other men who'd come into contact with my father. How had they felt about the boy-soldier and mascot in their midst? Why had they kept him? Were they trying to convince themselves that they hadn't corrupted their own humanity?

But Uncle and Auntie had died, as had Commander Lobe, many years before. And recently, just as a reconciliation between my father and his "stepsister" Mirdza seemed possible, she, too, passed away.

Trying to learn more about Jekabs Kulis, the soldier who had taken my father out of the firing line, I traced a family to New York, from where Kulis had written to my father in the 1950s. I tried to make contact by telephone. An elderly woman with a thick European accent picked up the receiver. When I mentioned who I was and what I was seeking, I heard her gasp before hastily denying any knowledge of my father.

"We are Czech Jews! Leave us alone!" she cried, before slamming down the telephone.

When I reported this to my father, he appeared resigned and advised me to leave them in peace. "What point would it serve?" he said. "Even if it is them, they are probably too old and sick to want to remember me now."

"The Kulises have probably never been able to forget you," I protested.

But my father was adamant. The trail went cold after that.

Although nobody has come forward with information, I suspect that there are individuals—descendants of soldiers and perhaps old soldiers themselves—in Europe and elsewhere who know something about the little mascot. For whatever reason they remain tight-lipped.

And what of the enigma of Slonim? In the end I learned from the work of the historian Andrew Ezergailis that the Eighteenth Battalion was in fact stationed in the town of Stolbtsi in Belarus, as we had suspected. Given its proximity—a day's journey—to Slonim, it was feasible that the Eighteenth had been there. But I was confronted with a greater problem: I learned that the presence of the Eighteenth in Belarus at the time of the Slonim massacre is mired in yet a wider controversy. Some historians have claimed that the battalion was there but suggest variable dates for the massacre itself. And while some suggest that it was an isolated incident, others have argued that the massacre persisted as a series of incidents for which the Eighteenth was responsible from the end of 1941 through most of 1942. According to some, even if the battalion was present, extermination duty was not necessarily one of their official duties. Whatever the truth behind these controversies, we will never know whether my father actually witnessed what happened at Slonim or whether it was one of the many unnamed massacres he saw the soldiers commit. What remains indisputable is that my father cannot lay to rest his sense of accountability both for what he remembers of that day and for what he does not.

And then there are our discoveries from our journey to Belarus.

The mystery of the dusty bag of photographs from my father's original home in Koidanov persists. Who are these people whose framed sepia faces stare out at us? Cousins, uncles, nieces, grandparents? It is as if they are pleading to be recognized and remembered. But we can only identify one half-torn image of a young woman, smiling shyly, who just might be Hana Gildenberg, my father's mother.

We had learned later from Erick that his father, Solomon Galperin, had returned to the family home, hoping to find his wife and children, including his son Ilya Galperin, my father. Solomon had stayed in Koidanov until the last years of his life, when he moved to Minsk, where he died in 1975. If my father had spoken sooner of his past, then father and son may have been reunited.

There were other painful memories and realities to be confronted. Alongside the potential rediscovery of a family home was the mass grave where my father had witnessed his family's extermination.

Still, I had learned something of my father's resilience in the past months. While what was happening to him was extracting a heavy emotional toll, he maintained that this would provide him with ballast for what lay ahead.

Sadly, too, the relationship between my father and Erick, his half brother, has waned. The exact reasons for this estrangement remain obscure. It may be the language barrier: my father's Russian is that of a child.

But it has also proved difficult for the two men, one in his seventies and one in his fifties, to overcome the tyranny of distance—physical and historical—that separates them, in order to forge an easy bond.

The situation is not made any easier by the fact that my father often returns to the question of "Panok," and again raises the possibility that he might have been born a Panok and not a Galperin. He does so despite the correlation of his recollections with Volodya's during our day in Koidanov.

Who was Elli, the woman who befriended me in Oxford? She suddenly disappeared without explanation from the city and without forwarding details. Her father was an Israeli intelligence agent: was he behind the break-in at my parents' home? No valuables were stolen, but my father's papers had been ransacked as if the intruder searched for something specific. The photograph of my father posing with the members of the Eighteenth Battalion, perhaps?

Was either Elli or her father connected to two men who later appeared on my parents' doorstep one morning, claiming to be war crimes investigators? They, too, had come seeking the photograph of my father with the soldiers. How had they known about it? And why had they refused to give my father their names?

Every effort I made to find answers to these mysteries left me stranded with only my intuitions and suspicions. However, the evidence that I did have was sufficient to support my father's version of his childhood, and I wanted public vindication for him.

Somewhat naively I encouraged my father to return to the Holocaust center in Melbourne armed with the new details garnered from our visit to Belarus and Latvia. I believed that the experience would be a positive one for him. He might now be able to present himself to his interviewers as legitimately Jewish, whatever that meant in this context, and be embraced by them.

It was not to be. Inexplicably, the male interviewer had become determinedly set against my father. In a public interview he stated that my father was not Jewish, that he did not have a Jewish heart, and that he had never lost his sense of loyalty to the Latvians above all else. Most disturbing of all, he cast doubt on the veracity of my father's story, de-

The official rejection of my father's application for assistance from the Claims Conference in New York, 1999, later rescinded after much struggle.

spite the plethora of evidence we now had. We decided to leave him to his insinuations.

In one final push for recognition, I turned to the Claims Conference in New York, the organization primarily responsible for evaluating claims of Holocaust suffering and awarding appropriate "compensation."

It, too, declined to recognize my father's experiences in the Holocaust. "How has your father suffered?" one of its representatives demanded of me. "Your father was not even in a concentration camp," she argued indignantly.

Then came its final, embittering decision that my father had volunteered for the SS.

Official verification from the Gilf Society.

After many months of argument and verification of my father's story by the Gilf Society in Minsk, the conference was eventually forced to overturn its verdict.

In the midst of this struggle my father remained stoic. But as the months passed, I learned from my mother that his insomnia had returned, fueled by nightmares from which he awoke disoriented and in a cold sweat. He had none of his usual appetite for food and had lost weight. It seemed that the past as well as his more recent experiences had worn him down; he could no longer be placated by the space and the sunshine, the bright optimism of the "lucky country."

My mother's health also continued to worry us. Finally, a diagnosis was reached: she was suffering from a rare form of cancer that doctors deemed unresponsive to the usual forms of treatment. Her condition fluctuated; for days and weeks on end she would be fine, and a stranger would never guess how unwell she actually was.

Then one day in September 2003 I received a call from my father. My mother's health had suddenly deteriorated and she had been admitted to the hospital. He couldn't bring himself to tell me that the prognosis was extremely poor. My mother's sister called me the following morning to tell me to come home as soon as I could.

That evening I caught a plane to Melbourne.

A month later my mother died.

A darkness, not threatening, but sad and bewildering, settled over our home. My father had lost his dearest friend and partner.

One evening, sitting in the blanketing gloom of the unlit kitchen, my father and I both succumbed to a lingering sense of guilt that had until then been too painful to broach: we wondered whether in some way his story had contributed to her death.

"Your mother was a practical woman," my father said, "and people mistook this for toughness. She wasn't. Your mother was too soft, too kind. She was exhausted by my story. It was too much for her."

During the weeks that followed, he gradually lost interest in the unanswered questions about his past, telling me that the search didn't seem worth it anymore.

"The pieces we have," he said, "we'll make do with them."

Two months later I decided to return to Oxford: we'd rattled around under the same roof for long enough, usually avoiding each other's company. I had an inexpressible anger and grief toward the world that had taken my mother and sensed I was not a person my father wanted to, or should, be around.

The morning of my departure arrived. I didn't know how long it would be until I saw my father again, and I wanted to make a gesture of conciliation. I found him seated at the kitchen table, browsing the morning paper, as was his habit.

"Dad," I said.

He looked up.

"Fancy a visit to Williamstown?"

"For what?"

I shrugged awkwardly, shifting from foot to foot as if I were an ungainly teenager. "Coffee, perhaps," I said. "Or lunch, or an ice cream. A strawberry one, even."

For the first time in a long while he smiled. It was at my mention of strawberry ice cream. He was silent for several moments, thinking over my offer.

"Okay, son," he said finally.

Later that morning we found ourselves sitting on the same bench I'd sat on with my mother six years earlier. It had been the morning after she'd seen the videotape of my father's interview and finally knew what had been bothering her husband so much.

Once again, the dinghies moored just offshore bobbed in the light breeze, the occasional ring of one of their bells punctuating the silence between me and my father.

For some time I'd wondered whether the search we had undertaken had brought us enough proof that the past had actually unfolded as my father had claimed—and the doubters be damned. Still, many questions remained unanswered, and I wondered if a resolution would ever be found. I worried that I'd misjudged the heavy toll memory would take on my father.

"Has this been worth it?" I asked.

"What would make it worth it? Who knows? I have a name." My father shrugged. "And the film clip as well. Now that your mother's gone," he added gloomily, "I ask myself that question every day."

He began to shake his head. "But the truth is, my story is all that I have now . . ."

My father paused before he continued.

"From that single moment when I opened my eyes and chose to live—without knowing clearly what that even meant—and stepped outside into the darkness, my life took an unimaginable turn. And look where I've ended up sixty years on. The other side of the world!"

My father rose and headed for the shore; for several minutes he watched a black swan walking on the beach. Then he returned to where I'd remained seated and stood in front of me, obscuring the sunlight and my view of the bay.

"I don't know what I lost," he said, without prompting. "How can you know the life you didn't live? I took the chance to survive and I've never railed against that. This is just the way that life turned out for me. Any number of times I could've been exposed or even let myself be discovered, but I made my survival into a companion, and it has stayed by my side all throughout my life."

"Would it have been better if you'd never spoken of the past?" I pressed my father.

"I honestly don't know, son," he said slowly. "Even after sixty years, it unsettled me in a way that I could never have imagined. I thought I was in charge of my life but it wasn't so. How I survived even now dictates my life, and all I can do is follow at a safe distance, chained to it. It's as if there are two persons in my body. There is the Alex everybody knows and there's another Alex who was a secret. They'll have to learn to accommodate each other again."

So I had my answers to questions I had harbored since that day at the Café Daquise in London, when my father had suddenly become a stranger to me.

There was no resolution, no absolution, no closure, no moving on, no getting over it, no pop-psychology solution. Only an accommodation of the past. My father had somehow known this all along.

I realized that I, too, had to find a way of living, comfortably or not, with this, my legacy.

ACKNOWLEDGMENTS

T his journey has been a long and difficult one. Without the support, advice, assistance, and, above all, the friendship of many, my father and I may not have reached this point.

Sarah Blair has supported me enormously throughout the writing of the book—typing and proofreading—and offering general advice and encouragement. I am deeply grateful to Sarah, and also to Jane Enright, who was similarly unstinting in her help. Thanks also to Luke Mason, who also pitched in with valued work on the manuscript early on in the process.

Robert Guinsler, my agent, has been very generous with his time. His sound advice and good humor have kept my spirits up during the darker moments of writing this book. The commitment of the editorial team at Penguin, in particular Hilary Redmon, was thorough and solid and always very reassuring. I am also especially grateful to Bernard Nyman for protecting the integrity of my work.

At the outset, I had little knowledge of the time and space of the world in which my father lived and moved. I listened to the stories and anecdotes of many who did share his world and my gratitude to them is immense—I am humbled by their lives. The research of countless historians also informed my general understanding of Europe at that time. Special note must be made of the scholarship of Professor Andrew

Ezergailis in his book *The Holocaust in Latvia*, which later helped me piece together some of the movements and identities of Latvian troops.

During the actual journeys to Belarus and Latvia I received invaluable support from many individuals and organizations. In particular I want to acknowledge the support of the Jewish World Congress, London; Frank and Galina Swartz of the East European Jewish Heritage Project in Minsk, who became generous friends and hosts to my mother and father during our time there; Frida Reizman from the Gilf Society in Belarus; the Latvia State Archive for Audiovisual Document in Riga; and Ryuta Akamatsu of Telesis Ltd, Japan.

In a project such as this, with its inevitably disheartening setbacks and periods of isolation, it was frequently the face of a friend and a kind word now and then or a laugh that made a world of difference. There are many dear people who did so for me: Gro Ween, wonderful Daphne Lennie, kind and generous Audrey and Michael Phillips, Jeffery Lies, Rachel Moseley and John Turner, Uma Bhattacharya, Jane Enright, Alan Russell, Lee Parsons, and Gordon Hickson. Distant friends, too, seemed close at hand and ever present in their support: dear Anne Rahilly, Janet Westwood, Peter Westwood, Lisa Reichenbach, Irene Kuijpers, William J. Holmes, Margaret Chu, Maria Norris, and Mary Ida Bagus and family.

And then there is Sim Tan, a great friend who lightened my load considerably.

Special thanks to Eiko and the late Takaaki Hosokawa for their considerable support and friendship during the past years and, similarly, the three branches of my family spread around the globe—the Kurzems in Australia, the Galperin family in Belarus, and the Krupitsky family in the United States.

Other kinds of help and care bestowed on me must be acknowledged. Thanks to Helen Beer for her information on Yiddish culture and to Heathcote Williams, a man of erudition and immense talent who took a strong interest in my father's story, and his partner, Diana, who opened her home to me.

Mention must also be made of every staff member at the Oxford Eye

Hospital where I received excellent and compassionate care from all quarters as they struggled to save my eyesight. They did! In particular, I wish to thank Miss Susan Downes, Mr. Paul Rosen, and Mr. John Salmon and their respective teams for holding back that dark prospect.

There are only two people remaining to thank. First, my very dear friend Alastair Phillips, who has shown faith in my ability to tell this story, even when I faltered. His support, encouragement, compassion, and care have greatly guided me.

And then last, but of course not least, there is my father, who entrusted me with his voice.

INDEX

Volhov area (Russia) (*cont.*)
  and researching Alex's story, 165
  Volodya with partisans in, 352

Wannsee Conference (1942), 168, 272
war crimes investigators, visit to
  Alex's home by, 390
war criminals, 234, 307–8. *See also
  specific people's names*
Wiesenthal Center, 308
Wilkomirski, Benjamin, 173–74, 175
Williamstown Beach (Melbourne,
  Australia)

Alex and Mark's visit to, 394–95
Mark's conversation with his
  mother at, 260–63
World War II
  Alex's feelings about, 197
  ending of, 197–98
  as Great Patriotic War, 267
  Latvia's role in, 159

yellow star, Jewish, 97, 131

Zakkini Brothers, 253